Isaiah 40—66

INTERPRETATION
A Bible Commentary for Teaching and Preaching

INTERPRETATION

A BIBLE COMMENTARY FOR TEACHING AND PREACHING

James Luther Mays, *Editor*
Patrick D. Miller, *Old Testament Editor*
Paul J. Achtemeier, *New Testament Editor*

PAUL D. HANSON

Isaiah 40–66

A Bible Commentary
for Teaching and Preaching

John Knox Press
LOUISVILLE

Library of Congress Cataloging-in-Publication Data

Hanson, Paul D., date
    Isaiah 40–66 / Paul D. Hanson.
        p.   cm. — (Interpretation, a Bible commentary for teaching and preaching)
    Includes bibliographical references (p.   ).
    ISBN 0-8042-3132-X (cloth : alk. paper)
    1. Bible. O.T. Isaiah XL–LXVI—Commentaries.   I. Title.
II. Series.
    BS1520.H36   1995
    224′.1077—dc20   95-5534

© copyright John Knox Press 1995
This book is printed on acid-free paper that meets the American National Standards Institute Z39.48 standard. ∞
95 96 97 98 99 00 01 02 03 04 — 10 9 8 7 6 5 4 3 2 1
Printed in the United States of America
John Knox Press
Louisville, Kentucky

SERIES PREFACE

This series of commentaries offers an interpretation of the books of the Bible. It is designed to meet the need of students, teachers, ministers, and priests for a contemporary expository commentary. These volumes will not replace the historical critical commentary or homiletical aids to preaching. The purpose of this series is rather to provide a third kind of resource, a commentary which presents the integrated result of historical and theological work with the biblical text.

An interpretation in the full sense of the term involves a text, an interpreter, and someone for whom the interpretation is made. Here, the text is what stands written in the Bible in its full identity as literature from the time of "the prophets and apostles," the literature which is read to inform, inspire, and guide the life of faith. The interpreters are scholars who seek to create an interpretation which is both faithful to the text and useful to the church. The series is written for those who teach, preach, and study the Bible in the community of faith.

The comment generally takes the form of expository essays. It is planned and written in the light of the needs and questions which arise in the use of the Bible as Holy Scripture. The insights and results of contemporary scholarly research are used for the sake of the exposition. The commentators write as exegetes and theologians. The task which they undertake is both to deal with what the texts say and to discern their meaning for faith and life. The exposition is the unified work of one interpreter.

The text on which the comment is based is the Revised Standard Version of the Bible and, since its appearance, the New Revised Standard Version. The general availability of these translations makes the printing of a text in the commentary unnecessary. The commentators have also had other current versions in view as they worked and refer to their readings where it is helpful. The text is divided into sections appropriate to the particular book; comment deals with passages as a whole, rather than proceeding word by word, or verse by verse.

Writers have planned their volumes in light of the requirements set by the exposition of the book assigned to them. Biblical books differ in character, content, and arrangement. They also differ in the way they have been and are used in the liturgy, thought, and devotion of the church. The distinctiveness and use of particular books have been taken into account in decisions about the approach, emphasis, and use of space in the commentaries. The goal has been to allow writers to develop the format which provides for the best presentation of their interpretation.

The result, writers and editors hope, is a commentary which both explains and applies, an interpretation which deals with both the meaning and the significance of biblical texts. Each commentary reflects, of course, the writer's own approach and perception of the church and world. It could and should not be otherwise. Every interpretation of any kind is individual in that sense; it is one reading of the text. But all who work at the interpretation of Scripture in the church need the help and stimulation of a colleague's reading and understanding of the text. If these volumes serve and encourage interpretation in that way, their preparation and publication will realize their purpose.

The Editors

PREFACE

Readers of the commentaries in this series are accustomed to finding an entire biblical book covered in one volume. In the present case they will find one half of a book interpreted, the other half having been treated in Christopher R. Seitz's previously published *Isaiah 1—39*. The editors of the series no doubt spent considerable time discussing this division, because good arguments can be made both for the present arrangement and for a unified treatment by one author. I did not participate in that discussion but merely accepted the assignment to write a commentary on chapters 40—66. Thus I am free to imagine that the discussion between the editors concluded like this: "Clearly, the substantive arguments end in a balance. So let us be guided by a very practical consideration. A single volume will be a cumbersome tome to carry and to use. We will divide it between chapter 39 and chapter 40."

What I like about this fanciful reconstruction of their decision is that it allows me to offer my equally unscientific explanation. The Book of Isaiah is like the wine brought in a carafe along with the chalice from which the guest is to drink. The guest assumed the chalice and carafe were of equal volume. But after the chalice was filled, half of the wine remained, so the guest requested a second chalice and offered it to a friend. Given the literary, historical, and theological richness of the Book of Isaiah, it seems appropriate that it spills over into two volumes.

I am sure, however, that Seitz will agree with me that our two volumes, while offered separately, belong together. The sixty-six chapters of the Book of Isaiah did not come together by accident. From the complementary sides of the division, we both point to broad themes that run throughout the book. Readers will discover other connections through their own study. Likewise, they will discover further subdivisions. Thematically, and perhaps even literarily, chapters 34—35 belong to chapters 40—55. But the editors chose wisely not to engage in a fragmentation that finally ends in confusion.

Some readers, on the other hand, may ask why the twofold division was chosen rather than a threefold one. After all, many scholars distinguish between Second Isaiah and Third Isaiah, with the division lying between chapter 55 and chapter 56. Again, I imagine the reason was the practical one of size, since substantive arguments again could weigh in either direction. As my commentary will point out, chapters 40—55 constitute one of the most unified, and beautiful, compositions in the entire Bible, whereas chapters 56—66 stylistically and in terms of tone stand quite apart. But here too there are exceptions, such as chapters 60—62, which are closely akin to chapters 40—55. We could continue thus in analyzing the architectonics of the Book of Isaiah, but further evidence would only corroborate what is already clear. To apply Buckminster Fuller's apt neologism, the book is characterized by *tensegrity*. The distinct parts are brought together into a whole that fascinates through its inner tensions and complex unity. But what do we expect of an earthly chalice that contains a Word that causes grass to wither and flower to fade and yet does not return empty until it accomplishes that for which God sent it?

My understanding of the concept of "compassionate justice" in Second Isaiah, which I first developed in *The People Called,* has been enriched by the dissertation research on *mišpāṭ* in the Book of Isaiah by Father Thomas L. Leclerc of Harvard University.

I count as one of my greatest blessings the honor of having studied under a teacher-scholar who was filled with a contagious fascination with the poetry of Second Isaiah. His range of knowledge was, and continues to be, daunting, but his pure faith and the dedication to his students that grew out of that faith radiated from a Center that few poets possessed sufficient gifts to describe. Frank Moore Cross counted Second Isaiah, and Job, among those few. I only hope that the inspiration he passed on to me is sufficiently alive to make my words worthy of the time and attention of the readers who open the pages of this commentary.

CONTENTS

PART ONE

Second Isaiah

Isaiah 40—55

Overview

The Historical Setting

Events moved at a dizzying speed for the Jewish people between 550 and 515 B.C.E., the period of thirty-five years that produced the twenty-seven chapters treated in this commentary. The crises of those years were of the magnitude that would have tested even the most robust and secure of communities. But the Jewish community of the latter half of the sixth century B.C.E. was neither robust nor secure. As a result of the devastating attack of the Babylonian armies earlier in that century, a large segment of the population of Judah now dwelled as captives and exiles along the banks of the Euphrates, surrounded by worshipers of Marduk and Nebo and the other members of the Babylonian pantheon.

Spiritual alienation did not necessarily imply economic hardship, however. The exiles, on balance, enjoyed better chances of prospering in commerce and trade than their kinsfolk who had remained on native soil. Whereas the Babylonians granted their captive guests considerable freedom to enter into business relationships, the people dwelling in Judah occupied a land that had been left in ruins both by the original Babylonian destruction and by successive waves of marauders, such as the Edomites, who swept over crippled Judah in search of plunder. But the economic and cultural opportunities that were opened up to the Jewish exiles did not remove the odium of captivity. Indeed, in the eyes of some, it added to national shame the threat of cultural and religious assimilation. The loss of native land could come to be attibuted to the powerlessness of Israel's

1

God to secure the safety and security of the nation, even as the opportunities for economic prosperity within the new land could be credited to the gods of that new land. Through this process of reevaluation, the Jewish community could easily lose its religious identity. And because its identity as a people was inextricably tied to its religious roots, extinction as a family that descended from Abraham and Sarah could rapidly follow.

This was the scene entered by the prophet variously called Deutero-Isaiah, Second Isaiah, the Prophet of the Exile, or the Prophet of Consolation. We know nothing concerning the personal life of this prophet, neither name nor gender nor social class. Although it is disputed by some scholars, most assume that Second Isaiah crafted the message found in Isaiah 40—55 (as well as chaps. 34—35) while living with the exiles in Babylon. Vivid descriptions of Babylonian cultic practices as well as announcements of Yahweh's coming to return the captives over a wilderness route to their native land argue for this setting. Beyond these bare facts, little more can be said about the prophet.

Actually, a caveat should be added. It is in relation specifically to the prophet's *external* life that we can say little. But sparsity yields to immense richness when one turns to the prophet's *inner* life of inspired reflection and creative imagination. On that level we find detailed commentary on the spiritual health of the Jewish community, on its relation to the customs and beliefs of the Babylonian hosts, and on the significance of the world events that were changing the face of world history.

How can we explain such a keen interest in world events and their impact on the Jewish community alongside virtual silence in the realm of biographical facts? The answer is to be found in the historical consciousness that was a central aspect of biblical prophecy that it inherited from even earlier Israelite religious sources. The prophets viewed the welfare and destiny of their people firmly within the context of world events. God's deliverance of Hebrew slaves from Egypt was a call to historical existence as a family within the family of the nations. The covenant that God concluded with the people entailed living in accord with divine commands amidst the day-to-day business of society and affairs of state. The welfare of Israel was thus tied up with economics, law, and international relations as well as with more explicitly religious matters. It is not surprising, given this historical groundedness of the prophetic perspective, that divine sanctions imposed in response to violations of the terms of the covenant commonly involved actions by foreign nations, even as divine deliverance of a chastened and repentant people was seen as a part of the reordering of historical relationships among the nations.

As with all of the prophets, so too with Second Isaiah it is mandatory that the interpreter be well aware of the historical and, to the extent possible, the social realities that the prophet is addressing. When the prophet asks the people to consider who it was that "gave up Jacob to the spoiler, and Israel to the robbers" (42:24) and then informs them that it was their own God Yahweh, it is necessary to recognize that the background is the destruction of Judah by the Babylonian armies in 586 B.C.E. Similarly, when the prophet introduces, in chapter 41:25, the theme of a conqueror stirred up by Yahweh to bring down rulers, one must understand the significance of the political revolution that was being fomented by Cyrus as he first consolidated the Medes and the Persians in 550 B.C.E., then in 546 B.C.E. moved on to defeat Croesus, the powerful king of the Lydian empire in Asia Minor, and finally brought dreaded Babylon to its knees in 539 B.C.E. It is important to be aware of the sharp contrast between the ruthless Babylonian policy of obliterating the culture of defeated peoples and Cyrus's policy of restoring captive peoples to their homelands and granting them the financial aid required to rebuild their economic, social, and religious institutions.

Second Isaiah's attentiveness to international affairs accordingly is based on the prophetic understanding of world events as the context of divine activity. World happenings are not arbitrary. Underlying the rise and fall of nations is providential direction. In fact, divine purpose is to be discerned on a cosmic scale, since humanity and creation in their entirety unfold within one drama, a drama ultimately redemptive but on the way toward that goal entailing judgment and the persistent threat of chaos.

If the description ended here, Second Isaiah could begin to look like a cosmic commentator describing world movements in cerebral detachment as deputy of a God "who sits above the circle of the earth, and its inhabitants are like grasshoppers" (40:22). But there is more to the picture of both prophet and God. For this we need to turn to the dilemma of the Jewish community in the second third of the sixth century B.C.E. and

3

examine the evidence found in Second Isaiah's message for the manner in which the prophet related personally to the existential concerns of the exiles.

The Personal Dimension of the Prophetic Message

An anonymous contemporary of Second Isaiah gave voice to the sadness and mental anguish of the Jewish people in the wake of the Babylonian destruction of Jerusalem:

> Judah has gone into exile with suffering
>   and hard servitude;
> she now lives among the nations,
>   and finds no resting place;
> her pursuers have all overtaken her
>   in the midst of her distress.
>
> (Lam. 1:3)

This was the Judah addressed by Second Isaiah, a community that saw added to its physical suffering the anguish of being caught in a crossfire of conflicting messages: Israel is a people chosen by a loving God who will care for all its needs. God's love has turned to wrath. Israel's God lacks the power to withstand the assaults of Babylon and its pantheon. God is punishing Israel for its sin. God no longer loves Israel. God does not care. What sort of response did this moment of crisis require? Some advised turning to other deities (cf. Jer. 44:16–18). Others thought blind fate determines the destiny of human beings, so the best course of action was to indulge in the moment, mindless of mercy or justice and free from fear of divine reprisal (Ezek. 8:7–12). Luck falls to the powerful, some seemed to be saying, so let's live the high life (Isa. 56:12).

Second Isaiah, far from being the detached analyst, was one who strove passionately for the preservation of the community from cynicism and despair with the conviction that life is not driven by arbitrary forces but is guided by a loving God who remains true to a universal plan of justice:

> I did not say to the offspring of Jacob,
>   "Seek me in chaos."
> I the LORD speak the truth,
>   I declare what is right.
>
> (Isa. 45:19)

4

But the task of convincing the people was vexed by serious problems. Many were convinced that cosmic forces more powerful than Yahweh determined destinies. So the prophet mounted an offensive in the form of mock trials in which Yahweh and the gods of the nations took the stand. Others were so paralyzed by their despair that they abandoned all hope for the end of captivity. To them the prophet described a God who, like a mother, cannot forsake her young. Thus a body of literature virtually bereft of the external facts of the lives of prophet and people is steeped in the dialogues of the heart that reveal a prophet intimately involved in the struggles of the people who reveals to them a God whose compassion leads to an equally passionate engagement with their needs. Adequate understanding of those dialogues, though, requires an accurate understanding of the worldview of Second Isaiah, specifically as it describes the relational webs that connect God, Israel, the nations, and the physical universe.

The Worldview of Second Isaiah

> [God] did not create it a chaos,
> [God] formed it to be inhabited!

Thus we read in 45:18 of God's creation of the heavens and the earth. The prophet is addressing an audience that has experienced life as chaos. The sacred center that formerly had held together an ordered universe, the temple in Jerusalem, was destroyed. The concentric circles of institutional structure that had unified the diverse spheres of human activity into a harmonious whole, namely, royal court, priesthood, and commerce, had ruptured. Rushing in to fill the void were looters, worshipers of pagan gods, and foreign armies coming to tear the Jewish people from their homeland. Finally, one morning, the followers of Yahweh woke up to see the sun rising not on the hills of Ephraim but on a land where Marduk and Nebo were worshiped. Confusion swamped the consciousness of many. Life no longer had a center but came to resemble the chaos poignantly described by William Butler Yeats:

> Things fall apart; the center cannot hold;
> Mere anarchy is loosed upon the world.

Amidst the confusion engulfing another civilization at a time closer to the modern world of Yeats, as pale-skinned invaders raped, pillaged, and slaughtered unsuspecting inhabitants of

5

native villages a Cheyenne chief offered his explanation of the erratic behavior of the aliens who had disrupted a carefully ordered way of life: "They are strange and do not seem to know where the center of the world is" (Berger, p. 111). The persistent hardships of Native Americans down to the present day stand as a stern reminder of the bitter fruits sown by communities that lose a sense of center and then go on to wreak havoc among other peoples.

Second Isaiah at that earlier epoch that produced our Scripture apparently realized that much was at stake as she or he sought to renew a sense of center within the foundering Jewish community. Here was a people with a destiny intertwined with the families of the world standing at a threshold that called for rigorous scrutiny of ancestral traditions within an alien setting. The resulting deconstruction and reconstruction of the monuments of the past issued forth in spiritual renewal rather than further confusion because the prophet held before the people a compelling vision of its identity, purpose, and place in creation. It was compelling because it was held together by a clearly identified holy Center: "I am the LORD, and there is no other" (45:5).

Second Isaiah presented God as a dynamic, destiny-shaping presence in the midst of human history. All that exists, from the heavenly bodies to the sphere inhabited by human beings, finds its being and purpose in relation to that Center. Because of the clarity with which Second Isaiah understood this cardinal fact of the ancestral faith, his message on its most fundamental level presents a comprehensive vision of the entire creation restored to its divinely intended wholeness accompanied by ongoing comment regarding the role that Israel was to play in the fulfillment of that vision. Elements that detract from and threaten the vision are also present in that message: godless tyrants, cowering disciples, rival deities. But from the clarity of the prophet's faith perspective, all of these are seen for what they ultimately are—nothingness, stuff destined to disappear before the eternal word of God.

At times our own perception of the prophet's central vision in Isaiah 40—55 becomes blurred amidst arguments between God and human beings, trials summoning gods, nations, and Israel, indictments and threats and complaints. But these are interpreted by Second Isaiah as the inevitable labor pains of the birth of the new creation. And that explains the connection between the prophet as visionary and the prophet as sober realist and keen observer of human affairs. Second Isaiah presents the vision of divine purpose not as an avenue of escape from the nitty-gritty of the world but as an invitation to join in the restoration of that world to a realm of universal justice and shalom.

This explains why we shall observe in Isaiah 40—55 a constant fluctuation between bold envisioning of God's order of righteous compassion and pragmatic description of the real-life situations of the people. Vision and realism create the bipolar field on which a lively dialectic is played out as the prophet struggles to break a people from bondage by shocking them out of deceptive and sterile ways of thinking. The rich repertoire of images and metaphors that the prophet brings into this struggle serves well the consciousness-raising intention that underlies the entire composition.

In a chaotic situation in which people were tempted either to throw out all forms of the past or to cling mindlessly to tradition out of fear of change, it was terribly important to maintain a comprehensive vision of reality ordered around one life-giving Center. A criterion for discerning truth and falsehood was sorely needed. In order for the community to survive the crosscurrents of inner questioning and external pressure, it needed to be able to distinguish between essential aspects of the faith that could revitalize the community, adiaphora that would prove useless against the forces of chaos on all sides, and discredited elements that undermined the spiritual health of the people. How did the prophet apply the God-centered vision to concrete problems?

As Second Isaiah sought to direct the attention of the community beyond tragedy to the restoration of a vital faith community, what was there to say about the institutions of kingship and temple? The answer could be discovered only in relation to the Center, that is, the God who was present with the people before the introduction of either temple or kingship and by whose assent both had entered into Israel's history. The covenant relationship had been cultivated for a time within the structures of those two institutions but was not dependent on them. Hence in 45:1–6 Second Isaiah, doubtless to the dismay of many contemporaries, could ascribe to a foreign ruler the titles and offices associated in Israel with Davidic kingship. What had been assigned to the Davidides were tasks and func-

7

tions, and tasks and functions under changed circumstances could be reassigned.

In a similar manner, the tabernacle, and somewhat later the temple, had served as a place chosen by God for rituals through which God could be present with the people. But God's presence, the exiles learned, could continue without a central sanctuary. As with the earliest Passover celebrations, so contemporary gatherings for worship and study could occur in homes, around common meals, and, finally, in synagogues scattered in different parts of the world.

"Do not remember the former things" (43:18). "Remember the former things" (46:9). The prophet could say both, because a living Center guided the people as they located themselves in relation to past and in anticipation of the future. Sometimes this dialectical response to tradition involved a simultaneous remembering and not remembering, as when the covenant promises made by God to David in an earlier era were expanded to apply to the entire community (55:3). For traditions were drawn not blindly or slavishly from the past but critically within the context of a living relationship that enabled the community to discern the God preserved in memory as living presence in bold new initiatives and forms not yet imagined.

It is Second Isaiah's dialectical relation to tradition that explains the juxtaposition of admonitions "to remember" and "not to remember" as well as allusions to the major Hebrew epic traditions found alongside audacious innovations. The effect of such dialectical interplays is to break people from their complacency and to heighten their awareness of God's presence in their present situation, an awareness, to be sure, guided and enriched by the memory embedded in the epic. What preserves this dialectic from lapsing into sheer contradiction is Second Isaiah's lucid attribution of all of life to the one divine source, that is, his recognition of life's living Center. The audacity that characterizes this prophecy can thus be traced to the profundity of the confession that lies at its heart: Once faith is sure of its grounding in the one true God, it is able to address every aspect of life boldly, freshly, and courageously.

Let us consider a few more examples of the way in which tradition is reshaped and brought to new life as Second Isaiah seeks to bring God's word to bear on contemporary realities. Themes from the Genesis creation story become the vehicles for describing the imminent renewal of Zion's "waste places"

8

2.

(51:3). Just the naming of Abraham, God's "friend" whom God led forth from a distant land, adds credibility to the divine announcement that God is gathering the scattered children of Israel from the far corners of the earth (41:8–10). So too the assurance of blessing to the exilic generation is placed upon solid rock by directing its attention "to Abraham your father and to Sarah who bore you" (51:2). The exodus of Hebrew slaves *3.* from Egypt itself becomes more than a memory of past deliverance; it becomes the description of deliverance lying just ahead

4. (43:2). Even the combat with the dragon Rahab through which Yahweh established creation out of chaos, after modulating into the deliverance of the Hebrew slaves at the sea, leads to a picture of the present generation of exiles ransomed from their captivity and returning in joy to Zion (51:9–11). Perhaps no passage demonstrates more clearly the dynamism that arises out of the prophet's grasp of the interconnectedness of all of reality grounded in its one source and Center than this last mentioned as it draws together into one redemptive movement the primordial, the historical, and the eschatological. All time and space finds its unity in the sole reality capable of holding together the whole.

All parts of Isaiah 40—55 can be viewed as aspects of the prophet's effort to call the people back to recognition of their Center. The plaguing doubt and despair generated by the Babylonian destruction of Judah in 586 B.C.E. are addressed head-on first by identifying Yahweh as the one who commissioned this terrible event and then by probing deeper to its underlying roots in Israel's rejection of God's just order. This courageous move maintains the moral grounding of all of life and directs Israel's attention to the covenant relation as that alone which can reestablish Israel's life upon a reliable foundation. The fierce attacks waged by Second Isaiah against the gods of the nations, especially the Babylonian gods, are likewise motivated by the purity of the prophet's focus on the Center. By turning attention to other forces, whether out of fear or in worship, Israel clouds its consciousness with lies. Second Isaiah is tireless in naming all such forces "nothingness."

The same courage that enables the prophet to deny any power to Bel (that is, Marduk) leads to frank recognition of the resounding success of Cyrus and a bold integration of that Persian's conquests into the universal plan of Yahweh. What Cyrus is accomplishing is God's purpose (46:8–11), including both his conquest of Babylon (48:14) and his repatriation of the Jews and other captive peoples (44:24—45:7).

What directs all of world history is captured succinctly in the divine word in 46:10: "My purpose shall stand, and I will fulfill my intention." Similarly, the first words of Second Isaiah, words directed by the universal Lord to divine messengers, announced that God's purpose had turned toward the ending of Israel's bondage. The message at the end is the same, describing the word that "shall accomplish that which I purpose, and succeed in the thing for which I sent it" (55:11). Beginning, middle, and end, Second Isaiah's message consistently describes how God was about to heal a torn creation and restore a broken community. The extent of the salvation that Second Isaiah saw radiating from the center of all reality is manifested in the role that redeemed Israel would play in the future era, the role of mediating God's order of compassionate justice *(mišpāṭ)* to the ends of the earth (42:1–4; 49:6). Nothing less than a universe restored to God's "covenant of peace" is what the prophet announces (54:10).

I have used the phrase "compassionate justice" to express Second Isaiah's dialectical understanding of God's nature, as manifested in Israel's experience. "Justice" *(mišpāṭ)* is associated in Second Isaiah with (1) the courtroom and (2) Yahweh as sovereign and the Servant as God's agent. While the courtroom revolves around disputation, Yahweh and the Servant *do* and *bring* justice in a matter that commends use of this phrase.

Although the picture of a cosmos restored to its divinely intended wholeness is lofty in concept, it does not slip into ethereal abstractions but is grounded always in the intimacy of a personal relationship. The Creator of the heavens and the earth who is the sovereign of all nations reveals the source of the divine initiative:

> Because you are precious in my sight,
> and honored, and I love you.
> (Isa. 43:4)

The majestic center of all creation is moved simultaneously by justice that cannot ignore evil and by love that cannot abandon the lost, even those lost in their own sin. The importance of Second Isaiah's choice of metaphors is seen once again in a passage that describes the limitless extent of God's compassion:

10

Can a woman forget her nursing child,
> or show no compassion for the child of her womb?
Even these may forget,
> yet I will not forget you.

(Isa. 49:15)

It is after such a profound sense of justice and love that Israel is to pattern its life as a people. The Servant of the Lord stands out as the most arresting metaphor of all for the individual and the community drawn into partnership with God in restoring all of creation to health through reconciliation with its Center.

The Literary Qualities of Second Isaiah

As already seen, the verve and audacity of Second Isaiah's visionary, God-centered worldview is enhanced by literary dimensions such as genre, poetic style, symbolism, and compositional structure.

What we have described as the dialectical relationship between old and new in the prophet's treatment of epic traditions finds its counterpart in the way in which poetic style and genres are developed. The poetic style is definitely archaizing. Frequently one finds a prosody characterized by parallelism and regularity of metric structure that resembles the earliest poetry of the Bible. The hymnic style of creating elaborate divine epithets through a string of participial clauses recalls a feature commonly found in the psalms. At the same time, however, the syntax has become more complex than in earlier poetry, and many stylistic features are novel. Old and new thus interact to create a sense of bold freshness that nevertheless preserves contact with antecedents.

The prophet's relation to the genres, or speech forms, utilized by earlier prophecy is also complex. The traditional elements of disputation, lament, judgment, and promise are all there, but they are often combined and transformed in daring new ways. The Servant of the Lord passages perhaps illustrate this point most vividly, for, while drawing on prophetic call narratives, laments, and assurances of salvation, they represent a new form that defies precise classification. Even on the formal level of literary genres one can thus hear the Lord's announcement, "I am about to do a new thing" (43:19).

So too with the overall compositional structure of Isaiah

11

40—55; attempts to analyze it by applying the templates of earlier genres, such as one finds in the important commentary of Claus Westermann, often end up being forced. The categories that may be helpful in studying Hosea and Amos do not always fit the material in these chapters. This is due in part to the new situation in which Israel finds itself. The settings in which the earlier prophets proclaimed their messages, such as temple and trial in the gates, disappeared with the institutions that hosted them. The new settings are in large part produced within the imagination of the prophet. They are not divorced from antecedents; witness the divine assembly background of 40:1–11. But they take flight in new directions on the wings of a prophet who dares to imagine the unprecedented, a community reconciled to its God and living in the world as agents of God's salvation. The old wineskins no longer were adequate, abetting the productions of new containers.

The other extreme, though, is correspondingly inappropriate. James Muilenburg, in a commentary that, again, is valuable for its insight, tears Second Isaiah from important roots when he describes a poet working with the complicated structures of a modern composer. Second Isaiah fits, rather, the description in Matthew 13:52 of the scribe trained for the kingdom of heaven, who, like the master of a household, "brings out of his treasure what is new and what is old."

Perhaps we can invoke the dialectical spirit of Second Isaiah in claiming that the contest between the atomizing form-critical approach of Westermann and the modernizing literary analysis of Muilenburg ends in a draw. Second Isaiah the poet, like Second Isaiah the thinker, draws on the old to create the new. The resulting literary product cannot be reduced to stanzas and movements any more than it can be boxed in trials, disputations, promises, threats, and exhortations. This behooves us to remain attentive to ways in which the prophet draws on older genres as well as ways in which she or he reshapes them to address a rapidly changing world.

On the level of overall structure, critics have long noted a seam between chapters 48 and 49. In 40—48, Jacob/Israel is addressed, replaced in 49—55 by Zion/Jerusalem (exceptions are found; e.g., 40:9). Subtle reasons exist for viewing the former half as the product of an earlier period in the prophet's career than the latter. For example, the sense of urgency and of imminent expectation seems to be heightened in chapters

49—55. At any rate, it is naive to expect that a prophet, one with as rich an imagination as Second Isaiah, will not have experienced development in outlook over a period of years.

What is more surprising than certain minor differences is the high degree of consistency in overall style and theme throughout the entire sixteen chapters. Few prophets, if any, have produced as homogeneous a composition. One can only admire the gifts of someone who can embrace the entire civilized world plus the vast reaches of the cosmos in one sublime poetic picture of divine majesty. Equally impressive is the power and integrity of the invitation conveyed by the prophet: Denounce self-deception, repudiate false gods, return to truth, face the facts of life openly, embrace justice, be moved by compassion, find the roots of all of life in the Center of all of life, the One who, though sitting above the circle of the earth and viewing its inhabitants like grasshoppers, nevertheless loves each of them as a mother loves the child of her womb! In a modern world in which persons often search in vain as they long for the insights of persons who possess both the inspired poetic imagination and the intellectual honesty to project reliable maps for life's journey, Second Isaiah arrives as a welcome pioneer. As one who has breathed deeply from the inspiration of this faithful prophet of God in the course of preparing this commentary, I can only plead that, whatever help my words may offer, they always be placed at a very lowly position on a desk or lap beneath a message beginning with the joyous words, "Comfort, O comfort my people, says your God."

Isaiah 40:1–11
A New Message for Israel

In the opening speech of the second major section of the Book of Isaiah, we find a message that is filled with drama, mystery, and hope. It presents a bold statement concerning the presence of God in the events of human history and thus addresses what over the centuries has remained one of the most important themes of Jewish and Christian theology. When one realizes that this speech was addressed to a people that had experienced the loss of nearly all of those structures and institu-

13

tions which give identity to a community, it assumes a poignancy especially for readers who face their own personal or corporate existence with apprehension or dread. The perennial doubt expressed by the protagonist in Archibald MacLeish's *J.B.* here is met frontally: "If God is God He is not good, If God is good He is not God" (MacLeish, pp. 11, 14). In the face of loss of temple, nationhood, and homeland, can a people confess the basic message reformulated in the table prayer, "God is good and God is great"?

Many of the readers who approach this text find that its meaning is obscured by a language and set of symbols belonging to a worldview vastly different from their own. What is the concept of God that stands behind the message of Isaiah 40? This question leaps out at us already in the first words, "Comfort, O comfort my people, says your God." The words of this classic lection from the Second Sunday of Advent (year B) elicit for many people a sense of awe. Others, however, may hear undertones resembling those encountered in the ancient collect that beseeches God for deliverance from the horn of the unicorn. In Isaiah 40, are we responding to pious phrases emptied of meaning and depending for emotional effect on the patina left by centuries of repetition? To whom is God speaking these words? It is often not even clear to readers or listeners that the twice-repeated word "comfort" is a plural imperative. To whom is this divine command being directed?

These questions arise from more than antiquarian curiosity. They bear on the specific theological meaning of the text, first of all as that meaning related to its original audience but also as it relates to those who read Scripture today with the expectation of hearing the living word of God.

Regarding the original audience, we must remember that many of the prophet's contemporaries were asking whether there was any source of comfort left for a people stripped of self-defense, vulnerable before their captors, bitter of soul as they mourned in a foreign land. In our time there is no lack of self-appointed messengers of God who offer lavish promises of healing and deliverance regardless of the gravity of the suffering or the prospects of relief. Biblical faith offers no comparably facile answers to the agonizing questions of life. In fact, the tradents who handed down the writings that became Scripture did not hesitate to include books such as Job and Ecclesiastes that sharpened rather than blunted the questions of suffering

14

and evil. How different from the cheap comfort of many tele-vangelists is the sermon of Qoheleth: "Again I saw all the op-pressions that are practiced under the sun. Look, the tears of the oppressed—with no one to comfort them! On the side of their oppressors there was power—with no one to comfort them" (Eccl. 4:1).

When the holy seers and prophets of Israel *did* proclaim a message of hope and comfort, they were engaging in something vastly different from cheap promises and wishful thinking; they were drawing from the depths of the Israelite covenant rela-tionship with the sovereign of the nations and discharging their duty as interpreters of the faith of Abraham and Moses. Specifi-cally, when Second Isaiah addresses a people mourning their loss of homeland and sacred shrines, he offers something dis-tinct from normal human condolences. He conveys a message as one commissioned by God to observe and then report on developments shaping the destiny of nations, events occurring within the sphere of divine providence. It is within the context of the prophetic office and the vocational understanding of Sec-ond Isaiah that we can begin to make sense of the words, "Com-fort, O comfort my people," and to understand the conceptual world they presuppose.

Finding language adequate to describe the ways of God is most difficult in every age. What we find in Isaiah 40 is a view of the divine realm that was widespread in the ancient Near East in biblical times. Well attested in the literature of both Mesopotamia and Canaan, it portrays the deliberations of an assembly of the gods that was believed to order and govern the universe. Within that assembly decisions were made that deter-mined the destiny of its august members as well as the fates of human beings. Thus in the Babylonian creation myth, *Enūma eliš*, the gods in executive session commission Marduk to repel the threat posed by the rebellious deity Tiamat and her hosts. Marduk's victory results in both the restoration of peace in heaven and the creation and ordering of human society.

Within the Old Testament, the deliberations of the divine council are portrayed at points where the ultimate meaning and cause of a particular happening or situation are sought. In I Kings 22:19–24 the situation involved is the course of a war between Israel and Syria. In the first two chapters of the Book of Job, the question at issue is the reason behind the sufferings of a righteous man. Closely related to our text in Isaiah 40 is the

15

account found earlier in Isaiah in chapter 6, where Isaiah of Jerusalem describes his experience of being commissioned a prophet as an event occurring within the divine council. These biblical applications of the council motif, while continuous with the general pattern found throughout much of the ancient world, also reveal one of those characteristics which set Israelite religion apart: Whereas the parallel texts outside the Bible depict various gods, identifying them by name and acknowledging their distinct realms of authority, the related passages in Hebrew Scripture subordinate the hosts of heaven to the one deity who exercises sole power and authority, the God of Israel. The question can easily follow, Why, then, did biblical authors continue to utilize the symbolism of the divine council?

On one level, this question can be answered historically. The earliest surviving manuscript tradition of Deuteronomy 32:8–9 describes an understanding of the divine realm that early Israel shared with neighboring cultures. Each nation had its patron deity. Collectively the gods of the nations constituted a divine council. Over the course of the centuries and as a result of the questions posed by interaction with other nations and their deities, the people of Israel were prodded into reflecting on the scope of their God's reign. Especially the exilic setting that forms the backdrop of Second Isaiah pressed this question with unprecedented urgency. Psalm 82, when contrasted with Deuteronomy 32:8–9, indicates where Israel emerged on the question of God's reign: Among the gods of the divine council, Israel's God alone proved to be committed to compassionate justice and protection of the vulnerable, with the result that all gods except Yahweh were stripped of their power, leaving one God alone as sovereign over the nations.

As interesting as is the historical explanation of why a council of divine beings remains in the biblical narrative even after their sovereign power has been removed, the theological dimension of the question is far more important. We know that while Israel drew generously upon the repertoire of mythic motifs of the wider culture, its borrowing was not indiscriminate. For example, the ubiquitous fertility aspects of the deity that lay at the heart of most ancient Near Eastern cults were rejected by the dominant religious groups within Israel. What theological significance, then, did ancient Israel recognize in the notion of the divine assembly that led to the preservation of this archaic motif?

16

To judge from hints both in Second Isaiah and in the other parts of Scripture with which Second Isaiah has closest affinities, especially the Psalter, the notion of the divine assembly, which on the surface may seem to compromise the First Commandment, has the opposite effect by being drawn into the exaltation of the sovereignty of the one true God. Later in Isaiah 40, God speaks thus:

> To whom then will you compare me,
>   or who is my equal? says the Holy One.
> Lift up your eyes on high and see:
>   Who created these?
> He who brings out their host and numbers them,
>   calling them all by name;
> because he is great in strength,
>   mighty in power,
>   not one is missing.
>
> (Isa. 40:25–26)

There is an abundance and extravagance to creation that is not limited to the mundane. And *all* of it redounds to the glory of the one God. God's sovereignty is not diminished by the presence of the divine assembly, whether its members are portrayed as the stars (40:26) or as executive members of a deliberating council (Isa. 6:1–9; 40:1–11; Job 1). The realms that serve God reach far beyond human ken. And that implies that there is a source of comfort even in a creation vast beyond human comprehension and in a world filled with awesome powers capable of deadly destruction. For ultimately there are not multiple powers that must be reckoned with, but only one Power, a gracious, just power whose nature comes to expression in acts of forgiveness and redemption.

The unity of all creation under the sovereign power of God is expressed powerfully by Psalm 148:

> Praise the LORD!
> Praise the LORD from the heavens;
>   praise him in the heights!
> Praise him, all his angels;
>   praise him, all his host!
> Praise him, sun and moon;
>   praise him, all you shining stars!
> Praise him, you highest heavens,
>   and you waters above the heavens!
> Let them praise the name of the LORD,
>   for he commanded and they were created.

17

> He established them forever and ever;
>> he fixed their bounds, which cannot be passed.
> Praise the LORD from the earth,
>> you sea monsters and all deeps,
> fire and hail, snow and frost,
>> stormy wind fulfilling his command!

Once again the reality of the heavenly hosts is not denied. Even the reality of the unruly chaos waters (cf. *tĕhôm* of Gen. 1:2 and Tiamat of Babylonian mythology) is not denied. But their sting is taken away, their bounds have been set, as they are drawn into the purposes of the one true God. Life no longer is pressed toward an abyss by whimsical, bickering gods. Life is firmly set within a universe governed by the just laws of the gracious sovereign of all.

We are now perhaps in a better position to understand those magisterial opening words of Second Isaiah, "Comfort, O comfort my people." As plural imperatives, they issue a command to those standing in attendance on the God of the universe, a command to speak words of comfort to the people of God, a people further specified as Jerusalem. Thus the sovereign of the world draws the sublime beings of heaven into the mission of comforting, pardoning, and redeeming the broken nation. In a world dreading the influences of various divine forces, some good, some evil, Israel receives the assurance that the heavenly beings constituting the divine council are participants in the redemptive drama of the one true God. As the divine hosts join in praise of God in Isaiah 6 and Psalm 148, so too those same hosts here receive God's command to bring a word of comfort and release to Israel. The anguishing human doubt expressed by Ecclesiastes is dispelled; there is comfort for the oppressed, the power of the oppressor is set aside. God reigns, and God is about to act on Israel's behalf.

In the sixth chapter of Isaiah, the beings attending upon God sing God's praise. In our passage, they obey God's command. The biblical authors are not timid when it comes to discerning the scope of God's authority. The universe teems with life, with monsters of sea and land, cherubim and seraphim, creatures in the netherworld and in heaven, all of them together forming an assembly subservient to God's will.

18

When Second Isaiah identifies the source of his message of consolation and hope, he traces it to nothing less than the nerve center of the universe, which is a place hardly dull and moribund but filled with action and power. In customary prophetic style, he becomes a messenger of the divine word by being drawn into this deliberative center. In contrast to the call narratives of Isaiah (chap. 6), Jeremiah (chap. 1), and Ezekiel (chaps. 1—3), however, the prophetic "I" recedes into the background, being overshadowed by the glory of God as in no other biblical depiction of the divine assembly. Even the sole first-person reference to the prophet in verse 6 is textually uncertain (see below). This magnification of the divine glory, however, does not diminish the persuasiveness of the prophet's message; rather, it enhances its intrinsic power through symbols that open up to the prophet's audience both the heavenly source of divine sovereignty and the presence of God in earthly agents and events.

Appropriately, then, Second Isaiah opens with a description of happenings in the divine assembly. This issues forth in a series of divine commands. First, the attendants in the assembly are commanded by God to "comfort, comfort my people, speak tenderly to Jerusalem." This word of comfort has specific content: The era of warfare under which Israel has suffered incalculable loss and shame has come to an end. Termination of conflict, however, is not attributed to luck or chance. It is given specific theological grounding: Peace has returned as a result of the restoration of a proper relation between Israel and her God, that is, "her iniquity is pardoned" (v. 2, RSV).

This tie between Second Isaiah's message of pardon and the theme of divine forgiveness is of fundamental significance in biblical faith. In the preexilic period the dominant message of the prophets was one of impending divine judgment, whereas prophets who were delivering promises of peace and prosperity repeatedly were dismissed as false messengers. "They have healed the wound of my people lightly, saying, 'Peace, peace,' when there is no peace," Jeremiah charges (Jer. 6:14, RSV). So, what is the difference between the message of peace proclaimed by Hananiah, which Jeremiah condemns as false, and the message of Second Isaiah? The answer to this question underscores the contextual nature of God's word in the Bible. In the case of Hananiah we find a prophet offering assurances to an unrepentant, unchastened, and arrogant people that they would not suffer divine judgment. Second Isaiah, in contrast, is addressing a people that has suffered grievously and through repentance has become receptive to God's word that "she has

19

received from the LORD's hand double for all her sins" (Isa. 40:2).

What is consistent throughout the history of biblical prophecy is God's steadfast commitment to the covenant relationship. Whether the divine response was in judgment or in forgiveness was inextricably bound up with the spiritual state of the people, as manifested both in their patterns of worship and in their response to God's will as formulated in the law (cf. Lam. 4:22). Although Second Isaiah portrays God as unrivaled in splendor, his God is not one who forces in place a plan of history but rather One who engages personally with Israel within the terms of an intimate bond. Thus both the moral character of reality and the profundity of divine love are upheld. Indeed, that Second Isaiah does not downplay the fact that Israel's defeat at the hands of the Babylonians was an act of divine judgment upon Israel's sin (42:24–25) contributes powerfully to the credibility of his announcement of salvation.

In contrast to the message of false prophets that Dietrich Bonhoeffer so aptly called "cheap grace" (p. 35), we find here what another author has called "severe mercy" (Vanauken). The deliverance that God prepares is not promised to a people whose love is as fleeting as the morning mist and who would promptly nullify divine blessing through persistence in sin, but to a people brought to its senses by facing up to the gravity of its iniquity and thus preparing for true deliverance through repentance.

The first divine command has placed Israel at a historical turning point. It is a turning point defined by divine initiative. And it reveals that a portal of hope has been opened up to Israel by the removal of the obstacle that had cut Israel off from its God, the obstacle of sin now swept away by divine forgiveness. At this turning point and through this portal, what will be the nature of the reentry of the divine healer and restorer?

Second Isaiah does not set forth the details of national reconstruction. Instead, he artfully unfolds a vision of the restoration of blessing in place of the chaos of warfare. This is not to say that he is a utopian dreamer either. At appropriate points he will not hesitate to relate his vision to the specific political realities of his day. For his God is not a God confined in ethereal splendor to the divine council, nor is his God a light only to the inner life of the individual. But lest the meaning of God's return to a repentant people be reduced to narrow human projects,

20

Second Isaiah sustains the cosmic scope of the divine command. In verse 3, we find ourselves still listening in on the proceedings of the divine assembly.

A second command is issued: Those attending upon the Lord are to prepare a way for God in the wilderness. As in the case of the divine assembly, here too we find the language of a common ancient Near Eastern motif, namely, the processional way along which the god, represented by the cult image, was carried in the central annual religious festival. But once again the very borrowing of the motif underscores the uniqueness of Israel's God. In Isaiah 46:7 our prophet gives a vivid portrait of the Babylonian procession in which Marduk was borne around the wall of the city and then returned to his resting place in the temple:

> They lift it to their shoulders, they carry it,
> they set it in its place, and it stands there;
> it cannot move from its place.

It is not a cult drama in which human attendants strain under the weight of their god and then return him to a dais from which he has no ability to move himself; it is, rather, a cosmic drama in which a way is prepared for the God who orders the heavens and unfolds a plan for all the nations of the earth. Much ink has been applied to the question of whether Second Isaiah was intending to give a literal description of the leveling and clearing that would create a highway through the rocks and crags of the wilderness. This line of inquiry fails to recognize that the narrative develops further a set of symbols depicting the divine provenance of Israel's deliverance. The restoration that Israel is about to experience is not the product of human endeavor but originates in God's gracious reentry into the life of the outcast nation. The nature of the symbolism and its intended force can be grasped by comparing verses 3 through 5 with Isaiah 34 and 35, two chapters that, on both stylistic and thematic grounds, are best attributed to Second Isaiah. After chapter 34 has depicted the collapse of the created order that provides the cosmic context for the calamity of Israel's past experience, chapter 35, again with cosmic embrace, portrays a restoration of creation to a beauty and splendor that both manifests the glory of God and sets the context for Israel's deliverance. Before Second Isaiah moves to explain how specific historical figures and events are parts of God's plan, he establishes with utmost clarity the universal scope of God's reign. What transpires on the historical plane is the aspect of a cosmic drama that is visible to human beings.

The second command culminates with an explicit formulation of the ultimate purpose and source of the impending turn of events: "The glory of the LORD shall be revealed, and all people shall see it together, for the mouth of the LORD has spoken" (v. 5). The concept of God's "glory" (Heb. *kābôd*) is theologically among the most important in Second Isaiah. It has a rich history in the faith of Israel. In the Priestly stratum of the Pentateuch, God's glory is closely associated with the tabernacle. It is the manifestation of God's presence, in the display of both wrath and favor. In Ezekiel, God's glory leaves the defiled temple and joins the exiles, until such time when it can return to the restored temple in Jerusalem.

Second Isaiah follows the clue of Isaiah of Jerusalem in drawing out another aspect of this theological concept. In the call narrative in chapter 6, Isaiah hears the praise of the seraphs: "The whole earth is full of [the LORD's] glory" (6:3). This is an expression of the universality of God's reign. Second Isaiah in turn recognizes that the preparation for the Lord's coming will have been accomplished when the universality of God's glory is recognized by all human beings, a theme revisited and embellished with vivid detail in the beautiful hymn in 42:10–12. At first blush one may get the picture of a rather disagreeable deity in 42:8 and 48:11 who insists, "My glory I give to no other." But this must be understood in relation to the polemic waged by the prophet against idolatry. To ascribe divine glory to anyone but the true God is to be received in the most egregious way. It is to become bound to deadly falsity. In contrast, to acknowledge the glory of the Lord is to be drawn to the truth that banishes all lies and restores health and harmony to all creation. The revealing of God's glory, and, correspondingly from the human side, the joyous acknowledgment of that glory, represents the revealing of the truth that alone can save an endangered world.

In 43:7, Second Isaiah will develop one other aspect of the concept of divine glory. Yahweh is pictured returning the scattered of Israel to their home, "whom I created for my glory." Israel's presence among the families of the nations is for the purpose of the revealing of this saving glory. Thus we begin to see the richness of the theme introduced at the end of the second command with the words, "The glory of the LORD shall be revealed, and all people shall see it together" (v. 5).

In verse 6 a third divine command is issued within the divine assembly. In contrast to the preceding two commands in which the imperative is directed to the divine attendants in the plural, here the imperative is in the singular. To whom is the command "Proclaim!" directed? The answer is contained in the next phrase, "And . . . asked," but unfortunately the versions are divided over the question of the pronoun governing this verb. The Isaiah scroll from Qumran reads, "And she asked," apparently referring to Jerusalem/Zion of verse 2. "And I asked" is the way the ancient translators rendered it in Greek. Although the evidence remains ambiguous, the majority of interpreters seem justified in preferring the first-person reference, especially if this passage is intended to describe the source of the prophet's authority in the divine council. As in Isaiah 6, the prophet speaks in the name of the Lord because he has been commissioned. Although silent to this point as he stands amidst the members of the divine council, he now responds to the one who has addressed him: "What shall I proclaim?"

If the ancient texts provided an equivalent to our quotation mark system, we would have a better clue to the next problem, namely, the identity of the speaker or speakers of the second half of verse 6 and verses 7–11. Although certainty again eludes us, it seems plausible to attribute verses 6*b* and 7 to the prophet, verse 8 to the heavenly voice that issued the command to the prophet in verse 6, and verses 9–11 to the prophet.

The prophet's initial response to the awesome spectacle of the divine assembly resembles that of Isaiah of Jerusalem, who cried, "Woe is me! For I am lost; for I am a man of unclean lips, and I dwell in the midst of a people of unclean lips; for my eyes have seen the King, the LORD of hosts!" (6:5, RSV). Second Isaiah borrows the language of lament familiar to us from the Psalter (cf. Ps. 90:5–6): "All flesh is grass." People of faith from Moses on have responded to an awareness of God's presence with this dread sense of unworthiness and nothingness. Whereas this sense of human fragility harbored by unfaith leads to despair, faith creates of it a portal for encounter with the one reality that does not fade like the flower. The divine herald picks up the prophet's lament and carries it the decisive step through that portal:

23

INTERPRETATION

> The grass withers, the flower fades;
> but the word of our God will stand forever.
>
> (Isa. 40:8)

Little wonder that the lesson concerning the transiency of all flesh strikes dread in the human heart as does nothing else. Human conquerors build their empires under the illusion of the durability of human fortifications and fortunes. The image of an awesome wind that reduces all to nothingness attacks the very heart of human schemes. Yet there is one group for whom that image contains the possibility of hope, namely, those who suffer under the brutal might of the oppressor. The announcement that "all flesh is grass" removes all distinctions in status and power. All human beings stand on equal footing as "grass." One distinction alone remains, that between those who open their hearts to God as deliverer and those who revile God as enemy and rival.

The prophet, representative of those looking in faith to God as deliverer, proceeds from the only secure basis for hope and assurance, the eternal word of God, and issues a command of his own. Zion/Jerusalem, the recipient of God's words of comfort in verse 1, is here commissioned to proclaim a joyous announcement to the rest of the land. The admonition attached to this commission, "Fear not!" is further indication of influence from the lament form found in the Psalms, and in Second Isaiah it becomes one of the marks of the oracle of salvation. Those who had cried out from their anguish to God for deliverance need fear no longer, for they are about to experience God's intervention on their behalf. No longer would earthly oppressors determine their fate. The barrier of sin that had cut them off from their source had been removed.

With the joyous announcement that Zion/Jerusalem is to shout forth from the heights, we come to the climactic point of the introductory unit of Second Isaiah: "Here is your God!" (v. 9). Here a word that strikes terror into the hearts of the ungodly becomes for repentant Israel a word addressing Israel's dilemma in exile with the joyous proclamation that Israel had not been abandoned to the oppressor but was under the loving care of a God both great and good.

24   The temptations of hopelessness and despair that plagued Israel in the aftermath of the Babylonian conquest fed on the twin doubts that perennially afflict those enduring grievous suf-

fering, the one questioning God's power to change the situation, the other calling into question God's goodness and love. With consummate skill, the announcement of God's advent is elaborated with two images, each image addressing one of the twin doubts of the exiles.

The first image addresses the fear that on foreign Babylonian soil the gods of Israel's conquerors were in power and that Yahweh had been stripped of his power. In verse 10, Israel's God is described with the imagery of the Divine Warrior, mighty and victorious as he comes to deliver his people. Verse 11 offers as counterpoint an equally vivid image speaking to those who felt that in their world of international upheaval, Israel could not expect from its God the loving care for which it longed so profoundly. It is the image of the shepherd who gives personal protection to every one of his sheep. "GOD comes with might, . . . he will gather the lambs in his arms." The God announced by the herald of good tidings was a God both *able* and *willing* to save. Israel need fear no longer!

The passage with which Second Isaiah opens his proclamation is about divine absence and divine presence. Israel knew what absence was about, having served its term like a prisoner removed from people and places Israel loved. Israel had been incarcerated in the gloom of warfare and desolation and hopelessness. In the bitterness of its laments, Israel had asked whether God cared any longer.

The transition from divine absence to divine presence was not an easy one. Great distances, awesome armies, and powerful rulers marked the landscape on which the Jewish exiles found themselves. The prophet did not call for human rearmament, whether in the military or moral sense of the word. The prophet directed the attention of the people to one reality, before whom all earthly powers were mere grass. Although glorious in power, this power before whom every power is nothing differs from them in another respect. God is a God of compassion, and he now addresses the people with forgiveness. And he promises to return to deliver them from their bondage. He will gather them and carry them and gently lead them like a shepherd.

There is nothing like beginning a message with basics. And nothing in human existence is as basic as divine absence and divine presence. Life with God has a center, has meaning, has a source of healing and reconciliation and great joy. Life with-

25

out God is doomed to confusion, futility, and finally the dread of eternal darkness.

The prophet begins with basics. There will be much to cover regarding all the obstacles that human beings set up to remove themselves from God's presence and the resistance they muster to avoid confessing that they are powerless to save themselves. The prophet will argue and plead and cajole; but all of this is done against the background of the opening scene of the drama, in which the God who has been absent is seen returning: "Here is your God!" It is the announcement that can transform the darkest tragedy into the deepest blessing.

Isaiah 40:12–31
An Argument with Doubt

Although Isaiah 40:12–31 forms a new unit, it is closely related to the preceding eleven verses. Verses 1–11 had announced a decisive turning point in the life of a broken and humiliated community. A debt of sin that had cut the people off from their source had been paid, the life-giving glory of the Lord was about to be revealed, and a lost nation was again to be gathered and shepherded. The major themes of Second Isaiah had been sounded like a brilliant blast of a trumpet in those verses. But the people who heard them doubtless found their minds simultaneously flooded with questions: Given the might of the Babylonian captors and the splendor of their gods, did the God of Israel possess the power to deliver? How could the glory of the Lord be revealed in a world dominated by emperors and their armies? The former of these two questions is addressed in, among other places, the section to which we now turn, 40:12–31. The latter question elicits the prophet's response in subsequent descriptions of the historical agent whom God was enlisting as the instrument of the divine glory.

Isaiah 40:12–31 is a disputation. That is, it addresses and argues with the doubts that impede an exiled people's embracing the message of God's imminent entry into their lives to restore their community to integrity in its homeland: "Given the daunting power of the empires and their rulers and deities, how can we believe that our God can accomplish our deliver-

26

ance? Given the complexity of the cosmos and its celestial hosts, can we really believe that *one* God controls our destiny?"

In characteristic disputational style, the prophet draws out his audience through a series of vivid rhetorical questions. One by one, the doubts that block their wholehearted affirmation are raised to consciousness and rigorously scrutinized. Verses 12–17 probe the divine assembly and the nations over which its members preside to determine whether Israel's God is merely one actor under the command of others. Verses 18–26 display Yahweh's rivals, the national idols, the rulers who represent them on earth, and the stars that manifest their celestial power, again with the intention of locating the *ultimate* determiner of creation's destiny. Finally, verses 27–31 bring the disputation to a climax by confronting the Jewish community explicitly with their questions of doubt and proclaiming boldly the sole sovereignty of God and God's abundant grace that makes available to those who transcend doubt through belief the power to persevere and to overcome.

Intellectual prowess and poetic eloquence are both manifested in 40:12–31. We encounter a philosophical mind equal to Job's in a series of rhetorical questions resembling those found in Job 38—41 (e.g., "Who determined [the earth's] measurements, . . . who shut in the sea with doors, . . . who has the wisdom to number the clouds?" Job 38:5, 8, 37). Nagging doubts that threaten to tear a people away from their spiritual roots are not dismissed with facile pronouncements. Rather, the prophet honors the integrity of their questions and meets the people where they are, inviting them to enter into a shared struggle to grasp the central mystery that unites all of life under one supernal hope and joy. For such a task the mode adopted by the prophet is a fitting one, the mode of a disputation or argument combining rigorous thought with poetic imagination.

The repertoire of Second Isaiah is not limited to this mode. In addressing the second nagging question regarding the manner in which the divine glory is manifested in the historical experiences of the people, he will switch to a more empirical approach, pointing to the campaign strategy and foreign policy of Cyrus as historical evidence of divine purpose and even presenting Cyrus's own propaganda as evidence of the instrumental role he was playing in God's plan for Israel. The immediate objective in 40:12–31, however, is to reopen the minds and hearts of the people to the incomparable majesty of God and to

27

restore their sense of location in a vast universe. For this purpose the prophet effectively applies the genre of the disputation.

The unity of Second Isaiah's vision is seen in the inseparability of creation and redemption in his thought. Opening the minds and hearts of the people to the possibility of deliverance from bondage begins with displaying the vastness of the universe as evidence of God's majesty and power. To contemplate the One who can weigh the mountains and measure the heavens is to lift the mind toward the One who alone is capable of returning a captive nation to its home. The actions described in verse 12 such as "measure" and "mark off with a span" draw on the images of cosmogony associated with the great creation myths of antiquity. Established already in the Genesis creation accounts and preserved all the way through the history of Jewish and Christian biblical interpretation is the confession that the designer of the universe is the savior of humanity. To begin hope for deliverance with a sense of reverence before the Creator creates a safeguard against idolatrously viewing God as an instrumental genie. Hope for the future ceases to hinge on hedged bets on potentially useful religious connections and is secured instead through reconciliation with the source of all being and well-being. Viewing the Jewish community's deliverance within the context of cosmic renewal also lifts the vision of the people above selfish preoccupation to vital concern for all of creation.

The kind of faith that allows a people to look to the future with hope must not be undermined by the reintroduction of polytheism. As soon as one's universe becomes populated with multiple gods or entities of any sort that are accorded the right to claim ultimate allegiance, faith fades off into doubt and moral chaos. In verses 13–20 the prophet therefore presses his audience further, challenging them to search their minds to see whether their concept of reality leaves any corner governed by rival deities. Is Yahweh, like the Babylonian patron god Marduk, dependent upon the advice of the god of wisdom, Ea (v. 13)? Is "the path of justice," which in Israel's moral universe is the "straight highway" that will permit the people to cross the wilderness on their homeward journey, given to God by a heavenly architect, a goddess akin to the Egyptian Ma'at (v. 14)? The prophet invites his audience to cleanse their minds of all such idolatry and to renew their sole commitment to the one true God.

28

For many of the exiles, it was not only the thought of rival deities that tore away at their faith. Something much more concrete loomed before them, the mighty empires, greatest among which was Babylon, ruthless conqueror and captor that had shattered the dreams of the descendants of Abraham, Isaac, and Jacob. The prophet moves from interrogatives to a series of audacious pronouncements that reapply the creation imagery of verse 12: The mighty nations are a mere drop in a bucket and dust on the scales, nothing before God, and thus nothing to be feared (vv. 15–17).

The diatribe against idols in verses 18–20 is frequently assigned by critics to a later hand. This may be due to the failure of modern, rational minds to grasp the significance of idols in antiquity. In the overall structure of the disputation, idols fit into a progression fully congruous with an ancient Near Eastern worldview. Having first described the created world under the major headings of the prevailing cosmology (cosmic waters—heavens—earth), the prophet next invoked the concept of a divine council as a heavenly decision-making body, followed by the nations, and now, in verses 18–20, by the idols that manifest the presence of the gods in the nations and their cults. The prophet knows that this will not be his sole discourse on the subject (cf. 44:9–20), and so his reference occupies the same brief space given to the other entities in his disputation. At any rate, far from giving the appearance of an interpolation, the mention of idols is essential to the argument, so prominently were divine images displayed in the religious ceremonies of the Babylonians. Later, in chapter 46, the prophet describes the procession of Bel (one of Marduk's names) and Nebo (Nabu, the Babylonian scribe deity) and cites a question asked by God that closely resembles 40:18: "To whom will you liken me and make me equal, and compare me, as though we were alike?" (46:5). This question is followed in 46:6–7 by a description of the artistry of the goldsmith and the securing of the idol in its place, again in close parallel to 40:18–20. In a litany of impediments to faith, it was thus natural for Second Isaiah to include idols, and to do so with the aid of a descriptive pattern he used elsewhere as well.

The staccato effect produced by the quick succession of questions in verse 21 suggests a mood of exasperation. The prophet seems incredulous that the people have so completely forgotten the fundamental teachings of their tradition as to fail

29

to supply clear answers to the series of questions in the disputation. The oneness and the incomparability of God are as old as creation and as simple as the First Commandment. Verse 22 captures in one unforgettable image the lesson that no member of the Israelite community should ever forget, that of the creator God seated above "the circle of the earth," from which perspective its inhabitants appear like grasshoppers. The way is thereby cleared to relativize the status of earthly rulers, who, far from being able to rival God in creative ability, are no more than the "naught and nothingness" that existed prior to creation! God has merely to blow upon them and they share the fate of the grass described earlier in verse 7.

Then what about the hosts of heaven, those astral deities believed then as now by many people to determine the fate of mortals? Like all other rivals, they too are located by the prophet among the objects that God has created (v. 26). The heavens are cleared of the myriad willful powers that cause people to live in the dread of superstition. One Being reigns supreme, the moral foundation of the world is secured, the people can hope again, *if* they embrace the ancient confession that there is no God save Yahweh and place their undivided trust in the loving and just sovereign of the universe.

The disputation, by advancing through the obstacles to faith, has prepared the way for the prophet's culminating confession in verses 27–31. It begins with words that indicate that the prophet must refute arguments arising from the people that would undercut the entire case built up in verses 12–26. Detractors maintain that God does not see, that God does not care, that God has no interest in the individual's right. We hear exasperation in the voice of the prophet: "Have you not known? Have you not heard?" (v. 21). After all, this godly person has used all of the eloquence and persuasiveness available to prove the point! But they do not get it. So he repeats the central confession again: "The LORD is the everlasting God, the Creator of the ends of the earth." Then the problem becomes clearer. They are looking for magic, not for miracle; for a genie, not for the Creator of the universe. Those looking for simple proofs need to hear one more truth about the Creator of the universe: "his understanding is unsearchable" (v. 28).

At this point only those with the faith to "wait for the LORD" are left in the prophet's audience. Those looking for immediate fixes, for magical cures, are off invoking the rows of idols that seek their business. But to those few who surrender their lives to the everlasting God, the prophet has concluding words of encouragement that surpass all of the cheap promises of the idol market: The one who does not faint or grow weary gives power to the faint and strengthens the powerless.

The prophet-poet, after having taken the intellectual and existential doubts of the people seriously, demolishing the credibility of all rivals and celebrating the incomparability of God, thus brings the disputation to a close with the most eloquent poetry of all. This is the poetry of empowerment for those who allow their vision to be corrected by the denunciation of all idols and the affirmation of the incomparable power and wisdom of God. It is the empowerment of those who center their lives not on their petty personal "gods" but on the Creator of the universe. Verses 27–31 summarize the cardinal points of the entire unit by juxtaposing the essential poles of the relationship between God and the community:

> The LORD is the everlasting God,
>   the Creator of the ends of the earth.
>   (Isa. 40:28)

> He gives power to the faint,
>   and strengthens the powerless.
>   (Isa. 40:29)

To have brought his audience to this point of affirmation is to have prepared them for everything that God will teach them in the messages that follow. The fundamental lesson that prepares the human heart for the entrance of God is the lesson of God's oneness and uniqueness. It is the lesson that cultivates out of human powerlessness not helplessness and despair but openness to the power that alone can save, God's power. It is the lesson that sweeps the universe clean of all distractions. It is the lesson reiterated by Kierkegaard, "The purity of heart is to will one thing." So long as the human heart harbors other ultimate loyalties besides God, it is lost in a sea of chaos. Augustine was one who spoke from personal experience: "Thou hast made us for Thyself and our hearts are restless till they rest in Thee" (*Confessions* 1.1).

Together, the two units of chapter 40 form a fitting introduction to the section of Scripture we call Second Isaiah. It is no surprise that these powerful words were chosen as an Advent lection by the early church, for they describe the heart of

31

biblical faith as the entry of God into the confusion of human affairs. Like the rush of a forceful storm wind, God's entry sweeps away every obstacle that stands between the community and its God, as tyrants fall like stubble and a way is made through the wilderness. Human images that make a mockery of the true God, distorted thinking that populates the universe with contentious powers, denial of the claims of justice arising from fear of aggressors and their armies—all such illegitimate claims to our hearts are removed to prepare for the entry of the only one deserving of awe and worship. The same divine breath that removes idols fills the purified heart with hope and a deep love for creation seen as God's domain. Second Isaiah, with the power of poetry, has begun well the task that will occupy him for the next fifteen chapters, the construction in words of a universe renewed and restored around its life-giving, loving Center.

At the same time that chapter 40 forms a fitting introduction to Second Isaiah, it can be viewed as a strategically placed epitome of the central message of the Book of Isaiah as a whole. If one theme can be identified as the cornerstone of the message of the eighth-century prophet Isaiah, it is the single-minded trust in God that banishes all false claimants to the human heart. Isaiah 2:5–22 witnesses the fall of all that proudly defies God, for "the LORD alone will be exalted in that day" (2:11). The invitation that Isaiah issued to the people rested on the foundation of God's sole reign:

> In returning and rest you shall be saved;
> in quietness and in trust shall be your strength.
> (Isa. 30:15)

Although the block of tradition commonly referred to as Third Isaiah (Isaiah 56—66) is darkened by the turmoil of a sharply divided community, the Advent theme of Isaiah 40 shines brightly at its center:

> See, your salvation comes;
> his reward is with him,
> and his recompense before him.
> (Isa. 62:11)

32   It is little wonder that the ancient church drew upon Isaiah 40 for one of its Advent lections. Its lesson remains the cardinal confession of biblical faith.

Isaiah 41:1–29
The Nations and Their Gods
in the Courtroom of History

Chapter 41 draws the attention of the prophet's audience to the drama of the courtroom. Twice the judicial assembly is called to order, first in verse 1 and again in verse 21, with the first session recording its judgment in verses 4*b*–5 and the second in verses 24 and 29. By simulating a type of legal proceeding that is familiar to his listeners, the prophet is able to raise from a fresh new angle the question of the obstacles standing in the way of Israel's placing sole trust in God, with focus this time specifically on the Babylonian cults and their gods. Within this forensic setting, where the contending parties are invited to present their cases for judgment, the foreign gods are portrayed as utterly helpless in word or deed, leading to the pronouncement that they are nothing, even as their works are nothing, and that anyone who lends credence to their arrogation to power is an abomination (vv. 24 and 29). Adding to the dramatic effect of the whole chapter is the skill with which Second Isaiah interlards the stages in the legal process with God's words of assurance and promises of salvation to the faithful community, words and promises that arise directly from the fact established by the trial proceedings: The rival gods—despite the heroic efforts of those who create their images and officiate over their rituals—are nothing, leaving God as the sole power in the universe.

The relation of chapter 41 to the preceding chapter offers a vivid illustration of the subtlety that characterizes the literary structure of Isaiah 40—55. For decades, scholars have divided over the question of whether the compositional technique of Second Isaiah is best described in terms of short, discrete units modeled after traditional genres (Westermann) or as one long, unified composition constructed out of strophes (Muilenburg). We have chosen a position that mediates between these extremes, arguing that Second Isaiah modeled much of what he wrote after conventional genres as a means of catching the

33

attention of his audience, but adding that he did so with a freedom that allowed him both to relate his message to concrete situations of his day and to create a thematic unity that carries the interest of readers from one section to the next (see our discussion of literary qualities, in Overview).

On one level the first verse of chapter 41 starts something new. After the final verses of chapter 40 have built up to a powerful climax, 41:1 introduces a new scene with the summons to the islands and the nations. But intonations from what preceded continue to reverberate in the new chapter. The connection can be seen by recalling 40:27, in which the people registered their complaint against God:

> My way is hidden from the LORD,
>   and my right *(mišpāṭ)* is disregarded by my God.

Half of the prophetic reply to this complaint was given in the disputation in 40:12–31, a reply summarized nicely in the verse that follows the complaint:

> Have you not known? Have you not heard?
> The LORD is the everlasting God,
>   the Creator of the ends of the earth.
>   (Isa. 40:28)

The disputation established God as the sovereign over all that exists by systematically refuting the claims of all rivals. But was such disputation sufficient to complete the reinstatement of Israel's right *(mišpāṭ)?* Does the fact that God rules over the heavens and the earth remove from Israel the oppression of exile and the pains of servitude under the Babylonian empire? A second argument needed to be added to the first, the argument that God, although exalted above all earthly powers, nevertheless is *personally* concerned with this specific people in their bondage. Therefore the people could be confident that even in Babylon their Lord remains the force directing the events of human history to accomplish their liberation.

This second half of Second Isaiah's reply to the people's complaint therefore provides a clear link with the first half by returning to the key word of 40:27:

> Let us together draw near for *judgment (mišpāṭ).*
>   (Isa. 41:1)

34

As God's sovereignty over all creation had been demonstrated in chapter 40, the prophet now seeks to establish that God was guiding the specific events of human history toward the goal of Israel's release. The rival deities, on the other hand, were utterly lacking in power to obstruct God's purposes. Whereas the prophet had utilized the genre of the disputation to establish the fact of God's universal sovereignty in the previous chapter, he now applies the trial speech to demonstrate how that sovereignty becomes active in the world of kings, slaves, and armies.

The first verse of chapter 41 gets right to the heart of the trial: The gods, represented here by their subject peoples, are summoned to court to defend their claims to divine power. The interrogation in verse 2 focuses specifically on the historical figure who was reshaping the political world of that time, Cyrus the Persian. Although Second Isaiah creates an aura of suspense by withholding explicit mention of his name until the propitious moment reached in the Cyrus oracle of 44:24—45:7, his listeners, and supposedly the gods being interrogated, could have no doubts regarding the referent. Cyrus, in the brief span of a decade beginning with his removal of rival claims to the Persian crown in 550 B.C.E., brought the region of the Euphrates under his control, attacked Sardis, and, after defeating King Croesus, added Lydia to his growing empire. Finally he went on to conquer territories as far to the east as Afghanistan.

By the time of this trial speech, anyone in the Western Mediterranean who possessed knowledge of political matters could see clearly that Cyrus's next move would be against Babylon. The priests of Marduk were no exception, for their king, Nabonidus, had abandoned their holy city to restore and develop the cult of the moon god Sin in the northern commercial center of Haran. In a time when the entire area from Egypt to India was being recast politically, every thoughtful mind must have turned to the question of the impact that such sweeping events would have on personal life and national destiny.

It is certain that Second Isaiah was among the reflective minds seeking to interpret the meaning of such unusual happenings. For community leaders of every age who bear a sense of responsibility for their people, the task of seeking meaning during times of fundamental change is a demanding one. The late church historian of the Nazi period, Klaus Scholder, reported in a lecture in Tübingen in 1982 that when Hitler defeated the French army and began the German occupation of France, Dietrich Bonhoeffer, at a gathering of church leaders in Berlin, raised the question of how such a turn of events should be interpreted theologically. Who was directing such an epoch-making change? What was Hitler's role here? What was the proper response of the church? Scholder even reports that Bonhoeffer for a short time pondered the unthinkable, namely, whether Hitler, through his stunning chain of successes, was manifesting a strange new act of God.

Second Isaiah was also witnessing earthshaking events. The foundations of the known world were collapsing, and new foundations were being laid by a military-political genius whose empire had already become the largest ever recorded in history. What was the significance of these events, politically, yes, but, even more important, theologically? What sort of force was determining the destiny of the nations? Were the battles between hostile armies reflecting the clash between rival gods? Were the Babylonian priests right as they abandoned their king and clamored to realign themselves on the side of the new political power, with the claim that it was their god Marduk who was directing the fate of the nations?

Second Isaiah, the prophet of uncommon poetic and imaginative power, chose the dramatic form of the trial to adjudicate these questions. With the same rigor that he applied in the preceding disputation, he presses the central question on the gods and nations gathered together for judgment:

> Who has roused a victor from the east,
>   summoned him to his service?
> He delivers up nations to him,
>   and tramples kings under foot;
> he makes them like dust with his sword,
>   like driven stubble with his bow.
> He pursues them and passes on safely,
>   scarcely touching the path with his feet.
> Who has performed and done this,
>   calling the generations from the beginning?
> (Isa. 41:2–4a)

Throughout the history of the great religions of the world, the crowning act in the human response to divine grace has been the doxological ascription of incomparable power and glory to God. In religions such as Judaism, Christianity, and Islam, however, faithfulness elicits a more mundane response as well, that of relating divine will to the everyday realities with which human beings must cope. It is a responsibility fraught with danger. What political regime has lacked its "prophet" to declare that its acts of aggression and brutality are an expression of ultimate purpose? Yet for the community of faith and its prophets to withdraw from the realm of politics and international affairs is to abdicate the world to the ruthless and ungodly devices of tyrants. Bonhoeffer, it could be argued, was obliged by his spiritual calling to address the events of his day in the light of his understanding of divine purpose. And although one can see the trap into which Nazi propaganda could easily have led him, as it had so many of his fellow theologians, Bonhoeffer possessed a sufficiently profound and informed theology of history to break through, in the midst of crisis, to prophetic clarity and faithful testimony unto death.

Second Isaiah was grounded as well in a theological perspective that was the legacy of centuries of prophetic reflection, action, and martyrdom. In chapter 40, we glimpsed something of that perspective in relation to his understanding of God's glory. We shall add to our knowledge of his perspective in discussing the Cyrus oracle and other passages. Second Isaiah measured the success of Cyrus against a very stringent set of criteria, against concepts such as God's universal justice, divine compassion, and the culmination of creation in doxology. We draw from Second Isaiah an enrichment of our own understanding of the relation of faith to politics, not by joining the parade of those who are quick to fit an international event or natural disaster into an eschatological timetable, but by seeking to understand the vision that Second Isaiah held for the healing of all creation, from the haunts of wilderness beasts to the family of human beings to the movements of the stars. For only a vision of creation's restoration that is graciously infused with a divine love that is lavish enough for the healing of all creatures is equal to the precarious task of interpreting historical events in relation to divine intention.

Endowed with the divine gift of prophetic vision, Second Isaiah reported words pronounced by the divine Judge in the tribunal of the nations:

> I, the LORD, am first,
> and will be with the last.
> (Isa. 41:4*b*)

With this terse pronouncement the nations (and their gods!) were left trembling. An editor saw fit at this point to insert a

37

fragment (vv. 6–7), likely taken from the disputation in chapter 40, to ridicule those who manufacture idols and then claim that the products of their hands guide the events of history! In its own way this editorial addition contributes to the force of the trial scene in the first section of chapter 41 by setting the stage for celebration of the only agent who provides a sure foundation for life in a precarious world.

Verses 8–11 are personal and intimate. The God who has been praised as creator of the universe and the determiner of all destinies now draws near to assure the exiled people that they are embraced in tender love. The enduring quality of the relationship is highlighted by reference to Israel's ancestors, Jacob/Israel and Abraham. The words used to describe that historical relationship give fullness to the picture of a covenant of steadfast love that endures even through crisis and adversity: "my servant," "whom I have chosen," "my friend." Perhaps the most perplexing of the doubts driving members of the community to ruinous relationships with pagan gods was the fear of abandonment, a perplexity known all too well from human relationships: "He just does not care about my feelings!" "It is as if I do not exist!" "What hurts most is her indifference!" The Book of Lamentations, a collection from the generation to which Second Isaiah belonged, agonizes over the dread possibility that God had abandoned Israel to hostile powers. It concludes with this impassioned plea:

> Why have you forgotten us completely?
>   Why have you forsaken us these many days?
> Restore us to yourself, O LORD, that we may be restored;
>   renew our days as of old—
> unless you have utterly rejected us *(mā'as)*,
>   and are angry with us beyond measure.
>
> (Lam. 5:20–22)

To such doubts, God offers direct reply through Second Isaiah: "I have not rejected you *(mā'as)*." This reply is then amplified by sublime words of assurance:

> Do not fear, for I am with you,
>   do not be afraid, for I am your God;
> I will strengthen you, I will help you,
>   I will uphold you with my victorious right hand.
>
> (Isa. 41:10)

38

Much of the drama of Scripture stems from its discursive style. Questions are posed, replies are given, issues are engaged, high points are reached. The Book of Lamentations ends with the questions raised by the Babylonian destruction of the Holy City pressed to their breaking point. Is it possible that God has utterly rejected God's people?

Second Isaiah does not end this section with the beautiful assurances of verse 10. The message will continue to wind its way through the contradictions and trials of human existence. But at this mid-point in an ongoing conversation, a people perplexed by adversity is granted a heartening promise from its Lord. In spite of the bafflement of exile and the intractable paradox of righteous suffering, they can hold true to faith in God and hope for the future. The God upon whom the universe depends and by whom the nations are directed is a God who reaches out in love to this people and addresses it in terms both personal and intimate: "Do not fear, for I am with you."

Second Isaiah has an uncanny way of getting to the heart of the matter. What is the object of the human heart's yearning, whether in the Persian period or in modern times? Is it not the desire for a sense that purpose underlies the sweep of history, purpose stemming from one who cares about me and about my family, my people, and finally the whole threatened, divided family of the nations living on this beautiful but endangered planet? To contribute generously to life, to live courageously in situations of crisis, to defend the rights of others even at the risk of hardship, these sterling human qualities usually can be traced to the quiet trust that the seeming fragmentation and turmoil of life are ultimately drawn together into a purposeful unity characterized by infinite love and justice.

Verse 21 opens the second trial found in chapter 41. The language is the technical jargon of the court of law: "Set forth your case," "bring your proofs," "tell us" (vv. 21–22). The issue again revolves around the claims advanced by the followers of Marduk, Nebo, and the other Babylonian gods that their deities are in charge of events past and events to come. The debate does not take the form of abstract philosophical argument over the relative merits of monotheism versus polytheism. It focuses, rather, on the question of which deity is involved in the happenings of human history. The personal dimension that came to the forefront in the preceding trial is thus again present here. "Tell us the former things . . . or declare to us the things to come" (v. 22). In other words, give some indication that you gods are concerned about the existence of us human beings. Offer some proof that you have an effect on history. There is a progression in the interrogation, culminating with a plea that they offer *anything* whatever as evidence: "Do good, or do harm . . ." (v. 23). The outcome of the questioning is emphatic, as indicated by the descriptions of what they offer: "nothing" at all, "delusion," "empty wind" (v. 29).

In contrast to the utter inertia of the false gods and their images, the living God is then described as one acting incisively in the specific events unfolding in the world:

> I stirred up one from the north, and he has come,
> from the rising of the sun he was summoned by name.
> (Isa. 41:25)

To *such* a God one can rightfully bring one's deepest concerns with the assurance of being answered!

In the two trials described in chapter 41, the prophet thus gives dramatic expression to the nature of the true God. God is not only an awesome cosmic power but an agent active in the concreteness of history to remove obstacles to social justice and to restore wholeness within the human family. Congruous with this divine character is the literary character of the prophet's message, born out of the audacity to express specific claims, concrete proclamations, and distinct promises. That message in turn challenges the audience to respond with equal audacity by building lives characterized by trust and hope for the future, a future secured by the power and love of the one true God.

Isaiah 42:1–9
Here Is My Servant

In 42:1–4, God introduces a Servant who is charged with a specific task and whose style of carrying it out is described. The scholarly debate over this text has been preoccupied with two questions, namely, the identity of the Servant and whether this Servant passage and related ones found in chapters 49, 50, and 52—53 stem from Second Isaiah or another hand.

40

The resulting literature that has accumulated generally offers dreary reading with little genuine insight. Although dozens of candidates have been advanced as the person or group designated as the Servant, the matter is as confused as ever. In the case of the question of authorship, the close thematic and stylistic connections between the Servant passages and the wider context suggest that we encounter here another instance of the theological imagination of Second Isaiah. That being the case, a more promising avenue opens up than the customary ones in pursuit of author and Servant's identity. It is the avenue of inquiry into the central themes of the Servant passages and their relation to the overall message of Second Isaiah. The result is a pleasant discovery: The meaning of the Servant passages, far from being withheld from the reader by the opacity of symbolism, unfolds precisely within the multivalence of that symbolism. The Servant, freed from the constraints of the positivistic quest, takes shape in the imagination as a catalyst for reflection on the nature of the response demanded of those who have received a call from God.

This fresh encounter with the symbolic power of the Servant image bears in turn on the question of the historical meaning of the passage by raising the probability that the original readers also found more than a biographical sketch of a particular person or group. We suspect that they also found in the description of the Servant's vocation an invitation to reflect on the responsibility of all those who acknowledge God's sovereignty and recognize the dependence of all creation on God's order of justice. It is reasonable to assume that such reflection could at times focus on godly individuals, at other times on the vocation of groups within the community or even on the ultimate purpose of the entire nation. Whether in relation to the historical meaning of this and the other Servant passages or to the question of contemporary theological significance, therefore, it seems in violation of the poetic tenor of the material to try to pin down the meaning of the Servant to one individual, one class, or, for that matter, one time.

Two principal themes accordingly emerge as the central foci of 42:1–4: the description of who the Servant is in relation to God and the task to which the Servant is appointed. 2.

The description of the Servant contains echoes of 41:8–10, a passage in which God turns to address Israel after having nullified the claims of the false gods and their protagonists:

Isa. 41:8–10	Isa. 42:1
You, Israel, my servant	Here is my servant
Whom I have chosen	My chosen
I will uphold you	Whom I uphold

In both cases we find title, formula of election, and assurance of divine support. In the former case, the Servant is explicitly identified with Israel, as is true also in the second of the so-called Servant passages in chapter 49. In this the first Servant Song, the referent is unspecified. What should be obvious through the comparison, however, is that the election is presented in terms apropos of both an individual such as prophet or king and the faithful community.

The task to which the Servant is called could not have been designated more clearly and emphatically than it is in 42:1–4: "to bring forth/establish *justice,* in truth, to the nations/in the earth." In our conflation of the threefold description of the Servant's task in these four verses we have italicized the key term that recurs in all three instances, *justice (mišpāṭ).* The concept *mišpāṭ* lies at the heart of Second Isaiah's message. Its meaning unfolds over the entire sweep of the prophet's proclamation, and it is best to treat each instance as it occurs in that unfolding. Before the present instance, *mišpāṭ* was presented in a disputation with the claim that it derives from no source other than the one true God ("who taught him the path of *mišpāṭ?*" 40:14). Further underlining the fact that there is no source of justice *(mišpāṭ)* save Yahweh is the claim in 40:23 that the sovereign of the universe "makes rulers *(šōpṭê)* of the earth as nothing" (Father Thomas L. Leclerc). In the complaint in 40:27, a people experiencing the collapse of their moral universe in the Babylonian conquest complain, "My *mišpāṭ* is disregarded by God," an assertion that evokes the prophet's assurance of God's presence in power for those who "wait for the LORD." Finally, the trial in 41:1 opens with a summons to the nations to gather together for *mišpāṭ.*

Mišpāṭ is the order of compassionate justice that God has created and upon which the wholeness of the universe depends. In Israel, God revealed *mišpāṭ* in the form of the *tôrāh* (note that in 42:4 *mišpāṭ* and *tôrāh* form a synonymous parallel). Those who repudiate God's *mišpāṭ* introduce evil into the world. God acts through God's servants to nullify the power of

42

evildoers and to restore the harmony that arises where God's *mišpāṭ* is acknowledged and observed.

Mišpāṭ is not a parochial concept. As seen in formulations of the blessings and curses of the covenant like Deuteronomy 28 and Hosea 4:1–3, the chaos or harmony that results from disobedience or obedience affects the entire universe, inclusive of human history and natural phenomena alike. The oracles of judgment against the nations found in Amos 1 and 2 further indicate that the domain of God is not circumscribed by the borders of Israel but extends to the surrounding nations.

Nowhere does the universality of God's domain of *mišpāṭ* come to clearer expression than in Psalm 82. Picking up on the motif of the assignment of the nations to the sons of the Most High *('elyôn)* found in Deuteronomy 32:8–9, Psalm 82 describes the mandate of each nation's deity in terms of responsibility for the administration of justice. Here the verbal form of the root *špṭ* is used:

> Give justice *(špṭ)* to the weak and the orphan;
>   maintain the right of the lowly and the destitute.
>   (Ps. 82:3)

Because the patron gods of the nations have failed to uphold justice and thereby threaten the universe with the specter of a return to primordial chaos ("all the foundations of the earth are shaken," Ps. 82:5), God asserts his power as defender of *mišpāṭ,* condemns the unjust gods, and assumes universal rule:

> Rise up, O God, judge *(špṭ)* the earth;
>   for all the nations belong to you!
>   (Ps. 82:8)

The frequent attempts to minimize or deny the universal dimension to Second Isaiah's concept of God's *mišpāṭ* display ignorance of the fact that by nature the biblical concept of divine justice bears universal connotations (cf. 42:1, "justice to the nations," and 42:4, "justice in the earth and the coastlands"). Especially in a prophet imbued with as deep a sense of God as creator of all that is, as was Second Isaiah, the emphasis on divine justice as the moral foundation upon which all reality rests seems intrinsic and essential to his message.

The description of a Servant whose task it is to bear witness to God's justice *(mišpāṭ)* in the earth is thus a description of the

43

raison d'être of those accepting the sovereignty of the one true God. It is a task only rarely discharged with unstinting devotion by those who come to be recognized as saints and martyrs. But even the example of those few renews the call that extends to all who look to the Creator of heaven and earth in worship. Rather than being a biographical description of one person in one place and time, the Servant thus is the description of the human being whom all who love God are challenged to become. Therefore it is important to take note of every detail in that description.

Verse 1 identifies *God* as the source of all that the Servant is and is called to do. Appropriately, therefore, the passage is in the divine first person. God presents the Servant in intimate terms: "Here is my servant." With equal clarity, the source of the Servant's strength is identified, for it is God who upholds him. On what basis is the Servant chosen? No mention is made of special human virtues or qualities. Again, the focus is exclusively on the divine initiator; the Servant is chosen because *God* delights in him. The Gospel writers found this passage helpful in explaining the nature of God's calling Jesus in the baptism in the Jordan. Mark describes the Spirit descending from heaven like a dove and a voice proclaiming: "You are my Son, the Beloved; with you I am well pleased" (Mark 1:11). In times when discipleship weighs heavily and the joy of living true to God's compassionate justice dims, remembering that the source of the vocation of those who love God is in God's *delight* can have an uplifting and empowering effect.

That the Servant is not left to his own cleverness is further emphasized by God's next pronouncement: "I have put my spirit upon him." The spirit in the Old Testament is the power and wisdom of God with which those called to serve are endowed (Isa. 11:2), including the judges of the League period, Israel's kings, and the prophets. Through the empowerment of God's spirit, weak and ordinary human beings rise up to accomplish daunting tasks on behalf of God's reign of justice, as seen in the case of Gideon (Judg. 6:34), David (II Sam. 23:2), and Ezekiel (Ezek. 8:3).

Only after the source of the Servant's call and strength is traced to God does the announcement move on to name the task, and it is well that the source has been so clearly identified, for the task is nothing less than to "bring forth justice to the

44

nations." The audacity of the assignment immediately raises the further question, How can that be accomplished?

When we recall one of the chief biblical contexts within which the notion of empowerment through the spirit of God is developed, namely, the context of Holy War, a means of accomplishing the task of bringing God's justice to the nations immediately suggests itself. Throughout biblical history and the history of the religions that fell heir to the biblical legacy—Judaism, Christianity, and Islam—Holy War has appealed to many as the most expedient means of bearing witness to God's universal reign. The Hasmoneans in their dedication to the principle of the *ḥerem,* the ban of all captives and booty, those followers of the Prophet Mohammed who interpreted one of the Pillars of Islam, *jihad,* in martial terms, and medieval Christians who sought to advance God's kingdom through the Crusades, each in turn set out to bring forth God's justice to the nations. In each case the result was bloodshed and a legacy of hatred that maintained the grip of war and terror on large segments of humanity.

The manner in which God intended the Servant to carry out the task of bringing forth justice to the nations stands emphatically in contrast to the manner of conflict and raw force:

> He will not cry or lift up his voice,
> or make it heard in the street;
> a bruised reed he will not break,
> and a dimly burning wick he will not quench;
> he will faithfully bring forth justice.
> (Isa. 42:2–3)

The style of witness of the Servant stands so starkly in contrast to the ways of the nations and their leaders that it must be regarded either as foolishness or as an intriguing alternative to a failed strategy. What sort of agent can this be, described in terms not of conqueror but of victim! Is it possible that the reign of justice can be promoted by submission and the express renunciation of force, even by special attention and care to fellow victims who are on the edge of collapse and death? Here we encounter one of the mysterious novelties of Second Isaiah's universal vision. It is pregnant with possibilities that have never been exhausted but nevertheless have inspired the godly of every age. The Servant does not cry out when oppressed, does

45

not move through the streets calling for pity, does not push aside the weak in the hope of winning conventional power to his cause. The Servant, rather, bears witness with quiet, patient gentleness, confident that the nations will be drawn to God's reign of justice not by dint of human force but by attraction to embodied compassion and righteousness. The source of that attraction is not within the Servant but points to the reality that transcends all flesh. To live consistently in the service of the justice of God is to pattern one's life on the nature of God. Only in this way is a mortal empowered faithfully to bring forth justice.

Gandhi-esque

Isaiah 42:5–8 gives the appearance of an addition provided by a disciple of Second Isaiah who wanted to make explicit one of the important interpretive possibilities implicit in the rich symbol of the Servant. Perhaps taking a cue from passages like 41:8–10 where the equation is made between the Servant and Israel, this disciple contributes to a tendency beginning with Second Isaiah himself (55:3) and later carried on by followers (61:1–2, 5–6; 65:13–16) to democratize the traditional offices of ancient Israel and to assign roles of responsibility to all members of the community. Additionally, he adds specificity to the task assigned to the Servant.

The new pronouncement is again in the first person of the deity. This time, however, it is not directed to an audience with the Servant as its subject but is spoken to the Servant himself. After God is identified as universal Creator using archaic language familiar from the Psalter, God gives assurance of his steadfast support of the Servant and then designates him with two unique phrases that are worthy of belonging to the Isaianic corpus by virtue of their enticing ambivalence:

> I have given you as a covenant to the people,
> a light to the nations.
>
> (Isa. 42:6b)

The referent of "people" *('am)* is most plausibly the same as that found in the preceding verse, namely, all the inhabitants of the earth, a meaning supported by the parallel "nations" that immediately follows. When we recall the universal dimension to the Servant's task in the preceding unit, the phrase strikes us as entirely befitting the spirit of Second Isaiah's vision. The community called and upheld by God, by discharging the patient faithful witness assigned to the Servant, becomes the instrument through which the nations are drawn into the covenant relationship marked by God's reign of justice, the covenant relationship of which Israel already had been a part because of God's gracious activity on Israel's behalf and which now was to be extended to the wider family of the nations. The parallel phrase "a light to the nations" amplifies this vision, that is, Israel is to become the instrument through which nations come to share the light of God's salvation.

The notion "covenant to the people" is so novel and expansive as to have elicited numerous scholarly attempts in the recent past to deny its universal implications, but similar passages in the Isaianic corpus advise against such attempts (e.g., Isa. 19:16–25). While it is true that this vision far outstrips the facts of Israel's subsequent history, it is of the very nature of religious symbolism to challenge faith with possibilities dismissed as utopian by prevailing thought.

"Covenant to the people" does not stand alone as a seemingly impossible vision but is accompanied in the Isaianic corpus by equally challenging notions: by the era in which the nation will not "learn war any more" (2:4), by a nation in which "your people shall all be righteous" (60:21), and by "new heavens and a new earth" (65:17). Nor does the Isaianic group stand alone among biblical traditions in encouraging the imagining of the humanly impossible, for visions of universal restoration and new creation are rooted in early Yahwistic notions such as the entitlement of every family to its patrimony and the restoration of pure social structures in the Jubilee year. To diminish the audacity of such biblical symbols is to encourage the atrophying of the human imagination that Carl Jung lamented as such a dreadful part of modernity.

Lest the vision be left in suspension like a glorious icon for decorative purposes only, verse 7 goes on to give *specificity* to the implications of the covenant as it reaches the nations. It makes clear that the order of God's justice involves healing of human illness and the reform of oppressive political structures. As God's covenant with Israel took shape in the form of God's actively getting involved in the plight of slaves in Egypt, so too the task of the servant people involves advocacy for those who suffer and are oppressed. Recognition of the reign of God's justice, while lifting the human heart to the heights of hymnic confession that follows directly in verse 8, demonstrates its integrity in the nitty-gritty affairs of everyday life. This is a lesson

47

reinforced by all of Israel's prophets, including the one who read a Servant Song in the synagogue of Nazareth (Luke 4:16–21) and described the judgment of the nations before the Son of Man (Matt. 25:31–46) as revolving around clothing, kindness, and hospitality.

Isaiah 42:10–17
The Lord Goes Forth like a Warrior

Interspersed throughout Second Isaiah are hymns, often coupled with announcements of the imminent activity of God directed toward deliverance of the people and the renewal of creation. While the style and the thematics of these hymns give every indication of composition by Second Isaiah, it is impossible to determine whether they originally functioned independently of their present literary context or were composed expressly as a part of the dramatic development of Isaiah 40—55. What is clear is that they contribute to the poetic beauty and the spiritual power of Second Isaiah's message, as is illustrated by the unit to which we now turn, 42:10–17.

We find ourselves in the sphere of temple worship with the intoning of the first verse:

> Sing to the LORD a new song,
>   his praise from the end of the earth!
>   (Isa. 42:10)

The unit 42:1–9 had ended with a divine promise: "new things I now declare." The inbreaking of the new that breaks the bonds of exile and heals the brokenness of both human community and nature is a central theme in Second Isaiah:

> Do not remember the former things,
>   or consider the things of old.
> I am about to do a new thing;
>   now it springs forth, do you not perceive it?
>   (Isa. 43:18–19)

> From this time forward I make you hear new things,
>   hidden things that you have not known.
>   (Isa. 48:6)

Because of the perennially ravaging effects of war, captivity, and homelessness, the people whom the prophet addressed were a people plagued with hopelessness regarding the future. Like a veil of gloom, it had closed in upon their consciousness, robbing them of their energy and thereby tightening the bonds that held them. With every passing year, Marduk seemed more powerful and Yahweh more incidental to the major events that were engulfing the Jewish community. The pragmatic response was accommodation to the new realities, including worship of the local gods and conformity to the customs of the land. Economic documents coming from Jewish businessmen of that time from Tel el Murassu on the Tigris River indicate that the monetary rewards accompanying accommodation were considerable. From many sides, therefore, the religion of Israel was being threatened with extinction. What was sure to seal its demise was the inertia of resignation.

"Sing to the LORD a *new* song." Second Isaiah was clearly aware of the antidote for inertia. After attacking the claims of the pagan gods by advancing "proofs" of the sole sovereignty of God, he invites the people to celebrate their confession under the inspiration of the spirit of God who was breathing new life into the community, into nature, and into the entire universe. This was not a timid invitation, for it was one that burst all bonds, spilling over from tiny Israel to the ends of the earth, from human tongues to the waves of the sea. All creatures were invited to discover their ultimate purpose in joining the faithful community in the most blessed of all acts, that of praising the loving, caring, acting Creator, the source of all that is.

As if to shake any lingering inertia out of the members of the community, the archaic image of God acting as Divine Warrior completes the hymnic introduction to this unit. We find it difficult to appreciate this image in the manner in which our ancient ancestors did, for in our time scientific theories have replaced the mythic cosmology of their worldview. We need to remember, however, that the threat to all that was good, from the greening of the earth in spring to the security and prosperity of the nation, was perceived as arising from unruly forces of chaos. Hope sprang from the image of an active God, engaging those threatening forces in order to restore order and renew creation. With the Divine Warrior's appearance came the fructifying rains, the birthing of cattle, the retreat of enemy forces, and the prosperity of the nation.

Perhaps it helps to picture the rousing of the Divine War-

49

rior as the reentry into society of awareness of the God who empowers the oppressed and who calls the family of nations to tender concern for nature and its delicate harmony. Our images for this source of hope in the face of inertia and despair, enriched as they are by many other biblical paradigms, will likely be less bellicose, but it is hoped that they will be no less effective than Second Isaiah's Divine Warrior in shaking us from our lethargy and opening us to the challenge to hear the *new* songs of people challenging their oppressors and to respond in praise and supportive action.

After hymnically introducing the deliverer God, the prophet changes to the most audacious of all prophetic modes, that of reporting the words of God in the first person. They are words just as arresting and powerful as were the words describing the arrival of the Divine Warrior:

> For a long time I have held my peace,
>   I have kept still and restrained myself;
> now I will cry out like a woman in labor,
>   I will gasp and pant.
> (Isa. 42:14)

How are we to understand these strange words which amount to a confession that God has remained aloof from the plight of the exiled people? The key to understanding is found in identifying the source of the language of verse 14 in the so-called communal laments of ancient Israel. For example, we hear the lament of the people in the following:

> Rouse yourself! Why do you sleep, O Lord?
>   Awake, do not cast us off forever!
> Why do you hide your face?
>   Why do you forget our affliction and oppression?
> (Ps. 44:23)

Elsewhere in the Isaianic corpus, we hear the people bitterly lamenting the destruction of all that was dear to them and then asking the Lord:

> After all this, will you restrain yourself, O LORD?
>   Will you keep silent, and punish us so severely?
> (Isa. 64:12)

50   In all ages, the most perplexing of all theological questions revolves around the presence of evil in a world supposedly governed by a just and loving God. The songs of lament in the

Psalms, in the Book of Lamentations, and in other parts of the Bible give free expression to the agonizing questions of people who feel themselves on the edge of bafflement or disbelief in the face of suffering that seems to make a mockery of the distinction between guilt and innocence:

> The tongue of the infant sticks to the roof of its
>   mouth for thirst;
> the children beg for food,
>   but no one gives them anything.
>
> (Lam. 4:4)

All the great world religions have had to deal with this question of theodicy. Commonly, evil and suffering have been explained through the denial of any significance to the realm of human experience. The spiritual realm transcends earthly existence. The tragedies experienced by human beings, therefore, do not raise questions about divine providence, for that providence applies only to the existence of the soul apart from the body. Within the religions that stem from the Bible, this "solution" took its extreme form in Gnostic cults. But its influence has gone much farther, reaching into many different movements and denominations in Judaism, Islam, and Christianity.

The denial of spiritual significance to earthly existence receives scant support from the biblical writings. God is encountered by the Hebrews as deliverer from their slavery. The prophets proclaim a religion fiercely dedicated to social justice. God's word does not hover over human misery to be contemplated only by the enlightened but becomes flesh and lives among ordinary people.

Second Isaiah stands squarely within the classical biblical position on this issue. God is not indifferent to the realm of human history. The question of theodicy demands a different answer than the denial of the reality of suffering. Human suffering, if it is to be explained, must be explained within the context of the divine-human relationship, not outside it. In 42:18–25, the unit immediately following the present one, Second Isaiah, with a courage matched only by Job, goes to the heart of the matter. That unit receives its fitting introduction in verses 14–17.

In their laments the people of Israel complained bitterly to God that God had kept still and restrained himself in the face of their terrible suffering. "I have," God now admits, "but no

51

longer will it be so." As the introductory scene from the divine council in chapter 40 indicated, a turning point in God's relationship with the people has occurred. The punishment is over. A word of comfort is to be spoken. Here that message is given new force and urgency with language taken from the delivery room. God, like a woman in the final throes of labor, can wait no longer:

> I will cry out like a woman in labor,
>   I will gasp and pant.
>
> (Isa. 42:14)

What follows is a picture of the transformation that occurs when God draws near. It conforms to a pattern found also in Isaiah 34—35, the pattern of removal of obstacles and re-creation. God leads the way, and in his train are the blind who regain their sight and form a pilgrimage of those who place their trust in God. Brought to shame are all who cling to idols and deny the reality of the one true God.

In the face of a growing sense among many people throughout the world today that political events and ecological developments both on the face of the earth and in the atmosphere are being swept by forces over which they have no control, Second Isaiah's vision of a people crying out to a God who responds incisively against structures of injustice and corruption must be recaptured. Human beings are not helpless! If they look beyond their own undeniably insufficient powers to the creative, redemptive power of God, they can become powerful agents in the transformation of human communities and nature alike. We can learn much about the power of God's word from the people of Poland whose resistance to a godless regime prepared them for the reconstruction of society in which they are now engaged, or from struggling Latin American communities that, in the face of daunting repression, risk security and safety to advance the biblical ideals of freedom, equality, and justice.

Isaiah 42:18–25
The Deaf Must Hear! The Blind Must See!

Second Isaiah was a prophet struggling for the heart of a people that had forsaken its source and was now lost amidst spiritual uncertainty and political confusion. The literary forms that he applied were well suited to his task. For example, the hymnic outpouring in 42:10–17 concluded with words drawn from the lament of the people, enabling the prophet to engage divine word with human word in one spirited dialogue. The same urgency and directness is encountered in the passage to which we now turn, 42:18–25.

In the disputation in 40:12–31, the complaint of the people was addressed and then refuted:

> Why do you say, O Jacob,
>   and speak, O Israel,
> "My way is hidden from the LORD,
>   and my right is disregarded by my God"?
>   (Isa. 40:27)

Isaiah 42:18 opens a new dialogue with the people with equally provocative words:

> Listen, you that are deaf;
>   and you that are blind, look up and see!

In the background of this introduction is another charge directed by the people to their God, namely, that God is deaf and blind to Israel's plight. Thus begins another disputation, conducted on the basis of a string of interrogatives that begin with "Who . . . ?" In effect, 42:18–25 is arguing, "Yes, indeed, deafness and blindness is the problem, but the record needs to be clarified as to who is afflicted with deafness and blindness. It is not God but Israel!"

Equally remarkable are specific epithets used for blind Israel, for they do not draw from the repertoire of negative images but consist of ones that call to mind faithfulness and obedience to God's will:

53

INTERPRETATION

> Who is blind but my *servant*,
> or deaf like my *messenger* whom I send?
>
> (Isa. 42:19)

Always lurking in the shadow of election to God's service is the sense of smug superiority. "As a called and ordained minister of the Word, I hereby declare to you the forgiveness of all your sins." What temptations to a false sense of importance can accompany such awesome authority in the life of a contemporary minister! Israel was no different from the modern servant of the Word. The prophets found it necessary to repeat their lessons regarding the true nature of servanthood and chosenness. Resting solely on divine grace, election carries with it solemn responsibilities, not special privileges.

The first "servant song," in 42:1–4, attributed servanthood to God's good pleasure. The same song emphatically disassociated empowerment by the spirit of God from human pride and identified its qualifications instead in terms of meekness, gentleness, and empathy for the weak. The prophetic lesson concerning servanthood is taken up again here. Far from being acclaimed as a superior specimen of the human race, the servant is described as deaf and blind, and this in spite of the fact that through the special events of Israel's history, much had been granted him to see and hear (v. 20). By this emphasis on the human frailty of the servant even more than the earlier description, attention comes to rest solely on God's grace as the source of hope for the future. True, God has delegated responsibilities to human beings. God, through the covenant with Israel, has drawn them, with their frailties, into a partnership. God's purpose in all of this remains constant, in harmony with the mission of the Servant in 42:1–4, namely, "to magnify his teaching and make it glorious" (v. 21). But look at the present state of this called people, this people with a mission, this people with a special covenant relationship of trust and responsibility: They are "robbed," "plundered," "trapped," "hidden in prisons." These words, drawn from the vocabulary of the individual laments, set up the shocking irony of a situation crying out to be addressed, and addressed with the kind of unembellished honesty that it is hoped could restore Israel to proper thinking in place of the self-deception that had set the stage for national catastrophe. How could the very people saved from slavery through an act of unmerited divine love now be consigned by

54

divine decree to loss of nationhood and bondage under another foreign power?

The prophet, in this barrage of interrogations, seems to be pressing Israel to the extremity where faith is either abandoned as unsustainable or reaffirmed on a far more profound level than was earlier possible. We are faced with the kind of lesson in true versus false faith that Søren Kierkegaard taught in *Fear and Trembling*, the lesson that was first taught to Abraham on Mount Moriah. Israel was being offered a new opportunity to confront reality. The prophet, with words that on the surface may sound uncommonly harsh, was God's chosen agent in the struggle for the heart of a wayward people. The prophet was seeking to draw the people to the new future intended for them by their loving God.

But the message would not be an easy one to hear. Honest confrontation with the errors of one's past is much more difficult than abiding in the protection of illusions that blame everyone else, including God, for one's difficulties and failures. Necessary is the willingness to look deeply into one's soul, even if that entails discovery of much that is shameful and reprehensible. If this is true in the case of the individual, it is equally true of a nation on a larger scale.

The next question directed by the prophet to the people is thus an inquiry to determine whether there is even an audience for the honest kind of dialogue that is to follow:

> Who among you will give heed to this,
>   who will attend and listen for the time to come?
>   (Isa. 42:23)

Then comes the question that pierces to the heart of the matter, testing the very foundations of biblical faith and pressing the age-old issue that divides the religions of the world: "Who brought on the calamity that destroyed temple and nation and thrust the people into exile?" In the face of a question like that, it becomes quite understandable that even the chosen servant is struck deaf and blind! For the lesson that is being taught is difficult in the extreme: Destruction and deliverance come from the same God!

Strict monotheism is a difficult doctrine to uphold, specifically because it seems to attribute evil deeds to a good God. Dualistic tendencies therefore arise in most religions, and, even within religions that uphold a lofty monotheism, folk beliefs often compromise the stringent views of belief in one God. It is convenient to attribute the good that happens in life to God and to blame other divine beings or demons or pernicious forces for all the rest.

Second Isaiah defends monotheism in its purest form, and hence he eschews facile answers in the area of theodicy. When one recalls the polytheism of his Babylonian setting, with its divine agents dividing up the various spheres of life, and the dualism of Zoroastrianism, with its attribution of good to Ahura Mazda and evil to Angra Mainyu, one is able to grasp the significance of Second Isaiah's confession in the sovereignty of the one God over *all* of life:

> I form light and create darkness,
> I make weal and create woe;
> I the LORD do all these things.
> (Isa. 45:7)

According to Second Isaiah, Israel would make no progress in understanding the tragedy of their past if they sought to locate the ultimate cause of their downfall in penultimate powers. They would have to come to realize that the one true God who created all that is, who delivered their ancestors from slavery, who loved the children of Zion as a woman loves her children, is also the one who poured out the heat of anger and fury of war upon this nation. For only if they came to that realization would they look deeply at the cause of their own tragedy, for there is a second half to the answer regarding the cause of Israel's calamity, one that points to the brokenness of a relationship that was intended for wholeness but had been perverted by sin into death:

> Who gave up Jacob to the spoiler,
> and Israel to the robbers?
> Was it not the LORD, against whom we have sinned,
> in whose ways they would not walk,
> and whose law they would not obey?
> (Isa. 42:24)

From a prophet who is commonly called "the prophet of comfort," these are unusually hard-hitting words. The final verse of the unit adds to the shock, for it observes that after the judgment of anger and war, Israel still "did not understand" or "take it to heart." One is reminded of the refrain of the folk song, "When will they ever learn?"

Harsh words! But harsh only in the sense of love seeking to break the prison of self-denial that holds captive a people and of faithfulness seeking to dispel the illusory pride that repudiates forgiveness and repentance and obedience as the way back to the life-giving relationship with God. In the case of stubbornness of heart, mercy must be severe or it is not mercy. If it chooses the pampering path of reinforcing the sinner's pride through dishonest indulgence, it is hastening the death of the soul. Second Isaiah, like Ezekiel a spokesman for the God who seeks not the death of the sinner but life through repentance, rejects the easy route to dialogue and insists on honesty. The record of Israel's tragedy had to be set straight before attention could turn to the possibility of healing: God had delivered Israel up to worldly powers because Israel had chosen to reject God rather than to live in loving obedience. Once this was acknowledged, the new invitation to turn away from death and to "listen for the time to come" could be renewed. A turning point was at hand. And it was Second Isaiah's willingness to speak the truth about Israel's past with honesty that allowed him, in the very next unit, to renew the invitation with confidence.

Second Isaiah thus has made another unforgettable point for all generations of the faithful. Only the servant who trusts the righteous compassion of God can speak of the "right hand" and the "left hand" of God with equal clarity: "[God] poured upon him the heat of his anger" (42:25), "You are precious in my sight, and honored, and I love you" (43:4). And only those who recognize God's word in both are able to confess that the one true God is sovereign over all of life, over joy and sorrow, over life and death, over wholeness and calamity, and to add to this confession with confidence that ultimately joy, life, and wholeness will prevail.

Taken together, the three sections of Isaiah 42 give dramatic expression to the prophet's understanding of the nature of the relationship between God and human beings. Here we find a servant whom God chooses to perform the most demanding task imaginable, to be the agent for the establishment of justice in the earth! This servant is characterized by remarkable self-restraint. Although burdened and abused, he does not bring attention to his plight by cries of self-pity. To such a person we readily attribute the epithet "godly," because we conceive of God as "slow to anger" and compassionate in seeking the resto-

57

ration of the lost. Indeed, such an understanding of God and the faithful servant is central to biblical faith.

But this chapter shows another side of the picture, namely, the relationship *between* the human and the divine members of the covenant. Here we see anything but stoic restraint. We see a God gasping and panting on behalf of a straying people, a people shouting back, a God accusing them of being deaf and blind and forcing them to acknowledge that it was their own Creator who gave them up to the destroyer.

When one remembers Abraham arguing with God and Job hurling his accusations heavenward only to be answered in kind, one realizes how biblical this frank relational quality is. God is not a Lord aloof in divine isolation and intentionally ignorant of human beings as they tread the precarious path between life in covenant and death through disobedience. God through the prophetic word tears into the sloth and complacency, the guilt and despair, that threaten to numb human beings to the only reality that is able to save. Both destruction and deliverance come from God, and both are dedicated to the same redemptive purpose.

At a recent gathering of people engaged in the healing professions, my pastor described a former parishioner who had suffered abuse at the hands of her father. For years she had been afflicted by mental distress that, only after considerable therapy, could be traced to anger toward *God* for not having protected her compounded with subconscious guilt for harboring that anger. Healing began when she was able to accept not as a contradiction of biblical faith but as a central tenet that it is proper to feel anger toward God. For then the victim becomes aware that God shares that anger and is present to channel it toward constructive action and healing.

In Second Isaiah, human beings express disappointment and anger to God and God displays freedom to express the same emotions and passions. Through the open expression of such genuine feelings both sides bring the fullness of their beings to the relationship. The way is thus prepared for a reconciliation and healing that affirms and restores the whole person rather than just the sanitized part that for many people constitutes a complete definition of "religious person."

Isaiah 43:1–7
You Are Precious in My Sight

The unit 43:1–7 lies close to the heart of Second Isaiah's message. It stands in marked contrast to the unit that preceded in 42:18–25. There Israel was described as blind and deaf to God's presence, and the relationship between God and people was described in terms of wrath and destruction. Following an emphatic disjunctive "But now . . . ," 43:1–7 unfolds a picture of divine deliverance and intimate communion that seems to contradict the harsh imagery of God as wrathful warrior and Israel as unrepentant rebel. Yet the two units, precisely in their stark contrast, depend on each other for proper interpretation.

The relationship established by God through an act of unmerited gracious deliverance was not one that could be treated with indifference or calculating selfishness. To pervert a call to witness on behalf of justice and mercy into license for self-indulgence and presumption of special privilege was to trifle with divine holiness. Such mockery of God elicited an incisive response aimed at breaking human smugness and restoring reverence before the Creator of all. It is not accidental, therefore, that one of the harshest descriptions of divine judgment in the Bible immediately precedes and leads into one of Scripture's purest descriptions of divine love. For love can flourish only where the partner is open, receptive, and loving in return. Love, after all, is not an imposition but an invitation to reciprocity.

Willingness to peer deeply into the heart of life calls for courage to recognize paradoxes that drive one to reflect beyond facile solutions and to recognize the light of revelation amidst seemingly imponderable mysteries. Second Isaiah peered deeply with remarkable honesty and thus spoke of the necessity of suffering as a prelude to healing, brokenness as the condition for restoration to wholeness, and power as breaking forth out of powerlessness.

The scholarly debate regarding the scope of the individual units in this part of Second Isaiah is far from settled. Is 43:1–7 the conclusion of a unit that begins in chapter 42? Is it a complete unit unto itself? Is the movement from the "blind and deaf" servant in 42:18–25 to the Israel embraced by God's love in 43:1–7 and back to the blind and deaf servant in 43:8–13 the result of editorial patchwork, intentional compositional technique, or some third cause? While such questions need to be addressed, they do not exhaust the inquiry called for by texts whose complexity and subtlety often are missed by rigidly formal methods of study. The unhappy result can be that "solutions" are imposed on texts that are intended to force a deeper level of analysis by means of the very tensions the critic has sought to eliminate through clever exegesis. Viewing the material through the rigid dichotomy of independent unit/long compositional whole, for example, can set up an artificial dichotomy that obscures paradoxes essential to Second Isaiah's theology. The literary technique of enveloping a sublime hymnic celebration of divine grace within disquieting descriptions of a loved one who spurns the divine lover and nevertheless is called upon to witness to divine grace, rather than being dismissed as inept editorializing by a dull disciple of the great prophet, is more appropriately understood as a skillful means of expressing the tragedy and the hope that coexist in the divine-human relationship. The poetically beautiful and theologically complex writings of Second Isaiah therefore call for a literary sensitivity that simultaneously recognizes the structural integrity of short units and the overarching themes that often weave these units together into longer compositions.

Turning specifically to 43:1–7, we first observe its intricate structure. It is framed (v. 1 and v. 7) with a depiction of God as creator of Israel. The next level of its envelope structure (vv. 1b–3 and vv. 5–6), introduced by the assurance "Do not fear," describes God's redemptive activity within history. Finally, lying at the heart of the hymn like a pearl in its shell, is a moving personal confession in which God reveals the basis for God's creative, redemptive acts on Israel's behalf: "Because you are precious in my sight, and honored, and I love you" (v. 4).

This beautiful confession, lying at the heart of 43:1–7, in turn provides the key that unlocks the meaning of the paradoxes created in the longer composition that runs from 42:18 to 43:15 by the juxtaposition of divine fury and divine grace: Both in the fury of God's wrath and in the merciful acts of divine deliverance, faith recognizes the presence of the God who wills only to love and to be loved in return.

The envelope structure of verses 1–7, then, is clearly more

than a literary device. It highlights the constancy of divine compassion as evidenced in the creation of Israel. As alpha and omega, God remains Creator "in the beginning" as well as "at the end of time." Simultaneously, 43:1–7 also develops along a temporal plane, thereby delineating how the Creator God is at the same time the God who can declare, "I have redeemed you . . . and called you by name" (v. 1). Because the Creator God is the God who enters history to establish a relationship with human beings and to heal their brokenness, the return to the theme of God as creator in verse 7 goes beyond the formulation of verse 1 by identifying the ultimate goal reached in the creative-redemptive activity of God: The people called together from the ends of the earth has been "created for my glory."

At this climactic point in the hymn the faithful community is reminded that, while it reaches its highest purpose in praise of God, it is not the creator of its own doxology. Praise of God, etched into the very foundation of the universe, antedates all human creativity and explains the purpose behind the origin of all living beings. This fundamental fact of life no doubt offended those exiles living in Babylon who viewed their own cleverness as the sole source of hope for a better future. They were no different from those people today who choose to bow before no power other than their own prideful hearts. Now as then, however, persons of faith look to God as the only One who can confer the gracious sensitivity that recognizes wholeness in submission to the transcendent source of life and sovereign over all creation. God's confession that we are precious in God's sight, even honored, and, most astonishing of all, *loved,* draws forth as its only fitting response the fervent desire to submit obediently to God's will and thereby to find genuine freedom and fulfillment.

Contradictory as they may seem on the face of things, expressions of divine anger, as genuinely as affirmations of divine steadfastness, reveal the commitment of God to authentic, reciprocating love. In contrast, divine tolerance of human arrogance would be no loving act at all, given the fact that life limited to human designs is doomed to emptiness. God's mercy comes to clear expression in harsh words that break the self-adulation of human pride and draw attention back to the covenant relationship as the only context for human happiness and genuine fulfillment.

61

As modern readers, we need to imagine ourselves in the

position of the original audience of Second Isaiah, for in hearing God's word spoken to our ancestors in the faith, our own lives become open to promises that are as valid today as they were during the days of Cyrus, king of Persia.

What was it for which the hearts of the exiles in Babylon longed? Many of the exiles were sorely mindful of their sins. They had the testimony of the prophets that it was their ingratitude and disobedience that had brought upon them the calamitous events that had robbed them of temple, land, and freedom. Now they needed a word of assurance, a promise that there was a future beyond the baffling suffering and shame they had suffered. But who could be trusted as the bearer of an authentic word of assurance? The prophets of weal—those crowd-pleasers like Hananiah who persisted with their extravagant promises of divine intervention even as the Babylonians were breaking through the last defenses of the city and subsequently had the nerve to renew their facile message amidst the ashes of smoldering Jerusalem—had completely lost their credibility. Who could be trusted to instruct the people regarding the future? The harsh lessons of the past gave the answer: The trustworthy ones were the spokespersons belonging to a prophetic tradition that had had the courage to proclaim that the source of the wrath that had befallen Israel was the very God who had called this people into existence. The word of God spoken by Second Isaiah could be regarded as an authentic word precisely because this same prophet had not flinched in responding to the question, "Who gave up Jacob to the spoiler?" with the answer, "Was it not the LORD, against whom we have sinned?" (42:24).

The judgment and the lessons drawn from it by the prophetic spokespersons of God had had the desired effect within the lives of some of the people. Like Jewish slaves at an earlier time in Egypt, a repentant people was receptive to God's new word. And to them, the aversive particle *but* carried with it the promise of a new beginning:

> But now thus says the LORD,
>   he who created you . . . .
>   (Isa. 43:1)

The silence of exile and despair thus was broken by the voice of the One who alone could reverse their fortune, "who created you . . . , who formed you." That word addressed the deepest longings of those who felt confused and threatened by the ruthless world powers that destroy all in their path:

> Do not fear, for I have redeemed you;
> I have called you by name, you are mine.
> (Isa. 43:1)

These words renewed an ancient promise. The attention of the people of Israel was thus directed beyond the immediate calamity that had befallen them, back to the beginning of the love relationship, to the point when they, in a situation much like the one in which they again found themselves, had been enslaved, without hope, without a future except the future of serving their oppressors. At that earlier time they had nothing and acknowledged it with a cry for mercy. God had heard their cry, had delivered them from their captors, and had drawn them into the personal relationship of the covenant that forever after would be called to mind by the divine promise, "I will be your God, and you shall be my people." Could it happen again? Memory opened up a glimmer of hope for the people in exile.

Further images were brought forth from that memory, images of a sinister nature: waters, rivers, fire, signs of the inimical forces of chaos that overwhelm human life and destroy all that breathes. What we encounter here is the language familiar to ancient peoples describing the ordeal, that is, the ancient judicial practice of casting the accused into the river or the fire to determine guilt or innocence. Even when the full force of evil assails the people, they could remain confident of final vindication, for their religious epic spoke of the God who heard the cry of slaves and delivered those who clung to God in hope.

The sole ground of Israel's confidence is stated clearly in verse 2: "I will be with you." From this most central of all biblical promises stems the divine epithet that is a gospel in brief: *Immanuel,* "God with us."

Second Isaiah in this passage is not debating an academic question. He is addressing a people whose harsh experiences threaten to deaden their hearts even to the possibility of deliverance from their distress, who ask, "Will not our hopes rise only to be dashed again against the realities of ruthless world powers?" It is easy to imagine how the minds of the listeners could have been overwhelmed by a thousand doubts. Were not the gods of Babylon and Persia demonstrably stronger, as

63

proven by recent events? The prophet had already addressed these doubts in his disputations, in which he had argued for the sole sovereignty of God over all spheres. These arguments would not be repeated here. The moment had been prepared for a far more revealing word, one spoken from the heart of God. After all arguments had been advanced, after all contestants in the debate had rested their cases, the human heart waited for a word spoken directly from the heart of the God who created all for the wholeness of love. After all disputations had been completed, only one word could satisfy the deepest yearning of the fearful heart, a word of assurance that the Creator of all, the ultimate cause behind all that is, *loves radically and unconditionally.* The reason this defeated people could hope for a future beyond tragedy is a remarkable promise, a promise filled with the creative power that belongs exclusively to the purest of all qualities, love:

> because you are precious in my sight,
> and honored, and I love you.
> (Isa. 43:4)

What do we make of these seven verses within our world of contentious powers and widespread human tragedy? One thing is sure: The significance of the metaphor of the ordeal is not limited in its effects to the ancient Babylonians and Israelites. Human beings of every age encounter the threat of final negation, death in its myriad forms, death to dreams, to hopes, to loved ones, to a future. In his time, Jesus renewed biblical tradition's honest acknowledgment of the threat of final annihilation by including among the petitions taught to his followers, "Deliver us from evil," that is, "from the time of trial," from encounter with that which can nullify life's meaning and destroy all hope and consign us to despair unto death. Jesus directed their attention toward God as the only one who could give hope to those recognizing the fragility and precariousness of life.

What answer does the contemporary clergyperson or teacher of religion or friend of a suffering one give to people as they encounter the forces of chaos in broken health, broken families, broken dreams, or broken political structures? From many pulpits these people hear learned discourses giving political and psychological advice. From many seminaries they hear erudite disputations, in our time directed less against pagan cults than against rival theological schools of thought. But the faithful continue to yearn for the authentic word of God until the true spokesperson of God dares to identify the source of the fractures that imperil life on all levels, namely, the rejection of God's sovereignty and the assignment of glory to penultimate powers. Happy is the repentant heart that is informed in words as moving and clear as Second Isaiah's that hope and healing are as close at hand as the next breath and that it is dependable because it comes as a gift from the Creator of the universe and the Redeemer of the oppressed of all ages. Happy is the responsive soul that recognizes the source of hope in a prophetic word that comes from the heart of God:

> because you are precious in my sight,
> and honored, and I love you.
> (Isa. 43:4)

Daily we hear moving testimony to the lostness of life without the assurance of love. On *CBS Evening News* on September 12, 1994, an eleven-year-old girl was asked to comment on the announcement that two of her classmates had killed an itinerant worker in cold blood. Thoughtfully she said through her deep sadness, "They needed someone who loved them and showed them that, someone that really cared about them." It was clear through her honest eyes and the conviction in her voice that she had someone who loved her. But tragically, two eleven-year-old boys had come abruptly to the end of their childhood because they had not received the gift of love. In our cities, whether large or small, thousands of young people are growing up without love and without hope in the world. W. H. Auden (pp. 245–47) summed it up well:

> Lost in a haunted wood,
> Children afraid of the night
> Who have never been happy or good.

Now as perhaps never before, people, whether they are conscious of it or not, are dying to hear the words of assurance that only God can give: "Because you are precious in my sight, and honored, and I love you." Here alone is a foundation upon which a life can be built. And it is a word that will be heard only if the people that has been brought from death to life by God's love will pass the message on, a people placed in the world for that purpose, a people, God declares,

65

> whom I created for my glory,
> whom I formed and made.
>
> (Isa. 43:7)

Isaiah 43:8–15
You Are My Witnesses

The passage in 43:8–15 depicts a judicial trial. At issue is the question of who among the rival deities rightfully could be declared the true God. It is the same question explored earlier by the prophet in the trials described in 41:1–5 and 41:21–29.

A legal trial calls for cross-questioning and for witnesses to testify for each side. Appropriately, the rival gods are invited to offer their credentials and to produce witnesses on their behalf. Israel's God also testifies and calls in witnesses. What is surprising, however, and what ties this passage to 42:18–25, is the designation of God's witnesses as the *deaf* and the *blind!*

In 42:18–25 deafness and blindness had symbolized the faithlessness of Israel. This was a people that had witnessed remarkable events over the course of its history and had drawn together an epic that taught it much about the character of the Creator-Redeemer God Yahweh. In other words, this was a people that was in a position to bear witness among the nations to God's mercy and justice. But Israel had failed to preserve the memory of God's gracious acts, instead manifesting an ignorance of life's meaning that was captured in the metaphors of deafness and blindness.

> He sees many things, but does not observe them;
> his ears are open, but he does not hear.
>
> (Isa. 42:20)

According to Second Isaiah, the result of Israel's unresponsiveness was the calamity of the Babylonian conquest, but even the harsh lessons of war did not seem to break Israel's obstinacy:

> It set him on fire all around,
> but he did not understand;
> it burned him, but he did not take it to heart.
>
> (Isa. 42:25)

Why, when God's claims to divinity had been called into question and placed on trial by the rival Babylonian deities, would God call upon this deaf and blind people as his witnesses? This is the paradox that lies at the heart of 43:8–15. Once again it is a paradox that is explained best by the larger context, especially the twin "blind and deaf" passages in 42:18–25 and 43:8–15 and the hymnic passage 43:1–7 that lies between them.

Why does God, in the time of the great trial among the gods, call upon such an unlikely witness as oft-faithless Israel? The paradox leads to the surprising answer: Because it is the likes of Israel that God uses as agents of healing and justice on earth! Terms such as *servant of the Lord* and *God's witness* commonly evoke images of uncommon virtue and saintly perfection. They are enough to banish from the thinking of an ordinary human being the thought that he or she might be called by God to witness or to serve. There is an arresting message in these passages specifically in their tension-filled interrelationship. Precisely the blind and deaf, stubborn and resistant people sentenced to punishment in chapter 42 are the ones to whom God declares in chapter 43, "You are my witnesses, and my servant whom I have chosen." How, in the span of a few verses, can the prophet move from a description of Israel as a people punished with fire and still resisting God's law to a divine commissioning of this same people as witness and chosen servant?

Intrinsic human virtue is clearly excluded as an explanation. Nor is there a hint anywhere of heroic self-improvement. The explanation lies alone in the audacity of the divine love as expressed in 43:4: "because you are precious in my sight, and honored, and I love you." As tempting as it is to resolve the paradox by assigning the three passages in this complex to different authors, or at least to very different moods of the same author, the essential theological point emerges from the biblical text only when the interplay of audacious divine love and infuriating human obstancy is allowed to work itself out in the humanly impossible phenomenon of faithful testimony coming precisely from the *blind and deaf* servant.

All of this is very much to the point of the trial in this passage. What kind of evidence counts here? After all the nations have assembled, the divine Judge scrutinizes the deities gathered for the trial and questions:

67

> Who among them declared this,
>   and foretold to us the former things?
> Let them bring their witnesses to justify them,
>   and let them hear and say, "It is true."
>
> (Isa. 43:9)

The evidence sought entails information provided by human beings about the relationship between the gods and their peoples. At issue is the presence, or absence, of those gods in the history of their nations. What counts in the trial is the testimony of human beings as to whether the stories of the great deeds and accomplishments of their gods are true or not. The judge is simply asking for human testimony from the subjects of the various national deities that the claims being made on their behalf are valid: "Let them hear and say, 'It is true.' "

Israel's validity as a witness in this trial does not depend on moral superiority relative to the peoples of the other nations. It is not human beings who are on trial here. Rather, the people of Israel are summoned to testify regarding their *God*. They are to attest to the fact that theirs is a God who has been present and active in history.

Although that role does not require heroic stature or saintly virtue, it does call for reliable memory. For Israel to have experienced God's presence in history and then lapse into the darkness of forgetfulness is the one thing that would ruin its validity as a witness in court. This being the case, the passionate tone of God's address to Israel in verse 4 takes on added meaning. God speaks thus to shock Israel back into memory of its past. "Because I love you" is the kind of language that can bring the unfaithful back to their senses. It can bring back to mind the long history of the covenant relationship. It can restore to the consciousness of the witness the astonishing realization that God has been present through everything, through good times as well as bad, in deliverance as well as in punishment. For Israel's God is Immanuel, "God with us." As a witness to this fact, Israel is called into the court.

God, present in the scene as both the judge and one of the defendants, can speak confidently precisely because God knows the one fact upon which the outcome of the entire judicial proceeding depends: God has indeed been present with this people. And through the appeal of God's servant, the prophet, the shroud of forgetfulness will be lifted from the nation's understanding, and they finally will step forth and declare, "It is true."

As for the other gods standing trial, they have been present with their people only as idols can be present, as burdens weighing on their subjects rather than uplifting them. Their witnesses may be better trained in the esoteric knowledge of their myths and rituals than the common people of Israel, they may be far more erudite in astrology and necromancy and soothsaying than the *blind and deaf* witnesses of the God of Israel, but their learned tongues carry little weight in court since they have witnessed nothing of the actual presence of their gods in the day-to-day affairs of the poor and needy of their people. Stammering Israel's testimony alone carries the weight of legitimate testimony, because Israel has witnessed its "Redeemer, the Holy One of Israel," present to deliver those in bondage and to comfort those who mourn. On the basis of that testimony, the Judge can hand down the verdict:

> Before me no god was formed,
>   nor shall there be any after me.
> I, I am the LORD,
>   and besides me there is no savior. . . .
> You are my witnesses.
>   (Isa. 43:10–12)

With these magisterial words monotheism enters the disarray of a world long mired in the confusion of contentious gods (cf. Psalm 82). It enters in full view of human beings amidst the stuff that comprises everyday life. It is born not as an abstract, philosophical concept but as the key that unlocks the meaning of the lives of ordinary people. The ultimate meaning of life has its source in the one God, the Creator and Redeemer of all that is, who draws creation to wholeness through the lure of unbounded love, communicated to all who will listen through words of the heart:

> Because you are precious in my sight,
>   and honored, and I love you. . . .
> You are my witnesses.
>   (Isa. 43:4, 12)

By standing witness before the nations to God's faithfulness, Israel's own heart undergoes transformation. The stubborn one gives up the blindness of pride and becomes open to the Re-

69

deemer, the Holy One in its midst. And that is the greatest miracle of all. For it breaks down the walls of resistance that have held Israel captive, walls far thicker than the fortifications of the Babylonians, the walls of pride and clouded understanding that block their vision from the only reality that can place meaning and health at the center of human existence. Once sin is forgiven, once divine mercy has been received, the rest is simple.

This fundamental lesson of life was manifested clearly in the life of Jesus, according to the story in Luke 5:17–26. Having seen the faith of those who were lowering the paralytic from the roof, Jesus pronounced the life-transforming words, "Friend, your sins are forgiven you." After this, as the skeptical witnesses came to realize with astonishment, the act of physical healing was easy by comparison. And once again, the deeper miracle of having spiritual vision restored was contagious, as new witnesses were drawn into the drama:

> Amazement seized all of them, and they glorified God and were filled with awe, saying, "We have seen strange things today." (Luke 5:26)

Healed of blindness and deafness and returning to faith and knowledge of God, Israel was ready to hear God's new promises:

> I will send to Babylon
> and break down all the bars.
> (Isa. 43:14)

With the covenant restored, God can move beyond the work so alien to God's nature, punishing those who stubbornly resist grace, and proceed to the task of restoring a nation to freedom and health. When a relationship gets back on track, the impossible suddenly becomes perfectly natural. The walls come tumbling down!

Here is a message as contemporary as any in the Bible. All the walls that make modern human beings captive seem frightening and insuperable until they look to the Holy One. Personal walls, such as addictions, destructive relationships, greed, and fear, hold destroying power over individuals and cannot be removed until the human heart opens to God's presence. This is a lesson that has been taught to millions by Alcoholics Anonymous. It is a lesson that is central to the gospel. It is a lesson that the church can proclaim with a joy that is shared in heaven.

70

The walls that tear apart the fabric of societies and vitiate efforts toward world peace are even more formidable. But as hard-thinking members of the Center for Strategic and International Studies in Washington have written, religion is the missing dimension that must be rethought in relation to the crises that face the nations of the world (Johnson and Sampson). In the world of international diplomacy as much as in the realm of personal relations, we must recapture a vision of the Holy One if terrible new catastrophes are to be averted. It is important to remember, when world history seems to spin out of the control of members of communities of faith, that Second Isaiah's message was not a timid one whispered only to kindred spirits but a bold one that addressed nations and world leaders. Second Isaiah, after all, was mindful of the universality of the reign of the "Creator of Israel." And that is a vision which we contemporary people of faith could do well to recapture if we are to carry on with the task of God's people of every age, the task of testifying on behalf of the God of universal peace and justice and declaring with a confidence drawn from accurate memory, "It is true."

Isaiah 43:16–21
I Am About to Do a New Thing

The unit 43:16–21 is a tightly knit proclamation of salvation. It begins with a divine self-introduction, proceeds immediately to describe God's act of deliverance, and ends with reference to the culmination of Israel's purpose in praise of God.

In the hymnic style that is reminiscent of many of the psalms, God's self-introduction takes the form of participles describing aspects of divine activity. Commonly these epithets allude to God's creative activity:

> Thus says God, the LORD,
> who created the heavens and stretched them out,
> who spread out the earth and what comes from it,
> who gives breath to the people upon it
> and spirit to whose who walk in it.
>
> (Isa. 42:5)

71

In 43:16 the reference is to God's saving activity in the historical realm. More specifically, God's activity is described with terms that unmistakably bring to mind the deliverance of the Hebrews from Egypt, that is to say, the exodus. Second Isaiah's hearers would feel immediately at home with words bringing with them a very familiar ring: "way in the sea," "chariot and horse," "army and warrior." We can even imagine that these words would have had a lulling effect, evoking the feelings of the "old-time religion" and giving comfort to a people battered on all sides by a threatening world filled with unfamiliar gods, rulers, languages, and customs.

There is nothing necessarily wrong with a strategic retreat from the hostile unknown to the comfort of the familiar, especially if one has been pushed to the extreme by the harsh blows of life and is in need of spiritual renewal. But such retreat, if it becomes a habit of mind and a permanent posture, becomes spiritual escapism and an abdication of one's vocation in the world of human experience and historical happenings.

Slumber and forgetfulness were not characteristics that Second Isaiah could accept as permanent facets of true faith. Specifically, he believed that the hour in which his listeners found themselves called for watchfulness. Destiny hung in the balance with earthshaking events unfolding around them. The Jewish community was being engulfed by international developments that threatened to obliterate its identity and vocation as God's people. Accordingly, right at the point when his audience would have begun to yield to the soothing effects of the recitation of the traditional images of the exodus, Second Isaiah introduces a clashing dissonance with the words:

> Do not remember the former things,
> or consider the things of old.
> (Isa. 43:18)

Has the prophet here introduced a glaring contradiction into the divine word? How does one reconcile a string of divine epithets that epitomize the core of Israel's historical memory and describe the moment of its birth in the exodus with a blunt command not to remember the events of the past?

It is simple-minded to dismiss this dissonance as a mere logical contradiction. First of all, memory of the community-building events of the past is of central theological importance to Second Isaiah. In his prophecy, participles recalling God's

72

past activity function to authenticate the contemporary reality of divine providence by underlining God's unwavering faithfulness. In the disputations, the very mark of true deity is consistency over the entire span of history in giving providential guidance to the affairs of human beings. That there is something more subtle than a glaring contradiction underlying the command "Do not remember" is also suggested by the presence of admonitions elsewhere in Second Isaiah specifically "to remember," as in 46:8–9:

> Remember this and consider . . . ;
> remember the former things of old.

What on the surface may seem like a contradiction is actually a very effective rhetorical device involving the technique of surprise that was in favor among Israel's prophets as it has been among most great rhetoricians. Under what circumstances should Israel not remember the former things? At the point where a nostalgic relation to tradition threatens to tie the people to their past and to stultify alertness to present realities, responsiveness to new opportunities, and the potential for growth into yet-unrealized possibilities. The prophet pictures Israel as standing on a threshold. Like the slaves in Egypt, the Jews in Babylon are in bondage to a foreign power. But we know from epigraphic evidence that many Jews were prospering in that environment. Evidence from within the Bible indicates that many were reluctant to return to the uncertainty of a destroyed homeland. Geographically, the way through the wilderness over which the exiles would have to pass was fraught with dangers and hazards. Now that the advent of Cyrus had lifted the shackles of imposed bondage and was holding out the promise of political release, the newest threat to freedom was the prison of the people's own lethargy, and one bar in that prison was the wistful sort of memory of the past that dulls one's alertness to the present. Israel needed to be shocked out of such lethargy. And Isaiah heard a God whose presence was not limited to the past but who was active in contemporary events say to Israel:

> I am about to do a new thing;
> now it springs forth, do you not perceive it?
>   (Isa. 43:19)

The God of Israel differed from the gods of Babylon especially in the manner in which the divine presence was encoun-

73

tered and experienced. The gods of Babylon were experienced in the cult through the myth ritual, that is to say, through the reenactment of their primordial acts of creation and ordering, acts changeless in character and ensconced in a universe characterized by the cycles of nature that were as timeless as the graven images through whom the gods were presented to the people in their temples and shrines. The God of Israel—though in certain periods also presented to the people in temple theophany (albeit not in the form of visible representation)—was encountered in the ever-changing events of history. Ironically, the recitation of past events can itself take on the qualities of timeless myth if it allows nostalgia to expel expectation of "new things." Memory itself therefore could become a conceptual blindfold if unenriched by awareness of the open-endedness of the divine-human relationship.

"Do not remember the former things. . . . I am about to do a new thing" is thus a poignant call to wake up to the contemporaneity of faith. It is a challenge to muster sufficient theological imagination to see how divine purpose is unfolding in profane political events. Second Isaiah will get very specific in meeting that challenge in chapters 44 and 45, first by removing obstacles to the kind of clear vision required by an existentially relevant faith and then by lifting up for theological interpretation and application the preeminent political event of his time, Cyrus's rise to preeminence. But Second Isaiah moves the present unit toward its conclusion by remaining within the metaphorical field introduced by the opening divine epithets, the field of exodus imagery.

What is the new thing that God is about to do? "Way in the wilderness" and "rivers in the desert" present images that call to mind the exodus, as if we have come full circle. Rather than prodding the attention of his audience forward, do not these images move them back into their wistful reflections on the past? Is not the prophet taking back the force of surprise just interjected by his admonition "Do not remember"? Is he not reasserting that God is about to return Israel to the exodus experience of its past?

A reading that is sensitive both to the rhetorical qualities of Second Isaiah's style and to the way in which he utilizes paradoxes to deepen his message will recognize that an appreciation of tradition is being combined with a daring openness to the future in verses 19–21. The God who here promises to accompany Israel in the potentially perilous happenings that it now faces is the same God who was faithful to Israel's ancestors in their flight from Egypt and their journey through the wilderness. But this is not a backward-looking reenactment of a past event trapping the community in an endless circle akin to the annual circumambulation of the Marduk priests around the walls of Babylon bearing the cult idols. For here Second Isaiah portrays a procession led by the God who acts in the events of history, a procession not circling the temple shrine but leading from political bondage to the dignity of rebuilding community on native soil. Second Isaiah grasps the essence of the exodus tradition to which his images allude by envisioning the unfolding of that tradition in the major happenings of his day. Religion, so often the tool of tyrants and oppressors, here becomes the agency of divine mercy and justice. The realm of the sacred, far from imposing the mold of the past on those suffering under the weight of the present, instead reveals to the people a vision of "the new thing" that God is doing to break them from their bondage. "Now it springs forth, do you not perceive it?" This presents a challenge. The people must be open to the possibility of change and receptive to the opportunity to begin anew. They must not succumb to lethargy. They must not be lulled by the comforts of their increasingly benign captivity. They must stand straight, with their senses keen to perceive the advent of the God who comes to deliver slaves, to heal the sick, and to restore to wholeness that which is broken.

The last two verses of 43:16–21 offer a reason why Israel must respond to God's initiative with clear vision and vitality. It is a reason that goes beyond the welfare of the human community. It has to do with a theme to which Second Isaiah returns repeatedly, the theme of the ultimate purpose of all creation. God is a creative, redemptive God. God is committed to the healing of the entire created order and to harmony in all its parts. God is committed to shalom. Second Isaiah again invokes an image. In Isaiah 34, which together with chapter 35 likely stems from Second Isaiah, the prophet projected a vivid image of chaos: jackals and ostriches prowling amidst the ruins of a world collapsed under the weight of the iniquity of its inhabitants. To portray the radical nature of the new thing that God purposes, Second Isaiah reintroduces the jackals and ostriches, this time themselves restored to beauty and wholeness and giving honor to their Creator! Even they have taken their place in a world abiding in shalom, a world in which God tenderly cares for the people whom God has chosen, a world—and now we come to the culminating act that gathers all creation up into one common purpose—in which Israel by its very existence bears witness to the one reason that gives eternal value to life:

> So that they might declare my praise.
> (Isa. 43:21)

It is remarkable how this prophet can keep coming back to the central issues of life and do so with a freshness and an originality that give no hint of repetitiveness. Nowhere either does he take recourse to obscure abstractions. His language is vivid and concrete. In 43:16–21 it projects images that evoke thoughts of all that threatens life and goodness, horse and chariot, army and warrior, mighty waters, wilderness and desert. Perhaps these are not the images native to our nightmares, where, depending upon where we live in a still-threatened world, we may see mushroom clouds, typhoon winds, devastating earthquakes, or riot police. But it does not require mental gymnastics for us to feel the impact of the message as we hear of the God who removes the terrors of war machines, who transforms a hostile world into an environment supporting the passage of those who are in bondage to freedom and restored dignity, and who completes love's pageant by lifting up a redeemed world into one harmonious chorus that experiences the most exquisite of all delights in acknowledging the source of its well-being by declaring God's praise.

Isaiah 43:22–28
The Burden of Your Sins

The last prophetic unit in chapter 43, consisting of verses 22–28, clearly places Second Isaiah within the prophetic tradition beginning with the courageous critics of nation and cult in the preexilic period. The epithet "prophet of comfort" that is often used for Second Isaiah, although capturing a central theme of his prophecy, is misleading if it suggests that the theme of divine judgment in response to human sin is neglected in this prophet's proclamation. The unit 43:22–28 is a trial speech that, together with 50:1–3, places *Israel* on trial before God, in contrast to the other trial speeches in Isaiah 40—55 in which the nations and their gods are summoned to face judgment. The lessons that emerge from this trial are continuous with those introduced in 42:18–25 where God was described as the one who consigned Israel to the ravages of war: (1) The consequences of breaking the covenant by abandoning God in favor of other allegiances are of such grave seriousness that it would be merciless for the prophet not to state them clearly; and (2) the depths of divine compassion are seen all the more clearly against the background of Israel's heinous sin, for, contrary to what might be expected, God remains committed to the restoration of Israel through repentance and forgiveness.

The passage opens with the kind of indictment that occupied a central position in the proclamation of the preexilic prophets, an indictment against forms of worship that serve to disguise the true character of the worshipers and thus are a travesty of the faithful response that is fitting in relation to the Creator of the universe. The indictment presents a pathetic picture: In response to the God who created all that is and to whom Israel owes not only its biological but its political existence as well, Israel responds with indifference and with complaints that God is wearisome. In a culture that expressed gratitude through gift giving and hospitality featuring well-prepared food, a central feature of religious life was the ceremonial offering of food to the one who deserved hospitality more than any other, the deity. In relation to this most traditional of all ancient religious practices, this trial determines that Israel did not even measure up to its pagan neighbors.

The second half of verse 23 reflects a persistent prophetic theme: that God does not place ritual sacrifices as a burdensome duty upon the community and in fact takes no pleasure in sacrifices that do not arise from the full response to divine grace that manifests itself above all in acts of kindness and justice. The meaning behind God's accusation that Israel has withheld offerings is clearly this: Israel's niggardliness is a sign of the deadness of its heart in what should be the most precious of all relationships; Israel is incapable of extending even the simple gesture of gratitude symbolized by food!

So accustomed have we grown to a religiosity stripped of all ritual and reduced to a list of rules of proper conduct that we

77

may be puzzled by the picture of a deity who expresses disappointment over a people that has not bought him "sweet cane" and "animal fat." We take offense at such a picture with the same indignation expressed by those who witnessed what they judged to be the wasteful extravagance of the woman who poured a jar of costly ointment on Jesus (Mark 14:3–9; Matt. 26:6–13; Luke 7:36–50). Is not religion's function to translate cane or fat or nard into cash for charity? Are not ritual acts such as sacrifice and anointing a waste of valuable resources?

The God portrayed by Second Isaiah and the Jesus portrayed by the Gospel writers do not corroborate this pragmatic attitude. They point to a dimension in religion that cannot be explained by public policy but only by the dynamics of personal relationship. What from a business point of view represents waste from a relational point of view is seen as the manifestation of friendship and love. The God of Isaiah 43 and the Jesus of the Gospels are moved by acts that have no significance except as expressions of tenderness and devotion.

Should we find it difficult to understand such ritual sides of religion, we might think for a moment of the flowers brought by the young person to the one whom he or she loves, flowers that cut deeply into the last dollars remaining in a flattened pocketbook, flowers that will fade with the morning sun, flowers that cannot feed the hungry or bring warmth to the homeless, flowers whose only purpose in life is to say, "I *love* you." Second Isaiah looks upon the tragedy of a broken relationship. He peers into the heart of a God who has done everything possible to create a life of blessing within the reciprocity of a relationship of trust. He portrays the sadness of the God who looks for evidence that the receiver feels some sense of gratitude, some small indication of genuine response, such as a piece of sweet cane! Instead, the only response of the people is more unfaithfulness, more sin, more iniquity.

The indictment in verses 22–24 interweaves two words, the thrice repeated verb "to weary" and the twice repeated verb "to burden." Although God has not wearied Israel with ritual demands for frankincense, Israel has been weary of God and has wearied God with its iniquities. Although God has not burdened Israel with offerings, Israel has burdened God with its sins. In response to the loving God, Israel's behavior is petty, paltry, pathetic! No human relationship could survive such indignities, which makes Israel's calloused affront of God utterly reprehensible.

The conclusion toward which the accusations are leading is reached in verses 26–28. But intervening at the central point in the trial speech is verse 25, which introduces a dissonance similar to that created by the hymn in 43:1–7 that is placed midway between the two attacks on Israel's spiritual blindness and deafness in 42:18–25 and 43:8–15. The purpose in both cases is the same, namely, to describe the mercy of God as utterly unexplainable on the basis of conventional rational considerations:

> I, I am He
>   who blots out your transgressions
>   for my own sake,
>   and I will not remember your sins.
>   (Isa. 43:25)

As the creation of humanity and the birth of Israel as a people are traceable alone to divine mercy, so too the possibility of rebirth rests solely on the still inexplicable, inexhaustible mercy of God. Should one try to find an explanation for such an enigma, verse 25 points to the riddle that lies at the heart of all of life, the mysterious divine "I" and the inscrutable "for my own sake."

Hope burns brightly solely because of divine love. But its brightness does not automatically banish the gloom that accompanies human rebellion against divine grace. Its brightness instead pierces through the gloom and thus appears all the more brilliant to the faithful and dreadful to those who persist in sin. Second Isaiah, consistently the master of contrasts, thus places at the heart of this trial speech the most fundamental fact of human existence, the divine grace that through forgiveness restores hope.

But the tragedy of human sin continues to mutilate God's creation, and therefore verse 26 returns to the language of the court of law. The powerful effect that Second Isaiah thus achieves is reminiscent of the rhetorical style of Hosea 6:1–5: "It is [the LORD] who has torn, and he will heal us" (Hos. 6:1). Although we are dealing with a conventional form of speech, its purpose cannot be mistaken. A people going to ruin through their indifference is placed in a setting where they must account for their behavior: "Accuse me," God says, "let us go to

79

trial." We witness love attempting to break through the walls of self-delusion and deception, seeking to drive a people stubbornly bent upon its own destruction to a moment of honest reckoning. "If you truly believe that I have dealt wrongly with you, Israel, accuse me. Speak openly, cry out, shout, break the silence that like a deadly poison slowly paralyzes and then kills the victim."

God reminds the people that it was precisely such stubborn persistence in sin that led to the destruction of their ancestors. By summoning the descendants of the tragic earlier generations to trial, God seeks to bring them back to their senses. We hear the pain and ardor of love in the accusation that the people have grown weary of their God, in the expression of bitter disappointment that they could not even show the smallest of tokens of appreciation by bringing the Creator of the universe a sweet cane, in the reminder that divine forgiveness even now waits for the reopening of their hearts to remorse and repentance.

The trial speech that concludes chapter 43 therefore in no way subtracts from the prophetic call for a faith that expresses itself in acts of mercy and justice. Rather, it peers deeply to the source of the life of compassion, integrity, and courageous righteousness, namely, a living relationship with God that reverberates with love's gifts, responsiveness, gratitude, and simple tokens of true friendship, gifts that give concrete expression to the otherwise elusive mystery of the bonds of compassion and the cords of love that can unite God and human beings in an authentic relationship that becomes the basis and model for all other relationships.

Isaiah 44:1–5
I Will Pour Out My Spirit

Attempts to establish divisions between prophetic units in Isaiah 40—55 remain far from definitive. It is very possible that unclarities that persist reflect an important structural feature of this material: Divisions often seem to be "soft" divisions. Although 44:1–5, for example, in one respect bears the characteristics of a self-contained oracle of salvation, in another respect it develops out of the preceding trial speech in 43:22–28. It is possible to read 44:1–5 in isolation, and the result is a beautiful message of assurance and promise. But that message is given a deeper dimension of meaning when it is seen to arise out of the tension between accusation and forgiveness that reverberates through the preceding verses. The dynamic relational quality of faith in God becomes strikingly vivid. Israel's God does not remain aloof in divine isolation as human beings tread the precarious path between life in covenant and death through apostasy. God through the prophetic word tears into the sloth and complacency that threatens to numb Israel to the reality of the living God in its midst.

In both the accusations and the assurances the intimately personal forms of address are used repeatedly: "Jacob . . . Israel." We have noted in 43:22–28 how God seeks to shock the community back to its senses. The rules of drawing room etiquette are suspended in favor of hard-hitting straight talk. Emotions are not hidden behind a facade of divine immutability. God shouts: "Accuse me. . . . Set forth your case" (43:26). At the same time, the irrepressible love of God comes to expression with equal passion: "I will not remember your sins" (43:25).

This lively tension which sets in motion energies that strike at the defenses of a halfhearted commitment is too highly charged to be contained within the confines of one trial speech. The concluding description of punishment in 43:28, while an entirely fitting climax to a courtroom scene, within the broader context of Second Isaiah's theology simply cannot end the matter. In 44:1–5 we seem to be overhearing the continuation of the conversations between the contestants on the courthouse steps. The judge has stepped down from the tribunal, deep human emotions having overcome the formalities of the legal process and leading instead to a personal appeal to the hearts of the convicted.

Whatever else they, in the confusion produced by their wavering devotion, may regard themselves to be, God addresses them with names that indicate who they really are when viewed from the perspective of the One who created them in love and redeemed them from bondage: "Jacob my servant, . . . Israel whom I have chosen" (v. 1). If only they could accept how special they are in the eyes of God, the beauty of

81

the covenant relationship would overcome all resistance and rebelliousness. This is not some recent infatuation, some serendipitous convergence of passing fancy.

The relationship of love that God describes runs deeper even than the great acts of deliverance such as the exodus. It is more basic than Israel's being established as a nation within the course of history. The relationship that unites Israel and its God is more ultimate than any temporal phenomenon. Those addressed by God belonged to the Lord already in the womb. They were born into the sustaining grace to which they owe everything. More ultimate than the episodes of their epic, more crucial than the nurturance of their families, more essential than the air they breathe, is the loving God who created them.

Divine love reaches out to renew the bonds of love by speaking a word addressing the confusion that prompts their wayward wandering: "Do not fear" (v. 2). What ultimately turns a people away from its life source? It is fear in the face of powers claiming to hold awesome power over them, chthonic and astral deities, fate, divine kings, demons of pestilence and destruction or the dread arising out of the guilt lodged in their own hearts. The people's surrender to false gods does not arise out of a pious response to an experience of the holy but out of a sense of defeat before the demonic. The only effective answer to such resignation to the forces of death is a word of assurance from the giver of life: "Do not fear."

In verse 3 an image is offered that promises to restore the life-affirming confidence in God's grace that can dispel human fear. It is the image of a wasteland, the same image that T. S. Eliot found fitting as a description of the desolation and emptiness that continue to afflict people today. Life that is cut off from God is like dry ground: barren, deadening, hopeless. Over this bleak and sterile landscape God promises to pour water and create streams. Again this image establishes a basis for renewed hope that runs deeper even than Israel's epic story of the exodus from Egypt. Second Isaiah's theology of creation reconnects a languishing people with its life source, the God whose spirit (rûaḥ) swept over the face of the waters on the first day of creation (Gen. 1:2) and whose breath brought the first human being into existence (Gen. 2:7). Like the first garden, the earth, refreshed with abundant waters, will soon flourish. The scene is even more idyllic when it describes the generations to come, for they will be filled with God's spirit (rûaḥ) and with God's

82

blessing. No longer cut off from God by their parents' negligence (43:27–28), these happy descendants will prosper like the plants of a paradisiacal garden.

The restoration of the vital lifeline of fellowship and blessing in place of the barriers of rejection and complacency would prompt a wholesome and joyous response. In place of pathetic complaints about God being a weariness and a bother will arise glad shouts reclaiming the names that celebrate the intimate kinship ties that bound God and people together in an earlier age: "I am the LORD's," "Jacob," "the LORD's." It seems altogether possible, both in the light of the universalistic tendencies discernible elsewhere in Second Isaiah and on the basis of the specific language of this passage, that the community envisioned for the new era extended beyond the traditional bounds of the Jewish nation. For the fourth in the series of designations, "[another will] adopt the name of Israel," utilizes the verb *(kin-nāh)* applied to Cyrus in the next chapter (45:4). When God's spirit is poured upon a languishing creation, the results are surprises that recall the innovations of the first creation. The barriers that separated human beings from God crumble as a relationship of wholehearted love arises from a barren wilderness of alienation and distrust, and the restoration of that primal relationship brings with it in turn the removal of barriers separating human beings from one another. Celebration of the creating and redeeming God becomes the grounds for the reunification of human being with human being, as those who were separated join together under the banner of the one true God.

The inspired visionary in a community of faith is a gift of God's spirit. Out of the ashes of judgment Second Isaiah is able to discern the creative activity of God, sweeping over the face of a desolate human landscape like the spirit of God sweeping over the face of the primordial waters. We must take care not to set artificial limits on Second Isaiah's message, for the meaning of these words is not determined by historical pragmatics alone. Second Isaiah dared to imagine a new world by drawing on the power of the story of creation. God was not limited to historical acts such as the exodus, in which a specific group of slaves were freed from bondage. God the Redeemer was at the same time God the Creator. What Second Isaiah dared to imagine was not only a second exodus, in which exiled Israel would return to its homeland, but a second creation, in which a lan-

83

guishing and divided humanity would be revivified by receiving the spirit that originally brought life out of the dust.

It was not only the exilic Jewish community of the Persian period or the Pentecost community of the time of Peter that existed like a desolate wasteland desperately in need of the life-giving breath of God. "Wasteland" is perhaps one of the most apt metaphors for our contemporary world. As South American rain forests are cut down leaving behind ashes and the extinction of countless species, as deserts advance on the continent of Africa cutting off sources of food to starving millions, as nations are balkanized into warring religious factions, as cities decay threatening a whole generation of youth with futility, as AIDS tears into the health of whole nations, human resources appear pitifully unequal to the challenge of restoring our planet to health. Hard-nosed pragmatists will deride suggestions that we turn to a transcendent reality for aid. But for those who can discern beneath the surface of human neglect a fundamental dislocation on the level of spiritual commitment, Second Isaiah's call to a moment of honest reckoning with the Creator of the universe rings out as the most pertinent message of our age. Indeed, it is a call that has pressing relevance for all areas of contemporary life, a fact that we can only illustrate by mention of one.

At the core of contemporary life a sickness spreads that involves the breakdown of healthy interpersonal relationships, whether between spouses, parents and children, friends, or business associates. Granted, the Bible must not be read naively as a primer in relational psychology. Nevertheless, on a level glimpsed clearly by true sages of the human condition, authentic relations are secured best when rooted in the kind of spirituality that is intimately acquainted with God's struggle for the human heart. One such modern sage is Dietrich Bonhoeffer, who derives from Luke 14:26 a model for human relationships based explicitly on God's love: "There can be no pure love of the world unless we love it with the love wherewith God loved in Jesus Christ" (p. 82). No parent in our modern world is able to avoid moments of anguish when a son or a daughter, emerging into adulthood, is caught up in a situation that cries out for parental counsel at the same time as defiance becomes the child's chosen means of securing space for growth. In such a dilemma the message of detachment or confusion that is com-

municated by silence is as inadequate as the message of conde-
scending certainty. In such a situation the relationship can be
saved from paralysis only if parent and child are aware of a
grounding in love and trust that runs far deeper than any difference in judgment or perception, and there is no grounding that
is more dependable in such times than a shared faith.

Awareness of the givenness of love's grounding creates a
safe space within which honest feelings can be aired from both
sides. Words do not crackle with ill-disguised anger but flow
naturally from a blending of love and honest concern, even
when they are challenging words rooted in deep convictions.
The God who is so honest as to expose disappointment over as
seemingly trivial a matter as the human being's failure to bring
"sweet cane" invites parent to express feelings of anxiety and
hurt and child to assert with integrity the need to build a personal moral universe. It is a precious moment indeed when
spirited discussion draws to a conclusion not necessarily with
agreement, or even with the verbalization of mutual gratitude,
but with a quiet understanding in which child is appreciative
of parent's expression of love through the honest articulation of
personal values and parent is respectful of child's desire to address life's issues with courage and integrity. In such a discussion there are not winning and losing sides but only the
reaffirmation of mutual respect based on love and trust. As a
result of such authentic communication, the names that signify
the relationship are celebrated, wonderful names like father
and mother, son and daughter, names that create a sense of
well-being and security, a sense that the world has a center, a
home to which one can always return and be welcomed, no
matter how far one strays, no matter how much one changes.

Too often, though, we forget how basic to human development is the most fundamental relationship of all, the one in
which human beings are reconciled with their divine parent.
Upon this relationship, this honest give-and-take of deep feelings predicated on divine love and trust, human beings are able
to model all other relationships with a sense of confidence. For
the nagging doubt that tears away at authentic relationships—
fear, fear of being misunderstood, of being rejected, of being
cut off—is removed. That fear disappears before the awareness
that those who are upheld first by God's grace are bonded by
ties that cannot be severed by human differences: "Do not fear,

85

O Jacob my servant, Jeshurun whom I have chosen" (v. 2). Such assurance alone can satisfy the thirst of a world that longs for restored relationships.

It is time for people of faith to reclaim with Second Isaiah the audacity to envision God's creative spirit being poured out on a world that resembles a wilderness. It is true that all the way from our individual lives to relations between the nations to the vast realm of nature we face conditions of drought, as if spring rains have been cut off and flowing streams have been dammed up. Lives have become arid and sterile. Relationships wither or turn into tensions and strife. Repeatedly we hear people remark about a troubled marriage, "But they both are such wonderful people!" In such cases it is most natural to yearn for the inbreaking of a transforming spirit, which, like "streams on the dry ground," will re-create life and hope, the renewal of a spirit of honest engagement with each other. Such yearning, according to Second Isaiah, is not empty dreaming, for it is induced by the Creator of us all. And the good news of Second Isaiah is this: The same God who creates that yearning for authenticity in the human heart is eager to satisfy it with the inpouring of the life-giving spirit, a spirit of reconciliation and new birth!

Isaiah 44:6–23
Besides Me There Is No God

The prophet has set before Israel God's promise of restoration to health. Although Israel's present condition could be compared to "dry ground," God was preparing to renew Israel with "living waters." Guided by a realism that ever stood guard against slipping into empty dreaming, however, Second Isaiah turns next to address an ever-present threat to the promise. The primary obstacle standing in the way of restoration was misplaced devotion.

In 44:6–23 the prophet therefore applies the genre of the trial speech to contend with idolatry, a theme earlier broached in 40:12–31 and 41:1–29. The structure of 44:6–23 is unique. After opening the trial with the interrogation of witnesses, the narrative turns to a vivid description of idol manufacturing in verses 9–20. This section gives the appearance of a document produced by the prosecution as evidence discrediting the trust-worthiness of the idols and their defenders by tracing the steps involved in the production of idols. The document moves all the way from step one, the sawing of a log in half (one half for firewood and the other for carving into a god!), to the final step, in which the artisan falls down before the idol in worship and prays, "Save me, for you are my god!" (v. 17).

The opening statement in verse 6 sets forth the theological tenet that underlies the entire trial process. The divine Judge speaks on his own behalf, since it is his authority that is in contention: "I am the first and I am the last; besides me there is no god." Here the monotheistic principle is stated with unam-biguous clarity, thereby marking the culminating stage in Is-rael's emergence from ancient Near Eastern polytheism to belief in one God as Creator and Ruler of the entire universe.

The interrogation of the rival gods and their witnesses that follows underlines the historical nature of Israelite religion and the central role played by the prophets as interpreters of his-tory. In the debate over which among the many claimants is the one true God, the realm that comes under rigorous scrutiny is the realm of human experience, that is, history. The myths of Babylon, with their description of heavenly events before the beginning of time and their ascription of daunting accomplish-ments of creation and combat to Marduk, certainly sounded impressive in the timeless realm of the temple cult. But in this trial the focus is on history. Who is the God that directs history and calls prophets to interpret for the people the relation of the bewildering realm of human events to divine purpose? This historical focus is entirely consistent with all that we know of Yahwism from the biblical period. Through the trials of the centuries, the faithful in Israel discerned God's presence in the events around them, events internal and events in which the leading actors were the rulers of mighty foreign empires.

The next passage that we shall examine, the so-called Cyrus oracle, is a perfect example of this historical perspective, for it interprets the significance for Israel's faith of the sea change in the Eastern Mediterranean caused by the conquests of Cyrus. It is noteworthy, therefore, that the Cyrus oracle begins with a contrast between the lying omens of the pagan diviners and the word of Israel's prophets which God confirms. In that oracle as in the present trial scene, the case is to be decided on the basis of evidence from history. And the people are not left out as passive observers. They are key actors in the court of law, as they were in 43:10. What they have experienced in the history of their nation constitutes the evidence that will determine the outcome of the trial. The Judge enjoins them: "Do not fear. . . . You are my witnesses!" (v. 8).

For exiled Jews immersed in the chaotic events that followed the destruction of Judah, to be sure, the evidence may not have been so clear. Determination of the destiny of nations seemed to have been taken from Yahweh by Marduk, whose armies had destroyed Jerusalem and its temple. Of that patron god the Babylonian choruses sang (*Enūma eliš* IV. 5–9; Pritchard, p. 66):

> Thou, Marduk, art the most honored of the great gods,
> Thy decree is unrivaled, thy word is Anu.
> From this day unchangeable shall be thy pronouncement.
> To raise or bring low—these shall be (in) thy hand.
> Thy utterance shall be true,
>   thy command shall be unimpeachable.

It is important to remember that the Jews in exile were living as a minority in the shadows of the great Marduk temples and amidst the sound and excitement of the Babylonian religious festivals. Polemic that was waged against the claims of the Marduk priests therefore was not the idle activity of sophists. It was a matter of life and death for a people threatened by assimilation into powerful pagan cults. It is within that context that we must understand the next twelve verses.

Most commentators treat 44:9–20 as secondary, inserted, along with several other passages attacking idols, at various points in the Second Isaiah corpus (40:12–31; 41:1–10; 46:1–13). It is true that verses 9–20 differ stylistically from the surrounding verses. But this may stem from the dramatic skill of Second Isaiah, who presents a captivating satire on idol making as, in effect, "Exhibit A" in this "trial of the gods." This interpretation is supported by the fact that the contrast between the true God and the false gods permeates the entire Second Isaiah corpus (Clifford, pp. 450–64).

The prophet who in references to the conquests of Cyrus revealed himself to be an astute observer of political events here betrays himself to be an equally diligent student of Babylonian religious practices. Cuneiform scholar Thorkild Jacobsen has recently described the contents of ancient Mesopotamian texts that depict the fashioning and dedication of an idol (Jacobsen 1987a, 15–32). They substantiate the verisimilitude of Second Isaiah's account. Among the features of the ancient texts are ritual denials by carpenter and goldsmith that they were the manufacturers of the idol. Thus the goldsmith: "The god Gushkinbanda, Ea of the goldsmiths, verily made it. I did not make it!" The carpenter makes similar denial. There follows a lengthy scene on a riverbank depicting the birth of the god from his father, the river god Ea, and his mother, the tamarisk.

True to the genre of satire and in keeping with his own polemical purposes, Second Isaiah does not describe the more subtle aspects of the ancient idol-making ritual found in the texts examined by Jacobsen, such as the appeal to the god to depart from its heavenly abode to enter the image and thus be present among human beings. Such phenomenological sensitivity would be too much to expect of one fighting against formidable odds to keep the people faithful to their God Yahweh. Rather, he draws from the idol ritual one major point: A god carved and gold-plated by artisans and borne on the shoulders of porters is a god neither capable of delivering a people from its bondage nor worthy of that people's devotion. And what is to be said about those who would defend such gods? Unlike members of the prophet's community who are witnesses taught by the events of their history, the witnesses of these gods "neither see nor know" (compare v. 9 with v. 8).

Having presented "Exhibit A" as a disclosure of the nature of the other gods, the prophet returns to the positive side of the contrast, the God who, unlike the "gods" fashioned by human beings, is the Creator of all human beings. That God appeals directly to the people in verses 21–22. Since it is clear in these two verses that God no longer speaks as a defendant in the case but as the Chief Justice, his words of admonition give the trial a new twist. The case of the other gods having collapsed, the trial moves its focus to the people Israel. Now *they* are on trial! Before *them* stands the choice of the life or death sentence. The basis of their response is to be remembering, not the kind of remembering that is bound to discredited human structures (43:18–19), but a remembering that calls to mind the foundational events that define their essential being, their origins in God the Creator and their forgiveness and release from bond-

89

age accomplished by that same God, their Redeemer. The choice that faces Israel could not be formulated more succinctly: "Remember these things, . . . return to me" (vv. 21–22).

For Second Isaiah, the restoration of Israel to the blessings of their covenant relationship with God was not a parochial matter. It was nothing less than a key to the restoration of harmony within the entire created order, for as witnesses to God's universal sovereignty Israel served as mediators of the shalom stemming from Torah obedience and extending to the entire cosmos. Fittingly, therefore, the trial ends with the courtroom filling with a hymn of praise joined by the heavens, the earth, the mountains, and every tree of the forest! The Jewish minority no longer stand alone as witnesses to the legitimacy of Yahweh's kingship. They are joined by witnesses spanning the entire creation! Second Isaiah thus concludes the passage on one of his favorite themes: There is a purpose in the creative, redemptive activity of God that transcends even the deliverance of the exiled community and the healing of a shattered world. Ultimately, all members of the created order will be united in what is their highest calling and the source of their sublimest pleasure, giving praise to the one true God.

For the person who is interested in the significance of biblical texts for modern experience, Isaiah 44:6–23 presents interesting questions. In a world that brings diverse religious groups into ever-closer contact with one another, the "trial of the gods" found here strikes one with particular poignancy. What light does the Bible shed on the relation of the Jew or the Christian to the Hindu? Do we find guidance here for our relation to Native American religions?

As in the case of all modern issues, the questions that exercise us are not identical to those which pressed themselves upon our ancestors. Nevertheless, the Bible often opens up avenues of thought that move us forward in our reflection. And Second Isaiah is a very wise tutor for the person asking, "What is the relation between God and the gods?"

It is tempting to answer with a quotation from this text: "I am the first and I am the last; besides me there is no god." And thus the problem of "God and gods" is decided. Our understanding of God is right, while the objects of devotion of all other peoples is idolatry.

There are reasons to believe that the monotheism of Second Isaiah is more subtle and profound. A disciple of his described the Jewish community as a people that "delight to draw near to God" (58:2). But their notion, that disciple maintained, was completely wrong. What they called worship was a matter of serving their own interests (58:3). Like the people of Jeremiah's time who felt immune to judgment because they could gather at the temple and chant, "The temple of the LORD, the temple of the LORD" (Jer. 7:4), these people had turned their faith into a mockery of God. Their religion was no more authentic than the idolatry of pagans (cf. Isa. 66:3).

Second Isaiah did not simply line up the nations and claim that Israel had all the truth about God, while all others were cut off from God. On the one hand, Second Isaiah had to struggle against idolatrous notions within the Jewish community. "Who gave up Jacob to the spoiler, and Israel to the robbers? Was it not the LORD?" (42:24). On the other hand, Second Isaiah announced that God had named Cyrus the Persian as his "shepherd" and his "anointed" (44:28; 45:1) and appointed him as the deliverer of the exiled Jews. The one true God, according to Second Isaiah, did not refrain from relating to a pagan king. To the contrary, after appointing Cyrus, God adds the motive: "so that you may know that it is I, the LORD, the God of Israel, who call you by your name" (45:3).

The God of Second Isaiah is a God whose rule spans the universe, a God breaking the narrow conceptions of Jew and Gentile alike. Second Isaiah is uncompromising in insisting that there is only one God. But he emphatically does not invite us to draw an equation between our concept of God and the reality of the universal God. Rather, he encourages us to be open to surprises concerning the one who may offer us instruction in God's mysterious saving ways in the world.

Is knowledge of God, then, unattainable? Second Isaiah concurs with all of Israel's prophets in pointing to the kind of knowledge that is true, it is knowledge of God's will *(tôrāh)* and willingness to obey it. And this is where the witness of Israel takes on importance vis-à-vis the nations. Not in assuming the posture of superior knowledge of divine mysteries but in faithfully bringing forth justice to the nations (42:1–4) is Israel present in the world as God's chosen people. Accordingly, the distinction that is of foremost importance to Second Isaiah is the distinction between idol worshipers (within and without Israel) and those who uphold justice and mercy. It is in giving a faithful example of justice and mercy that Israel becomes "a covenant to the people, a light to the nations," and a witness to the God who calls the entire human family to righteousness and blessing. His "trial of the gods" therefore is set before us, not as an inducement to use our confessions to diminish the dignity and integrity of others, but to help us to distinguish between mockery of God and true piety. It would be interesting to know how the prophet who recognized the will of God in the conquests of the Persian Cyrus might have responded to the prayer of the king who, just a few years before Second Isaiah wrote his satire on the idols, prayed thus to his god Marduk (Jacobsen 1987a, p. 29):

> Without Thee, Lord, what has existence?
> For the king Thou lovest, whose name Thou didst call
> who pleaseth Thee, Thou advancest his fame,
> Thou assignest him a straightforward path.
>
> I am a prince Thou favorest, a creature of Thine hands.
> Thou madest me, entrusted to me the kingship over all
>   people.
> Of Thy grace, O Lord, who providest for all of them,
> cause me to love Thy exalted rule.
> Let fear of Thy godhead be in my heart,
> grant me what seemeth good to Thee.
> Thou wilt do, verily, what profiteth me.

Granted, it would have been harder to be charitable to the king who destroyed the temple than to the one who ordered its rebuilding! When we remember, however, that Second Isaiah shared the view of his prophetic colleagues that God commissioned foreign kings not only to deliver a repentant Israel but also to punish an idolatrous people, it no longer becomes absurd to think that he might have detected the openness even of Nebuchadnezzar to the guiding hand of the universal God.

Of course, we benefit from insights that were perhaps not available to Second Isaiah. We know that the Babylonians did not simply identify Marduk with a block of wood any more than does the Hindu draw such naive equations. We know that images of the same deity were found in many different Babylonian temples. And in dedication ceremonies, their priests prayed for the heavenly god to make him or herself present to the people in the idol. But perhaps our insights can be enriched by no source as profound as the words of the prophet who could capture the true relationship between the one God and all mortals in an image as sublime as this:

[God is the one] who sits above the circle of the earth,
  and its inhabitants are like grasshoppers;
who stretches out the heavens like a curtain,
  and spreads them like a tent to live in;
who brings princes to naught,
  and makes the rulers of the earth as nothing.

(Isa. 40:22)

Isaiah 44:24—45:7
Cyrus, My Anointed

The cities of Judah lay in ruins. Even the once magnificent emblem of the national cult, the Jerusalem temple, had not been spared. The leaders of Judah, together with a major segment of the populace, now lived as exiles in the land of the Babylonian conquerors and witnessed the processions of the victorious god, Marduk. How could a spokesperson of Israel's God Yahweh explain a world situation that seemingly was under the control of the patron deity of the Babylonian empire?

Many among the conquered Jews responded to the new situation by transferring their allegiance from Yahweh to the gods of the conquerors (cf. Jer. 44:15–19; Ezek. 8:7–18). In so doing, they were guided by the prevailing view in the ancient Near East that the defeat of a state indicated the decline of that state's sponsoring deity in the assembly of the gods. This view is illustrated graphically by the lament written in the wake of the Gutian destruction of the Third Dynasty of Ur. Ningal, Mother Goddess of Ur, concedes that gods more powerful than she have led to her defeat (Pritchard, p. 460):

Verily Anu has cursed my city,
  my city verily has been destroyed;
Verily Enlil has turned inimical to my house,
  by the pickaxe verily it has been *torn up*.

Her decline is painfully symbolized by the construction of the sanctuary of the victorious god on the site of her destroyed temple ("in the place of my house a strange house is being erected." Ningal suffers the disgrace of banishment (Pritchard, p. 461):

Woe is me, I am one who has been exiled from the city,
  I am one who has found no rest.

93

The national humiliation that accompanies military defeat inevitably leads to a deep questioning of prevailing religious beliefs. This is especially the case when the stature of a deity is equated with the wealth and the military success of that deity's favored nation. In the cultures surrounding Israel, cult and nation were inseparable. It is thus understandable that faith in Marduk, Amun Re, and the Olympian gods disappeared when their empires collapsed.

A repudiation of this linkage of the destiny of patron god to the fate of his client nation arose among the Gnostics on the basis of their disassociating pure deity from the material universe of possessions and human politics. But Gnosticism in its various forms proved to be no more satisfying to the human religious quest than the nation cults. While the yoking of deity with state was judged harshly by time, so was the dissolving of all ties between religion and historical experience. Gnostic sects thus died along with the cults of city-states and empires.

The faith of Israel explored a daring alternative to both nation-cult identification and Gnostic withdrawal. That Yahweh was involved in the events of history was a theological inference drawn by the Hebrews already in the exodus from Egypt. The prophets cultivated further the tradition of examining human experience in relation to divine purpose. Accordingly, the denigration of the material world promoted by gnosticism failed to take root in the religious communities growing out of the Bible.

The prophets, however, did not embrace the popular view of the great cultures surrounding Israel that the interests of a god coincided with the interests of the nation or city-state. While God acted on behalf of Israel's ancestors in Egypt and continued to be active in the events of Israel's history, the divine purpose was not guided by a nationalistic agenda but by a universal plan of justice. The moral norms that Israel extrapolated from its perception of God's interaction with human beings were norms that transcended the self-interests of any clan or nation. The Hebrew slaves were delivered, not because God loved Hebrews and hated Egyptians, but because God loved justice and hated oppression. From that experience the religious leaders of Israel inferred laws protecting the weak and poor and opposing exploitation and claims of special privilege.

94

As the leaders of the Jewish community increasingly were drawn into the vortex of international events, they found it necessary to extend inchoate moral principles beyond their

rather parochial beginnings. Amos stood fast against King Jero-
boam's attempt to equate religious faith with the interests of
state (Amos 7:10–17). For the God he served was the sovereign
Creator of the universe whose purposes were not guided by
favoritism but by impartial justice:

> The Lord, GOD of hosts,
> he who touches the earth and it melts,
>   and all who live in it mourn,
> and all of it rises like the Nile,
>   and sinks again, like the Nile of Egypt;
> who builds his upper chambers in the heavens,
>   and founds his vault upon the earth;
> who calls for the waters of the sea,
>   and pours them out upon the surface of the earth—
> the LORD is his name.
> Are you not like the Ethiopians to me,
>   O people of Israel? says the LORD.
> Did I not bring Israel up from the land of Egypt,
>   and the Philistines from Caphtor and the Arameans from
>   Kir?
> The eyes of the Lord GOD are upon the sinful kingdom,
>   and I will destroy it from the face of the earth
>   —except that I will not utterly destroy the house of
>   Jacob,
>   says the LORD.
>   (Amos 9:5–8)

The consistently moral understanding of divine purpose
that led Amos, and after him Isaiah and Jeremiah, to present
God's plan of universal justice to king and people was the same
understanding that guided Second Isaiah as he faced the doubts
of a people experiencing the apparent victory first of the empire of Marduk and then of Ahura Mazda. What room was left
for Yahweh, the God of Israel, in such sweeping world events?

For Second Isaiah that question was addressed by seeking
to discern how those events were serving God's universal plan
of justice and God's relentless opposition to oppression. The
argument that the Babylonian conquest of Judah had cast doubt
on Yahweh's sovereignty was an argument taken from the pa-
ganism of the nation-cults and was invalid within a prophetic
tradition that had consistently argued that God would enlist a
foreign power to punish a nation that had broken the terms of
its covenant with God by repudiating justice and mercy. What
the prophets had done in every other historical context Second
Isaiah would do now: He would interpret the events that were

95

unfolding in the world in relation to the universal moral purposes of the one true God.

Such interpretation, to be sure, represents an awesome challenge. Appropriately, the prophet begins by focusing on the one who is both the purpose and the source of proper interpretation of events in relation to divine providence. Such focusing is accomplished in the form of a hymn invoking Yahweh as Israel's Creator and Redeemer. In a world replete with competing deities, this hymn celebrates the Lord "who made all things" (44:24).

Noteworthy is the way in which this focus on the universal God is maintained throughout the entire oracle. In the first half (44:24–28) the technique used involves an unbroken chain of participial clauses that elaborate on the initial "I am the LORD" by proclaiming how everything, from the creation of the heavens to the specific details of the career of Cyrus, radiates from one purposeful center. In the second half of the oracle (45:1–7), the focus on the one true God is sustained by a chain of first-person pronouncements in which God, in the course of addressing Cyrus, explains how even this pagan conqueror is serving God's purpose. The rapid succession of three "I's" in the climactic verse 7 draws the entire proclamation into one remarkable universal confession.

In looking more closely at the first half of the oracle in 44:24–28, we note that the long series of participial clauses radiating from the divine self-introduction forms a single sentence. Its portrait of Yahweh's activities spans heaven and earth and encompasses creation and redemption. Moreover, the progression is suggestive of a meaningful order in God's interacting with human beings. Once the foundational confession has been made that God is both Israel's Redeemer and the Creator of all that is, the oracle turns to the question of how a human community can be enabled to understand the relation of divine purpose to the ambiguities of history. Here too the sovereignty of God is upheld: It is only because God has chosen to communicate with the human community through divinely appointed mediators that such understanding can be gained.

But in a world in which scores of self-proclaimed messengers are encountered speaking the "words" of a diverse array of deities, how can one distinguish between true and false prophets? Here too the faithful can rely upon God,

> who frustrates the omens of liars,
>   and makes fools of diviners;
> who turns back the wise,
>   and makes their knowledge foolish.
>   (Isa. 44:25)

The prophet is confident that the soothsayers and diviners and
sages of the other gods will be discredited on the basis of their
own words, which will not withstand the test of true prophecy,
that is, being confirmed by the events of history (Deut. 18:21–
22). More important than discrediting false prophets, however,
is affirming the dependable source of the words Israel is to trust,
the God

> who confirms the word of his servant,
>   and fulfills the prediction of his messengers.
>   (Isa. 44:26)

Critical to the preservation of a faithful community in the
midst of revolutionary change is the proclamation of those
called to deliver the message given to them by God. Who are
they? How can they be identified? How can a community be
confident that it includes faithful interpreters of divine will?
The answer of this oracle to these questions is clear: The same
God who directs the events of creation and history according
to a universal purpose will provide trustworthy interpreters.
Certainly this does not dispel all questions, but it does point
clearly to the heart of the matter: As in all other matters, so too
in the matter of understanding world events God will provide.

Having thus related the prophetic word to the source of all
reality, the oracle moves on to proclaim the message addressing
Israel's specific situation and point in time, for God is not only
cosmic Creator but the caring God redemptively active in the
lives of human beings. That message has a noteworthy ordering
of its own: At the beginning (44:26*b*), God announces the restoration of Jerusalem and the cities of Judah; at the end (44:28*b*),
God repeats the promise concerning Jerusalem and extends it
to include the rebuilding of the temple. Framed by this inclusion are two further promises: God names the agent of this
redemptive work, "Cyrus my shepherd," as the one who would
"carry out all my purpose," and says to the deep, "Be dry—I will
dry up your rivers." The individual parts of this intricate structure need to be examined more closely.

97

Crucial to Second Isaiah's message is the promise that decimated Judah and Jerusalem and their pillaged temple would be restored. The wholeness that God intended for his creatures was not a nebulous bliss located outside time and corporal existence. It entailed transformation of political structures that earlier had imposed exile upon a defeated nation and restoration of economic, political, and religious infrastructures enabling a people to resume its life and mission within the family of nations.

Although envisioning the restoration of real institutions and structures, this message could still amount to little more than empty dreaming if it had no chance of becoming a reality. But Second Isaiah was not an empty dreamer. Convinced that God was the sovereign Lord of all reality, he scanned the world stage for signs of God's activity in a process of discernment that combined deep faith with critical-historical knowledge. Recognizing that the people through repentance had opened their lives to God's mercy, he inquired whether there was evidence in world events of the one whom God would use as agent of Israel's restoration. His scrutiny led to an answer, which he presented boldly to his audience: *Cyrus* was the one chosen by God for this specific task!

The significance of this conclusion for biblical faith is great. Of those bearing the responsibility of preserving the classical confessions of a religious community is required more than repetition of hallowed texts. Upon them rests the challenge to relate those texts and their warnings and promises to the actual events of history. They must be able to reply to those desiring to know where and how God is present in contemporary events. They must be able to guide people who order their lives after God's will to a fitting response to the alternatives presented by the world of politics and economics.

Second Isaiah did not play it safe by hiding behind theological generalities. He responded with specificity and poignancy: God has chosen *Cyrus*. While it is difficult to fathom the complexity involved in prophetic inspiration, we can be aided by knowledge of what Second Isaiah saw on the world stage. He saw a skilled political-military leader who seemed to be guided not by delight in cruelty toward subject peoples but by an enlightened policy that viewed concern for their well-being as consonant with his own political objectives. He saw the speed with which Cyrus integrated Media and Persia into one kingdom and the incisiveness with which he defeated Croesus of Lydia in 546 B.C.E. He witnessed the banishment of ruthless tyrants and the ascent of a humane statesman. Well aware of the prophetic tradition that both ascribed to Babylon the limited divine assignment of punishing apostate Judah and threatened it with judgment for being driven by hubris to claim godlike sovereignty (cf. Isa. 14:4*b*–21; 21:1–10), Second Isaiah interpreted Cyrus's victorious entry into Babylon in 539 B.C.E. as evidence of divine commission. This explains his ascription to the Persian conqueror of a title widely used in the ancient Near East to designate kings: "He is my shepherd, and he shall carry out all my purpose" (44:28). We shall return to Second Isaiah's understanding of Cyrus's role when we discuss the second half of the oracle, 45:1–7. But first we shall consider the second divine pronouncement framed by the promise of restoration to Judah/Jerusalem and the temple: "who says to the deep, 'Be dry—I will dry up your rivers' " (44:27).

Conceptually we perhaps feel equipped to grasp the meaning of Second Isaiah's identification of Cyrus as an agent of divine purpose. But our modern minds tend to be baffled by the divine command to "the deep" *(haṣṣûlāh)* to "be dry." *Ṣûlāh,* the Hebrew noun here translated "the deep," together with the variant *měṣûlāh,* has strong mythic connotations. In Job 41:31–32, in parallel with *těhôm,* it designates the dwelling place of the mythical creature Leviathan. *Těhôm* in turn is related etymologically to a primordial "cousin" of Leviathan named Tiamat, the adversary of Marduk in the Babylonian creation myth. In early Israel's application of the cosmogonic myth to its epic, Yahweh the Warrior casts his adversary into the depths *(měṣôlōt,* in parallel with *těhōmōt,* Exod. 15:5).

The disposition of the primordial waters is enshrouded in ambiguity in ancient Near Eastern myth. In one aspect (as destructive floodwaters and saltwater tides), they are dread foes of human civilization and must be subdued by the god overseeing the order and prosperity of a culture. As subterranean sweet waters, however, they are regarded as essential to life and become one of the chief benefits accompanying the champion god's victory. Both aspects echo through the Hebrew Bible: the threatening aspect, for example, in Exodus 15; Isaiah 51:10; and Psalm 104:5–9; and the life-giving aspect in Genesis 2:10–14 and Ezekiel 47. At other times the ambiguity is preserved, as in the recasting of a Baal hymn in Psalm 29.

Closely related to the primordial waters in both of their guises is the temple. In the Babylonian creation myth, Marduk's defeat of Tiamat and his beneficent ordering of creation are commemorated in the construction of a temple (*Enūma eliš* VI. 47–120; Pritchard, pp. 68–69). In Ugaritic mythology, which is our closest source for the religious views of the Canaanites, Baal's victory over Yamm ("Sea") is similarly rewarded with the construction of a temple (Text 51 [IIAB]; Pritchard, pp. 131–35). Baal's temple vividly illustrates the ambiguity enshrouding the primordial waters. It symbolizes the defeat of Sea; yet its construction includes a window related to Baal's function as the Cloud Rider who brings the life-giving rains. In Ugaritic mythology the tent sanctuary of the father of the gods, El, in turn is located over the "double deep," again underlining the connection between sanctuary and primordial water. When the Sumerian king Gudea of Lagash received plans for a new temple from his god Ningirsu in a dream, these plans included water vases from which "sparkling waters flow and flow" (Jacobsen, p. 339). And it is noteworthy that in the Babylonian creation epic, when Ea, god of fresh waters, slayed Apsu (the god of primordial waters), he built his temple "upon Apsu." It was in the heart of Apsu in turn that Marduk was born to Ea and his wife Damkina (*Enūma eliš* I.51–82; Pritchard, pp. 61–62).

But does such ancient myth have any bearing on Second Isaiah's thought? There is reason to think that it does. In 51:9–11 we shall see how the cosmogonic myth that recounts the defeat of the ancient primordial adversary is related to both the exodus and the promised return to Zion. What at first seems to be a disconnected reference to "the deep" in the Cyrus oracle in the light of mythopoeic background reveals itself to be an ancient aspect of temple ideology.

No nation could be restored and no temple could be rebuilt if the arcane forces that threaten order and harmony on their most fundamental level were not incisively subdued. For in the ancient's imagination, there lurked beneath the surface of political programs and rebuilding projects inimical foes, mysterious and often malevolent in character. People with an ethical bent tend to ascribe the word "evil" to such forces; those who have a metaphysical orientation may designate them chaos. But they underlie every human project like heat generated by the friction between tectonic plates, ready to lash out without warning with deadly impact.

100

We may not be able to embrace the particular mythopoeic worldview that produced the imagery of Second Isaiah. But we may be in danger of underestimating the challenges that face every age if we do not reflect on the significance of the fact that chaotic forces persist in undoing projects undertaken by human communities. Second Isaiah was aware of the limits of human power. In the destruction of Jerusalem and the desecration of the temple, he recognized powers of superhuman stature. He dared to promise the rebuilding of Jerusalem and the refounding of the temple because at the heart of the word he received from God he heard God's command disarming such powers and removing their dominion: "Be dry!"

The second half of the Cyrus oracle (45:1–7) concentrates on the evidence within the realm of human history for the changes God was effecting on the most fundamental level of reality. And it revolves around the political-military leader who was dazzling the ancient world with his success, Cyrus.

It is instructive to place alongside the words about Cyrus in Isaiah 45:1–7 the words that Cyrus himself commissioned as an explanation of his plan of conquest. After condemning the reigning king of Babylon (i.e., Nabonidus) for spurning Marduk and oppressing the people, he speaks of his own commission (Pritchard, p. 315):

> Marduk . . . on account of (the fact that) the sanctuaries of all their settlements were in ruins and the inhabitants of Sumer and Akkad had become like (living) dead, turned back (his countenance), [his] an[ger] [abated] and he had mercy (upon them). He scanned and looked (through) all the countries, searching for a righteous ruler willing to lead him (i.e. Marduk) (in the annual procession). (Then) he pronounced the name of Cyrus, king of Anshan, declared him (lit.: pronounced [his] name) to be(come) the ruler of all the world.

Second Isaiah changes one important detail by reporting that *Yahweh* rather than Marduk is the God who called Cyrus: "I call you by your name, I surname you" (45:4). The phrase that follows indicates, however, that Second Isaiah was not naive but fully aware that his Yahwistic perspective was not shared by Cyrus: ". . . though you do not know me." And he concurs completely with the Cyrus inscription regarding the effects of the divine commission. Of Marduk the Cyrus text says, "He made him set out on the road to Babylon going at his side like a real friend." In the opening verses of Isaiah 45, Yahweh refers

101

to Cyrus, "whose right hand I have grasped," and promises, "I will go before you."

While we can only speculate over whether Second Isaiah knew of the Cyrus cylinder inscription, it seems likely that the gist of the Cyrus propaganda was familiar to him. It also seems likely that Second Isaiah was impressed with Cyrus's piety, described thus in the inscription (Pritchard, p. 315):

> And he (Cyrus) did always endeavor to treat according to justice the black-headed whom he (Marduk) has made him conquer. Marduk, the great lord, a protector of his people/worshippers, beheld with pleasure his (i.e. Cyrus') good deeds and his upright mind (lit.: heart).

Cyrus, in other words, probably impressed the prophet of Yahweh as an appropriate instrument of divine mercy, even as the ruthless Nebuchadnezzar had appeared to earlier prophets to be an appropriate instrument of divine judgment. Throughout the changing applications of the prophetic vision, however, one underlying theological principle remained consistent: Whoever the agent called by God, one ultimate purpose was served:

> That they may know, from the rising of the sun
> and from the west, that there is no one besides me.
> (Isa. 45:6)

The Cyrus oracle ends with a verse that has evoked considerable debate:

> I form light and create darkness,
> I make weal and create woe,
> I the LORD do all these things.
> (Isa. 45:7)

In the mind of the prophet may have been the dualism inherent in Cyrus's Persian religious background, according to which light/weal and darkness/woe were the domains of separate gods. The more important point of reference, however, is perhaps to be found in the complexity of the message of Second Isaiah. On the one hand, this prophet proclaimed God's imminent salvation: "I will turn the darkness before them into light" (42:16). On the other hand, he pointed to Yahweh as the one who had turned upon the nation in fiery judgment (42:24–25). Can the agent of light and the agent of darkness be the same being? According to the prevailing view in antiquity, such vacil-

102

lation in the fate of a nation was due to conflicts between gods of light and darkness, weal and woe. On the most basic level, reality was not unified, but divided.

Actually, the contest with dualism strikes even closer to the heart of Second Isaiah's message. We noted above that the announcement of the rebuilding of the temple included a divine word commanding "the deep" to "be dry." Even in the world of Second Isaiah, governed by the one sovereign God of the universe ("besides me there is no god," 44:6), the persistent powers of unruly chaos had to be addressed (in this regard, see Levenson).

All of the above is not to diminish the significance of the summary statement in 45:7. It remains climactic, but less so in a systematic way than in the manner of an urgent, perhaps even defiant cry of faith. Much there is in the experience of individual people of faith and communities of faith that suggests that reality on the most fundamental level is fractured into contending centers of power. All theodicies attempting to defend the ways of God notwithstanding, there persists the sense that the innocent suffer unjustly, and even if one were to grant the category of disciplinary punishment, limits are transgressed that seem to call into question the belief that a God of mercy is sufficiently powerful to vindicate the righteous.

Second Isaiah, witness to the destruction of Zion before pagan hosts, was not one to offer facile explanations for the persistence of evil. His view of reality was complex enough to include a vision of God as dragon slayer (51:9*b*) and of "the deep" as something requiring decisive divine action. Isaiah 45:7, far from denying the contradictions of life, holds up to them a defiant *nevertheless*. It gleams, with Job 19:25, as a jewel in the crown of the martyr who upholds faith in the God of mercy and justice at times when experience commends obeisance to a closet of trifling deities. It is not a scientific conclusion undergirded by positive proof but an audacious confession drawn through rigorous scrutiny guided by the confessions of faith. While unsatisfying to the positivist, and perhaps illusionary to the cynic, it is a proclamation that plays a more important function than explaining the past; it becomes a creative element in creating a future, a future not subject to the changing whims of blind fates but directed by the God of justice and compassion who addresses each heart yearning for wholeness with a defiantly hopeful word:

103

> I form light and create darkness,
> I make weal and create woe;
> I the LORD do all these things.

The word of God proclaimed by the prophet in 44:24—45:7 to a community questioning whether there was a future to live for is as powerful today as it was in the sixth century B.C.E. And it is as desperately needed. As wave after wave of violence passes over cities devastated by war, for example, good people ask whether God has forsaken them, whether the forces of evil or the hand of blind fate has assumed control of their lives. How easy in such a situation to succumb to despair. And despair is precisely the enemy that can destroy the future.

It is nothing short of miraculous to witness the presence of persons and communities of hope even in such situations of doom. And indeed, it is hope based on trust in the final victory of justice over evil that preserves the possibility of change. As dubious as it may seem to the unbelieving, the confession of the prophet rings with clarity even today within the hearts of the faithful as they stand up defiantly to the forces of chaos:

> I form light and create darkness,
> I make weal and create woe.

It is a harsh aspect of faith to accept that the God of love and justice not only allows woe but creates it! How much simpler to claim that the source of darkness is some other sinister, evil power. But those who share the tenacious faith of the prophet can hold to this severe confession because of their unswerving conviction that God's final plan is light and weal. This empowers them to seek out the human evils that afflict their communities. And it allows them, in the places where others see only the gloom of war, to recognize rays of light.

Václav Havel saw rays of light within an oppressive totalitarian state. The source of the light was the God of justice proclaimed courageously by his church throughout the long years of persecution and political repression under Communism. That light exposed for him the evil that he had to fight and gave him the weapons of truth and justice with which to carry on the battle. And the light prevailed and continues to guide him as he continues the struggle for the welfare of his people.

Nelson Mandela saw rays of light even in his jail cell. He did not succumb to the persecution of the powerful foes of justice

104

or to the prevailing doubts of the world whether the powerful grip of apartheid could be broken. His faith was grounded so deeply that no human counter-proofs were considered valid. And when the time for deliverance arrived, a seemingly hopeless situation was transformed into one open to reform and reconciliation and justice with a speed that astonished the world.

In the changes that have occurred in Eastern Europe and South Africa, people of faith see the activity of the God of justice who calls servants like Václav Havel and Nelson Mandela to specific tasks. And the faith that leads them to interpret world events is biblical through and through. It is the faith of Second Isaiah. It is a faith not only helpful in interpreting past events but in equipping people to deal with present crises. It is a faith that is neither cynical nor utopian. It is realistic in that it recognizes as the arena of God's engagement this world of society, economics, and politics. It is realistic in that it sees as God's agents actual human beings, with their full range of strengths and weaknesses. It is realistic in that it accepts the responsibility of every person of faith to contribute to God's plan of compassionate righteousness. But above all, it is hopeful, because it looks to God as the loving purpose that will never forsake those who seek to serve God by loving justice.

Biblical faith thus gives to communities of faith today a particular perspective from which to view the events of their society and world. Whether the concern is an urban community ravaged by crime and drugs, a country suffering from devastating drought and starvation, or a state controlled by a corrupt military junta that refuses to accept egalitarian principles, God's people will cling to their faith in God's providence and act with the courage that belongs to those who know that they are secure in God's love, whether in victory or in death.

Isaiah 45:8–13
Will You Question Me?

After an announcement of such profound significance as 105 that contained in the Cyrus oracle, it seems appropriate that the prophet break forth in a song celebrating the source of the deliverance to come. After subjecting the world events of his time to critical scrutiny and identifying the historical agent of God's saving activity, the prophet adopts the mode of speech that is more fitting than any other in dealing with the purposefulness of life, the mode of praise. The whole natural order, here represented by the heavens, the skies, and the earth, is invited to join in the act of restoring wholeness. The hymn concludes with the words of the One from whom all salvation and righteousness comes: "I the LORD have created it" (v. 8).

The progression of the chapter, however, gives one the impression that moments of celebration in praise of the Creator are snatched from a life filled most of the time with tasks far more mundane and personally far less rewarding than worship. For in 45:9–13 we find harsh words of woe and disputation. The prophet's audacious words about Cyrus seem to have been met with refutation. The exact nature of the objections are not given. Perhaps opponents of the prophet took offense at the identification of a foreign king as the anointed of Yahweh. Would not the God of Israel see fit to call a Davidide to the task of returning the exiles to their land and rebuilding the temple? Does not the naming of Cyrus as God's messiah prove that the words the prophet attributed to Yahweh were lying words?

Second Isaiah is so confident that the words he has delivered were from God that he replies with an incisive refutation of his opponents. Verses 9 and 10 are introduced with woe, conjuring up images of the lament intoned at a funeral service. The opponents are a sad lot! Their view of reality is totally distorted. They are like clay on the potter's wheel objecting to the design of the potter, or like an infant breaking through the birth canal with protests against the father and the mother. In verses 11–13 a divine word draws from the absurdity of such presumptiveness a sharp reproval of those who question that God's saving activity on behalf of Israel was a world-encompassing event. They needed to call to mind that God was the Creator of the earth and its inhabitants and of the heavens and their hosts. Questioning that God was the one behind the astonishing success of Cyrus was the product of a puny faith. The antidote was an awakening to the majesty of one who both stretched out the heavens and at the same time cared for the small exiled community. Yes, Cyrus, the daunting conqueror, is in the service of the one true God. "He shall build my city and set my exiles free." From the perspective of worldly wisdom, this all seems absurd. From the perspective of faith, it all flows from the mystery of grace: "not for price or reward." Gratuitous! That is simply the way the God of love is!

This passage, which the prophet found necessary to add when he encountered opposition to his message, forms a meaningful complement to the Cyrus oracle. We are often tempted to regard the Bible as a compendium of timeless principles, infallible truths stemming from a world unflawed by ambiguities that plague us. In Second Isaiah we encounter one whose faith gives him the courage to struggle both with the ambiguities of history and with the opposition of those who refuse to accept his message. In the midst of the fray he sings praises to God. Then he persists in his mission of guiding the people to whom God has given him as a comforter and guide. The word of God mediated to human beings through Second Isaiah is a word at the center of life, the kind of life we know all too well, life desperately in need of the faithfulness of one whose life is utterly given to the Creator of the heavens and the earth and the Redeemer of people in exile. Amidst the din and distractions of day-to-day affairs, through words both harsh and comforting, we too need to be reminded of our source!

Isaiah 45:14–19
The Mystery and Mercy of God

In 45:14–19 we find further exploration of the relation of Israel and Israel's God to the nations and their gods. Since these verses cover several different themes, many scholars regard them as a collection of loosely connected sayings from later writers. The fact that the context within which these themes become comprehensible is the thought world of Second Isaiah suggests an alternative view: We here encounter the prophet adding details to his portrait of the God who directs history and cosmos according to a righteous plan.

Verse 14 cannot be understood apart from its exilic setting where the identity of the Jewish community had suffered a shattering blow through defeat by the armies of pagan conquerors. Spoken to a nation enjoying imperial dominion, the promise of the wealth of the nations easily could abet smugness. But

107

for a people tempted to think that their contribution to the human family had been extinguished by their public humiliation, this verse constitutes a source of hope: The present world structures that bind the faithful followers of Yahweh in subjugation are not permanent but passing. Relationships will be set aright. In fact, a great reversal will occur in which the terror of the oppressor will be transformed into universal acknowledgment of the uniqueness of Israel's God.

We cannot deny that a great temptation hovers over a verse like this. It can so easily be enlisted to justify national self-aggrandizement through the confusion of God's purpose with political stratagems and God's reign with nationalistic ideology. History is so replete with the cruelty and destruction wrought by claims of *Gott mit uns* that we must take care to recognize the precise meaning of this and other passages that depict the submission of the nations.

The key is found in the last bicolon of this long verse where the ingathering peoples make a confession:

> God is with you alone, and there is no other;
> there is no god besides him.

Pride, in the form of self-centeredness that blinds individuals and nations to the integrity of others, is a particularly potent temptation in the lives of those who believe that God gathers for God's purposes a covenant community. It is therefore essential that the vision of all nations united in confessing faith in the God who is Creator of all be preserved from degradation into self-serving nationalistic pride. Israel is not to seek personal gain and fame from its testimony to this God but is to remain true to its calling as a servant people. The pilgrimage of the nations to Zion does not reflect Israel's superiority within the human family but is a demonstration of the universal sovereignty of the one true God. By responding to the light of truth to which Israel bears witness, the peoples of the world find their own true home in fellowship with the living God. While the fine line between religious arrogance and faithful confession must be drawn by every generation anew, Second Isaiah's nuanced formulation gives it a classical form.

Verse 15 adds an irony that is absolutely essential if the balance between clear testimony and proper humility is to be maintained. It makes a remarkable confession: "Truly, you are a God who hides himself." The one God who is Creator of all that exists does not exhibit divine power in the manner of a pompous potentate but rather in the quiet way of the Servant (cf. 42:2). As seen in God's commissioning of Cyrus (45:4), God's mystery is never surrendered so as to fall under the control of mortals. God's sovereignty is preserved, God's nature is revealed to those of God's choosing, God's ways forever surpass human understanding. But this hiddenness of God is finally an aspect of God's mercy. This irony is expressed beautifully by Jesus in a prayer in Luke's Gospel:

> I thank you, Father, Lord of heaven and earth, because you have hidden these things from the wise and the intelligent and have revealed them to infants; yes, Father, for such was your gracious will. (Luke 10:21)

God's hiddenness is a hiddenness in mercy, making God's presence available only to those whose hearts are properly prepared. The God who "hides himself" is thus the God who is discovered by the humble and contrite, those broken in spirit and open to God's gracious deliverance. Verse 15 thus concludes with the essential other half of the confession: "O God of Israel, the Savior."

Once again we see that Second Isaiah avoids utopian dreaming by describing the tragic nature of history. While envisioning the day when God's universal reign would be acknowledged by the nations, Second Isaiah is aware that even as God's "messiah" Cyrus does not know the One whom he serves, so too the nations still refuse the light that God has revealed to the tiny exiled nation. The epithet that the prophet uses for God in this context, therefore, is very significant, "the Savior." The importance of Israel's preserving its identity as a people of God extends beyond its own destiny to the hope of all nations. Israel's very existence is living testimony to the fact that the Creator is Redeemer, that the awesome ruler of the universe is the loving God who saves the poor and the oppressed.

For Israel to hide its confession out of a sense of diffidence before the world powers would not be an act of kindness toward the other nations. There were doubtless romantics in every age who argued that other cultures would be happiest if left to their own cults. Verse 16 unmasks such naive romanticism with a word about the actual condition in which the peoples of the world live, in shame and confusion due to their worship of gods who are unable to save, being mere idols. The repetition of the

109

words "put to shame and confounded" in verses 16 and 17 portrays vividly the lost condition of the nations of the world. Israel's story is therefore not property to be enjoyed self-indulgently. "Israel is saved by the LORD" is intended to become a word of hope for all peoples. Respect for the integrity of other nations was not to be confused with a denial of the presence in the world of a God who redeems the oppressed from whatever binds them, especially idols that cannot save.

Lest the subtle nuance intended by the statement that God is a God who hides himself be distorted by further claims that nothing can be known of that God's purpose thereby leaving human life in a state of chaos, the prophet adds another divine word. After an elaborate hymnic introduction that stresses the orderliness of creation, God says,

> I did not speak in secret,
> in a land of darkness;
> I did not say to the offspring of Jacob,
> "Seek me in chaos."
> I the LORD speak the truth,
> I declare what is right.
> (Isa. 45:19)

Although in essence God is a God of ineffable mystery, in reality God has not left human beings to grope in darkness but has spoken clearly of life's purpose. In saving a band of slaves, in revealing *tôrāh*, in guiding a nation through the perils of history, God has spoken with an incisiveness that will be acknowledged by all who are open to the truth. In creating the world and filling it with inhabitants, God did not create it for chaos. God established it with a good plan in mind. Even when God was obliged by *love* to respond to persistent, self-destructive apostasy with the harsh word of punishment, prophets were present to draw the distinction between chaos and discipline. Essential to God's plan, therefore, was the witness of those who would speak the truth of God by telling the story of how they were "saved by the LORD" and thereby delivered from shame and confusion. For it was a story intended for all peoples.

Stories of the history of Christian missions are known to all of us. In recent times it has become popular to decry the insensitivity of missionaries to native populations and to document the intertwining of religious with imperialistic objectives. Those who have personal acquaintance with missionaries know another side of the story, the side of personal sacrifice, of commitment and respect, of empowerment of indigenous leaders. The "Christian century" did not culminate in the envisioned goal of universal acknowledgment of God and his Christ. We must therefore continue to struggle with Second Isaiah's paradoxical reading of history and relate it to two dangers that lurk in the unfolding histories of our own religious communities. One is to claim our confessions as license for arrogance and national or denominational pride. The other is to say that our religious epic is of parochial interest only. Between these dangers stand two words that guard our destiny like the seraphim at the gates of Eden:

> Truly, you are a God who hides himself.
> (Isa. 45:15)

> I did not speak in secret. . . .
> I the LORD speak the truth.
> (Isa. 45:19)

Isaiah 45:20–25
Every Knee Shall Bow

In 45:20–25, Second Isaiah still has his eye on a world in which earlier power relationships are being overturned by the lightning-swift advances of Cyrus. God is portrayed as the heavenly judge summoning the survivors of the crisis to trial. The prospects for the defendants appear bleak from the outset: As in 45:16, they come from the ranks of those whose knowledge is distorted by following idols.

The divine Judge bases the case on the evidence of history. We can assume that those who have mediated God's interpretive word are the servants and messengers referred to in 44:26. The evidence is to be held up to public scrutiny in the court. The defendants are to present their case. Can they give evidence that their religious officials have provided an interpretation of history that makes sense out of the earthshaking events that were unfolding? Alas, their counsel fails to build a defensible case. The defeat of the Medes and the Lydians and the Babylonians is just that, defeat, since the gods upon whom they depend for protection are idols that cannot save.

111

The survivors of one nation present an exception: "In the LORD all the offspring of Israel shall triumph and glory" (v. 25). How can that be? Was not Israel defeated as well? The difference lies in this: Israel, when true to its confession that "only in the LORD . . . are righteousness and strength," recognizes that all world events unfold according to God's redemptive purpose. History is not guided by blind fate. It is not influenced by the gods carried about by priests. History is under the providence of the only God who is "a righteous God and a Savior." To acknowledge the reign of that God is to pass through defeat to salvation and glory, for it is to unite the will of a people with the will of the Sovereign of the universe.

Suddenly the focus turns back to the indicted nations. The trial is interrupted with a remarkable invitation coming from the Judge: "Turn to me and be saved, all the ends of the earth!" (v. 22). Salvation is not intended for the faithful survivors of Israel alone. All the survivors of the nations, all those who seek in vain to defend themselves on the basis of their cult gods, can be delivered from their ignorance and share in the saving knowledge that there is only one true God. Israel's faith is not a parochial matter at all but part of a universal drama that will culminate when God's word is fulfilled:

> To me every knee shall bow,
> every tongue shall swear.
> (Isa. 45:23)

Here, finally, is the standard that can guide the one who, with fear and trembling, seeks to find the proper posture before God in awareness of the diversity represented by the nations with their various cults and beliefs. The starting point in dealing with the perplexing questions of world events and the relations between the world's religions is awe before the Creator of all. It is the awe that is evoked in unexpected places, in Albert Einstein as he encounters the statistically improbable order of the universe, in astronauts as they look back upon mother earth, and in the mother and father as they hold the newborn child.

To this awesome standard the apostle Paul appealed in a community that was being torn asunder by disputes over dietary laws and Sabbath observance. What image could he invoke that might help these quibbling human beings to distinguish between petty parochial matters and essential matters of faith? The apostle turned to our passage in Isaiah:

112

Why do you pass judgment on your brother or sister? Or you, why do you despise your brother or sister? For we will all stand before the judgment seat of God. For it is written,

"As I live, says the Lord, every knee shall bow to me,
and every tongue shall give praise to God."

(Rom. 14:10–11)

Isaiah 46:1–13
Gods That Are Carried
or the God Who Carries?

Modern readers of the Bible, faced with yet another of Second Isaiah's tirades against idols, may begin to share the weariness of the beasts obliged to bear the cult objects in chapter 46. The ubiquity of such polemic, however, illustrates the intensity of the threat posed by the gods of Babylon to the people living in exile. The Yahwistic confessions of Israel stood as an exception to the traditional beliefs of Mesopotamia. To rest the case for one's God on evidence from the ambiguous realm of history rather than on the eternal myth and ritual of temple priests and the exalted science of astrologers ran counter to the prevailing orthodoxy. Second Isaiah returned repeatedly to the issue of the idols because it represented a deadly threat to the spiritual existence of the exilic community.

What could become tedious repetition, however, is lightened by the exquisite literary qualities of chapter 46. The chapter opens with a snapshot of a cult procession, that central part of the annual New Year's festival in which the cult objects were carried forth from the temple to circumambulate the walls of the city. The color and pageantry of the cult procession can be compared to that seen today in the Mardi Gras celebrations of Freiburg or New Orleans. It is with such a comparison in mind that we can appreciate Second Isaiah's stinging satire.

The throngs of worshipers line the streets in an enthusiastic show of reverence and gratitude to the gods that are responsible for the safety and prosperity of their worshipers. But look! The beasts carrying the high gods of the Babylonian cult, Marduk (the creator god of the central myth *Enūma eliš*, here

bearing one of his traditional titles Bel) and Nebo (god of wisdom and patron of scribes), are stumbling and falling under
their loads. The gods, who are supposed to save their devotees,
cannot save themselves. Dependent on the conveyance of animals, they fall when their weight becomes too great for the
weary beasts.

In verse 3 the true God speaks. The first word in a speech
that extends through the rest of the chapter is an imperative,
"Listen!" The same imperative introduces the concluding section of the speech (vv. 12–13). And in between is repeated
another imperative, "Remember!" (vv. 8 and 9). A carefully
structured lesson, built upon listening and remembering, is thus
presented in contrast to the ridiculous picture of idols borne
and carried on stumbling beasts.

The contrast is poignantly presented through the repetition
of the words "borne" and "carried." In the case of Yahweh, it
is not the god who is borne and carried but the people who are
borne and carried by God! Where did that occur? In Israel's
history, from its birth in the exodus down through future generations, even to old age. The passive voice suddenly is transformed into the active in a staccato conveying the initiative of
Israel's God:

> I have made, and I will bear;
> I will carry and will save.
> (Isa. 46:4)

The choice has been placed before people: the passive gods
of Babylon or the active God of the universe. Just in case they
still have not gotten the point, the contrast is drawn once more
in verses 5–7. Folks accumulate gold and silver, they hire a
goldsmith. The first of the four verbs depicting God's activity in
verse 4b appears again, but instead of describing the God who
makes all that exists, it describes the goldsmith who makes
metal into a god! Before such a product these folks fall down and
worship.

In a continuation of the technique of satirizing through
repetition of vocabulary, we next find Yahweh's "I will bear; I
will carry and will save" of verse 4 turned into a very different
application of the same three Hebrew words in verse 7: The idol
worshipers *bear* upon their shoulders the god the goldsmith
made, they *carry* it, and for good measure, they secure it in its

114

place from which it cannot move and from which "it does not answer or *save* anyone from trouble."

What is the central factor involved in the decision placed before the remnant of Israel of choosing between the God who acts and the gods who are a burden upon their worshipers? The next two imperatives give the answer: "Remember, . . . remember!" God commands. Israel's hope lies in their remembering, their remembering "the former things of old," the chapters in their history that reveal God's involvement in their life at its every stage, all of which taken together reveals a pattern summed up by God in verse 10 with the words, "My purpose shall stand, and I will fulfill my intention." Then in an illustration of the contemporary extension of that pattern, God alludes to Cyrus, "the man for my purpose from a far country" (v. 11). The heart of Yahwism is again revealed as deep faith in God's gracious care combined with a critical scrutiny of history, both past and present.

The pattern of divine guidance in past and present provides the basis for a bold promise to those who have been engulfed by the uncertainties of life as a conquered people surrounded by the apparently victorious gods:

> I bring near my deliverance, it is not far off,
>   and my salvation will not tarry;
> I will put salvation in Zion,
>   for Israel my glory.
>
> (Isa. 46:13)

The importance of hope is never more apparent than in times of deep crisis. Nothing less was at stake than remnant Israel's identity as a people and their divine commission to be a light to the nations. The kind of hope presented by the prophet is not of the dreamy, wishful-thinking sort. Second Isaiah does not deny the tragedy of conquest and exile but interprets them as evidence of divine judgment. And that evidence the prophet integrates into all of the other evidence preserved by memory, all the way from the exodus of slaves from Egypt to the astoundingly swift rise of Cyrus. The principle underlying this interpretation of history and enabling the prophet to discern a creative, redemptive pattern is theological. It revolves around faith in the divine promise, "I have planned, and I will do it" (v. 11).

115

Hope guided by faith and informed by a critical interpretation of history continues to be the legacy of Second Isaiah to communities of faith and discernment. It preserves those communities in times of trial by allowing them to see beyond tragedy and empowers them to be agents of divine purpose in acts of deliverance and salvation. The profundity of Second Isaiah's historical theology is evident in choice of vocabulary. The word commonly translated "deliverance" in verse 13 has the root meaning of "righteousness." The divine purpose that faith discerns through remembering is the fulfillment in human history of God's *righteousness.* Hope is possible in a troubled world because faith enables us to recognize that the destiny of the universe is determined neither by human potentates, nor by whimsical principalities, nor by blind fate, but by the God, known through communal memory to be just and compassionate, who answers the cries of the oppressed in acts of deliverance.

Our world offers as many glistening, golden idols as did the ancient world of Babylon. Their promises include material gain, self-indulgent sensual pleasures, feelings of superiority, and peer group affirmation. But in the moment of deepest need, they are silent as they weigh down upon their devotees with crushing, ruthless force. In contrast, the promise of the Lord abides: "I will carry and will save."

Isaiah 47:1–15
The Fall of Babylon and the Failure of the Human Illusion

In the previous chapter the prophet described a remarkable phenomenon. The gods of the empire that had defeated and exiled the remnant of Israel "themselves go into captivity" (46:2). Marduk (alias Bel) and Nebo, the gods responsible for the security of Babylon, are portrayed as helpless "burdens on weary animals" (46:1). Like all idols, they are unable to "save anyone from trouble" (46:7). Against this pathetic picture is projected the one Creator and Redeemer, who commands Cyrus according to an eternal purpose and promises Israel, "My salvation will not tarry" (46:13).

116

Following chapter 46, the present chapter forms the second panel of a diptych. Abandoned by her gods, mistress Babylon is portrayed sitting in mourning and shame in the dust. This is the outcome of the three themes covered in chapter 46, the captivity of Babylon's gods, the commissioning of Cyrus by the only true God, and God's promise to deliver Israel.

The connection between the defeat of a city-state's gods and its downfall is portrayed nowhere more vividly in ancient literature than in the Lament of Ur, where Ningal, lacking home or even place to sit, cries:

> [*Woe is me*, my city] which no longer exists—
> I am not its queen;
> [O Nanna], Ur which no longer exists—
> I am not its mistress. (ll. 286–87)

> I, Ningal—I am one who has been exiled from the house,
> I am one who has found no dwelling place. (l. 307)
> (Pritchard, pp. 460–61)

Thus the fall of the Third Dynasty of Ur was traced back to the fall of its divine sponsors. Similarly and in keeping with the mythopoeic worldview of ancient Mesopotamia, once Babylon's gods had been captured, the "virgin daughter Babylon" was doomed.

Equally close is the connection between God's calling "a bird of prey from the east, the man for my purpose" in 46:11 and the ruin of Babylon portrayed in this chapter. In 539 B.C.E., Cyrus's general Gobryas entered the gates of that ancient, proud city, to be followed shortly after by the Persian conqueror himself.

The promise of deliverance to Israel in 46:13 is in similar fashion complemented by the defeat of Babylon described in chapter 47. Not only was Israel's release impossible so long as Babylon was allowed to maintain its ruthless imperial policies. Chapter 47 looks deeper to explain how Babylon's initial victory over Judah and its subsequent fall to Cyrus were two aspects of one divine plan. The symmetry achieved by Second Isaiah in these two chapters thus matches the artistic balance of a medieval altar painter.

The portrait of the virgin daughter Babylon is patterned after the familiar biblical motif of reversal. Hannah had exulted in the Lord:

117

> The bows of the mighty are broken,
> but the feeble gird on strength.
> Those who were full have hired themselves out for bread,
> but those who were hungry are fat with spoil. . . .
> The LORD makes poor and makes rich;
> he brings low, he also exalts.
> He raises up the poor from the dust;
> he lifts the needy from the ash heap,
> to make them sit with princes
> and inherit a seat of honor.
>
> (I Sam. 2:4–5a, 7–8)

The very thought of Babylon struck horror into the hearts of those who had experienced the devastation of Judah and Jerusalem and the shame of exile. The dominant image was of a ruthless, arrogant queen whose love of luxury was matched only by her lust for cruelty. Exalted upon her throne and veiled in regal finery, she shouted out her orders to her slaves. The psalmist captured this terror in an epithet: "O daughter Babylon, you devastator!" (Ps. 137:8).

In what has been variously called a taunt, a mock lament, and a salvation oracle, and in actuality creatively combines elements of each of these, the prophet takes the harsh commands of the queen and directs them back to her. *She* has become the slave, reduced to sitting in the dust, grinding the meal, with her peasant's garb rolled up and her arms and legs bared for heavy labor.

Suddenly, in verses 3b and 4, the voice of another royal figure is heard, explaining that the descent of the queen is not due to fate or misfortune but to a divine decree. In her ruthlessness and arrogance, daughter Babylon has violated a higher law that respects no special exemptions: "I will take vengeance, and I will spare no one" (v. 3b). Who is that royal figure? "Our Redeemer—the LORD of hosts is his name—is the Holy One of Israel" (v. 4).

With this epithet we are introduced to authentic authority, not the kind that rules whimsically for personal vanity, but one whose rule is committed to redemption, the one under whose command are all the hosts of heaven, the one whose very nature defines holiness as the law of creation.

From this point on we know that the address to the daughter Babylon is not coming from a mortal whose misery is producing wishful delusions. We realize that the command is from the God of the universe. We know that when this God pro-

118

claims, "You shall no more be called the mistress of kingdoms," a turn of history is imminent (v. 5).

More. An explanation of the ultimate reason for that turn is given. The ascendancy of Babylon was merely one stage in God's universal plan. For reasons already given in 42:24–25, God had chosen Babylon to punish wayward Israel. But Babylon took this as license to vaunt its power as if it were personal possession and not delegated authority: "You showed them no mercy; on the aged you made your yoke exceedingly heavy" (v. 6). The drive behind this cruelty is immediately identified: "You said, 'I shall be mistress forever' " (v. 7).

The God who guides the historical destiny of nations chooses agents of divine purpose. They are servants. They are commissioned for specific tasks. They may be members of the Jewish community. They may be Assyrian kings or Babylonian rulers. They may be followers of Assur, Marduk, Amun Re, or Ahura Mazda. But whoever they are, they are not masters or mistresses acting on their own authority and ruling forever. There is but one Forever: "For I am God, and there is no other" (46:9).

Daughter Babylon, nonetheless, defiantly seizes the exclusive prerogative of God: "I am, and there is no one besides me" (47:8 and 10). She claims exemption from the moral law that has been placed over all human beings: "I shall not sit as a widow or know the loss of children" (v. 8). She thus sets her authority over against the authority expressed in verse 3, "I will take vengeance, and I will spare *no one.*"

This is high drama at its best! The queen's challenge is met head-on:

> Both these things shall come upon you
>   in a moment, in one day:
> the loss of children and widowhood
>   shall come upon you in full measure.
>   (Isa. 47:9)

Lest the entire drama seem artificially loaded in favor of Israel, we need to pause to consider the basis upon which daughter Babylon is able to make her claims. No culture (although Egypt and China could claim great achievements of their own) could rival the accomplishments of Babylon in ancient scientific study. Especially impressive were the advances made by Babylon's astronomers, and ancient savants were

119

equally impressed by Babylonian advances in other areas such as sorcery and enchantments.

The central argument coming from the side of Israel's God relates specifically to Babylon's highest achievements: "Your wisdom and your knowledge led you astray" (v. 10). The best that that culture had produced contained the roots of its undoing! How can that be?

Verses 12–15 drive home the point. Babylon ironically is invited to stake its future on its scientific achievements:

> Stand fast in your enchantments
> and your many sorceries,
> with which you have labored from your youth;
> perhaps you may be able to succeed,
> perhaps you may inspire terror.
> (Isa. 47:12)

There is only one problem with this. Those who would save the nation are incapable of saving themselves:

> They all wander about in their own paths;
> there is no one to save you.
> (Isa. 47:15)

This is not a chapter notable for its tolerance of all philosophical points of view. It is not a place to turn for a celebration of the human being as center of the universe and source of all things needed for human well-being. Here the finest and highest in human accomplishment is held up to scrutiny and found wanting. Here the claim is made that the noblest and the best that civilization can offer is ultimately incapable of securing safety and happiness. Chapter 47 of Isaiah introduces the daunting "in spite of" that anticipates Kierkegaard's "either/or." *In spite of* the highest achievements of science, the most advanced accomplishments of civilization, humanity is doomed if it does not recognize an "infinite qualitative distinction" between what is human and what is divine. Without the clear understanding of that distinction, humanity is doomed. There is but one authentic reference point when it comes down to the meaning and destiny of life. "Our Redeemer—the LORD of hosts is his name—is the Holy One of Israel" (v. 4).

Chapter 47 illustrates how unified the Book of Isaiah is when it comes to central themes, in spite of undeniable differences in authorship and social context. For Isaiah of Jerusalem everything that mattered came down to one contest, the contest between human pride and trust in God. All human haughtiness was doomed to disaster. Security was to be found alone in acknowledging one holy Center to all of reality:

> For thus says the Lord GOD, the Holy One of Israel:
> In returning and rest you shall be saved;
>   in quietness and in trust shall be your strength.
> (Isa. 30:15)

The tragedy of life comes in defiant human insistence on self-sufficiency:

> But you refused and said,
> "No! We will flee upon horses."
> (Isa. 30:15–16)

The Babylonians of Second Isaiah's time had lifted human accomplishment to a hitherto unheard of plane. Their security was not to be based on anything as crude as horses or chariots but on "the study of heavens." But Second Isaiah applied the religious principle of his teacher and came up with the same conclusion: Trust placed on any human achievement is ultimately misplaced when it comes to destiny.

It is not a facile move, but a fundamentally sound one, to go from Isaiah of Jerusalem's condemnation of Egyptian horses to Second Isaiah's condemnation of Babylonian astrology to the contemporary prophet's condemnation of the modern trust of our versions of salvation based on science and technology. Science holds our great potential if it acknowledges its role of servant in relation to the only One capable of redeeming and delivering human beings from their delusions of grandeur. The basic temptation facing humanity has not changed over the millennia. It is the claim made by the virgin daughter Babylon:

> I am, and there is no one besides me.
> (Isa. 47:8)

The finest minds of our scientific communities are pushing the frontiers of knowledge farther than ever before. From the intricate microcosm of DNA to the vast macrocosm of the expanding universe, we are experiencing an explosion of knowledge that makes our civilization equivalent to that of ancient Babylon or the world of the Enlightenment. The riddle of science is this: It can be as readily applied to the ruin of human life as to its improvement. Communities of faith are as useless as some ancient totem if they fail to pronounce the fundamental

121

prophetic judgment on every arrogation of human knowledge to divine status:

> Your wisdom and your knowledge
>   led you astray,
> and you said in your heart,
>   "I am, and there is no one besides me."
>   (Isa. 47:10)

There is a counter-claim. It runs against the grain of all human pride. It claims that only by acknowledging the source of human knowledge in a higher authority can understanding become a blessing to humanity. That is a severe claim. It touches on a dimension we should prefer to avoid. It touches on our ultimate commitment. Rather than admit our dependence on a greater reality, rather than acknowledge that our knowledge is powerless to save us, rather than humbly allowing our science to be subservient to the purpose of the only deliverer, we follow in the tradition of the Babylonians who "wander about in their own paths." To the extent that pride determines our ultimate commitment, we fall under the judgment of Israel's prophets, "There is no one to save you" (47:15).

Isaiah 48:1–22
The Promise of God and the Problems of His People

Form criticism is a method of interpretation that seeks to shed light on the meaning of a biblical text by determining the literary type to which it belongs and the social setting from which it accordingly stems. Its accomplishments are considerable. The significance, for example, of a composer's choosing a lament in one case and a satirical love song in another must be considered by the sensitive interpreter.

But any method runs up against limits. Isaiah 48 offers a good example. Claus Westermann, in his application of form-critical types to this chapter, encounters a difficulty. The chapter as it stands intersperses words of salvation to Israel with harsh charges against her. Westermann finds this to be a violation of form-critical principles. A passage must be either a salvation word or a judgment word. His solution is to remove the last clause of verse 1, as well as verses 4, 5*b*, 7*b*, and 8–10*b*. What remains of verses 1–11 constitutes a positive message appropriate to the culmination of the chapter in verses 20–21. He is equally pleased that the excised verses taken together create a consistently harsh word of accusation, which he attributes to a separate author (Westermann, pp. 195f.).

If one pays more attention to the text than to the canons of a modern method of interpretation, a different understanding of Isaiah 48 commends itself. The words of accusation are carefully woven into the fabric of what proves to be a carefully nuanced message. Second Isaiah emerges as a much more subtle thinker than Westermann's form-critically correct prophet who is incapable of complex thought.

In Isaiah 48 the prophet addresses a human condition that is filled with ambiguity. Even the promises of God at a time of renewed hope retain a bittersweet quality given the inconsistency of human commitment. The ebb and flow of this chapter skillfully reflect the prophet's realistic awareness of the convolution of the human response to divine initiative. Any attempt to sort out pure promise from pure judgment tears apart a skillfully balanced message. We encounter a prophet who uses genres creatively and independently in service of a divine address that is not formally prepackaged but relates sensitively to every new situation.

This nuanced understanding of the chapter's message explains its opening address, "Hear this, O house of Jacob." It echoes the address to Mistress Babylon in verse 8 of the previous chapter, "Hear this, you lover of pleasures." It is true that the following oppositional clauses are positive in tone:

> who are called by the name of Israel,
>   and who came forth from the loins of Judah;
> who swear by the name of the LORD,
>   and invoke the God of Israel.
>
> (Isa. 48:1)

But the phrase that concludes this verse, "but not in truth or right," is not the bungling addition of a later editor but precisely the main point, since it indicates that Israel, in spite of its covenantal background, has come precariously close to matching

123

the self-delusions of Babylon. As verse 2 goes on to clarify, distinctions in name alone will not save ("they call themselves after the holy city"). The essence of Yahwistic faith is not in facile nominalism. Nor is it in superstitious notions of security ("and lean on the God of Israel"). The "Hear this" with which God addresses Israel is no less a word of warning than the "Hear this" addressed in the previous chapter to Babylon.

Verses 3–4 deny Israel any excuses for their insolence. They are not without knowledge. God has accompanied their experiences as a people with interpretive words. We can assume that reference is being made here to God's speaking through the prophets, for, as declared in chapter 44, Israel's God is the One

> who confirms the word of his servant,
> and fulfills the prediction of his messengers.
> (Isa. 44:26)

God's involvement in human history, however, is not locked into a primordial template. We noted earlier that Second Isaiah both appeals to "former things" and announces God's doing "new things." The past is a faithful witness to God's purpose, for God is not whimsical but trustworthy. But God is ever creative in opening up unheard-of possibilities. How otherwise could Israel hope to be delivered from the mightiest empire in the world?

Obstinate Israel is shocked into alertness to God's presence by the juxtaposition of "former things" and "new things," this time in the same passage. No excuses! They have already heard the "former things." But no complacency either, lest they say, "I already knew them" (vv. 6–7). And lest Israel forget what holds such dialectics together and what preserves hope even in the face of human treachery, verses 9–13 state explicitly that it is for the sake of the One who is the first and the last, the Creator of the heavens and the earth.

In verses 14–16 the people are invited to assemble and hear. In contrast to the esoteric manticism of the Babylonian religion which excluded participation of common folk from the process of religious interpretation, prophetic faith is held up to public scrutiny and discussion. God's commissioning of Cyrus to remove the yoke of Babylon is put forward as the specific manner in which God is present in the contemporary world. This is true to the nature of God acting within the processes of human history to accomplish the divine plan:

124

From the beginning I have not spoken in secret,
from the time it came to be I have been there.
(Isa. 48:16)

The blunt warnings and the bold promises, the appeals to former things and to new things, the reference to the divine commission of Cyrus and the impending fall of Babylon—all of these themes that constitute the warp and woof of chapter 48 are directed to a specific goal. It unfolds rapidly in the remaining verses of the chapter.

Verses 17–18, introduced with a messenger formula and the familiar epithets "LORD," "Redeemer," and "Holy One of Israel," make a passionate appeal to the heart of Israel: "O that you had paid attention to my commandments!" The depth of feeling resembles Christ's sorrowful "Jerusalem, Jerusalem." All the suffering and destruction could have been avoided. God does not desire judgment but prosperity.

The culminating summons and invitation in verses 20–21 indicate, however, that the people are not to get mired in self-pity but are to take the preceding instructions as a call to immediate obedience and response. The command is specific, it is bold, and it has tremendous political, economic, and personal implications. The people are to break up their households, pull up their roots, pack up, set forth from Babylon in unwavering trust that God has already acted:

The LORD has redeemed his servant Jacob!
(Isa. 48:20)

This is a notable case where remembering "former things" is appropriate. The God who much earlier had accompanied the Hebrew slaves in their flight from bondage in Egypt and had led them through the desert and had provided water for their thirst would accompany the present generation of exiles on their homeward journey. In empowering Cyrus to remove the yoke of Babylon, God had opened up a new future for Israel. Now that future demanded their response in obedience and faith. The next move was theirs!

Under conditions that were precarious, in a situation in which matters no doubt were very ambiguous, some responded to Second Isaiah's summons and returned. In many ways this chapter prepared them for what was to come more thoroughly than any other passage in Isaiah 40—55, for its warnings that the promises of God are ever threatened by the obstinacy and rebelliousness would continue to be painfully relevant in years and decades to come. Fortunate it is that they had chapter 48 in a form characterized by Second Isaiah's bold realism rather than in the expurgated form of modern critics. For as we shall see in chapters 56—66, the promise did not unfold in a dream-like romance but in the bitter struggles that are ever a part of the human condition. Second Isaiah saw with uncommon lucidity that the miracle of divine grace does not come in the miraculous removal of all obstacles but in the fact that through all life's trials God remains true to the nature that God revealed throughout Israel's history:

> From the beginning I have not spoken in secret,
> from the time it came to be I have been there.
> (Isa. 48:16)

Isaiah 49:1–13
The Servant and the Salvation of the World

The preceding chapter opened with a command to Israel to listen and then delved into the convolutions of Israel's stinting response to God's initiatives in its past. Foreign nations came into that discussion only as they impinged on Israelite history.

In contrast, chapter 49 opens with a command to foreign peoples to listen and then describes Servant Israel as one bearing a commission that extends beyond domestic affairs to the welfare of the nations. Taken together, 49:1–6 and chapter 48 construct a pattern that is basic to Second Isaiah's thought. Israel is precious to God and the object of God's compassionate justice. But Israel's responsibilities extend beyond its borders to reach out to the nations of the earth.

The struggle for the heart of Israel in chapter 48 thus relates directly to the daunting task assigned to Servant Israel in chapter 49. By being a faithful partner in the covenant relationship with Yahweh, Israel equips itself to be an instrument of God's saving acts on behalf of the whole world.

The complementary themes of inner-community health and international relations provide the warp and woof of chap-

NB.

126

ter 49. The summons to the peoples of the world to listen to the Servant's description of his call indicates from the start that this figure is of more than parochial interest. God's plan is a universal plan, and the community that responds in obedience to God's call becomes a part of a redemptive process that embraces *all* peoples. This is something the nations need to hear about!

Second Isaiah does not tire of reminding his audience that God's plan is not something newly concocted or something constantly fluctuating with the pulsations of human history. God's plan is eternal, and all that happens does so in response to divine purpose. This explains the Servant's attribution of his call in this passage to a period before his birth. In regard to both the source of the call and its universal dimensions, verse 5 resembles the call that came to the prophet Jeremiah:

> Before I formed you in the womb I knew you,
> and before you were born I consecrated you;
> I appointed you a prophet to the nations.
> (Jer. 1:5)

Of course, God draws different types of agents into the divine purpose for the world, with assignments commensurate with their particular abilities. Cyrus was called to use his statecraft and military prowess for the release of the exiles and the rebuilding of Jerusalem (44:28; 45:13). Verse 2, in contrast, specifies the "weapon" of the Servant, it being the same one with which the earlier prophets were equipped, namely, the word of God. In a world in which the rise and fall of nations appears to be determined not by prophetic pronouncements but by imperial armies, this may seem like a feeble piece of equipment.

Not so according to the similes adopted by the Servant, who likens his linguistic gifts to "a sharp sword" and "a polished arrow." The biographies of other bearers of God's word, such as Elijah, Amos, and Jeremiah, indicate that delivery of the divine word often brought the verbal "swords and arrows" of the prophets into conflict with the metal swords and arrows of kings. The second halves of the two bicola in this verse thus acknowledge another gracious gift from the divine commander, protection.

The word of commission itself comes with directness and brevity matching that of a polished arrow:

127

> You are my servant,
>> Israel, in whom I will be glorified.
>>> (Isa. 49:3)

Commentary on this verse commonly gets bogged down in debating whether "Israel" is original to the text or a later addition. Metrical considerations, the attributes that seem to refer to an individual (vv. 1, 2, 4, 5), and reference to the Servant having been sent *to* Israel (v. 6) have been used as evidence to support the deletion of "Israel" and the interpretation of the passage as the commissioning of an individual.

Advocates of a collective interpretation, on the other hand, have pointed to passages in Second Isaiah in which the nation or people Israel is designated as "servant." In commenting on 42:1-4, we drew attention to the parallelism between 41:8-10 and 42:1 and concluded that a sharp distinction between individual and community is alien to Second Isaiah's thought. The evidence when taken as a whole suggests that the Servant of Yahweh is a metaphor richly multivalent in meaning. At times the prophet whom we call Second Isaiah seems to identify with the Servant personally. At other times the lives of figures like Jeremiah and Elijah seem to add color to this mysterious figure. Israel in its rare times of obedience to God's will, and especially the faithful remnant within the Israelite community, contributed features to the portrait of the Servant. Above all, however, it is important to recognize the eschatological dimension in this metaphor. The Servant is both faithful individual and obedient community in the era in which God's plan begins to unfold among those identifying completely with God's will.

The most important benefit of breaking out of the impasse of trying to decide between individual and collective interpretations remains to be mentioned. It returns the focus of interpretation back to the final phrase of the verse which thematically is climactic: "in whom I will be glorified." All that the Servant is and will become is to one purpose alone, that God be glorified. While this purpose represents the highest calling of every individual, it is most obviously the one to which God's people is called. The manner in which God is glorified is especially noteworthy, namely, through redeeming Israel (44:23). By responding in obedience and praise, Israel allows its life to be drawn into its ultimate purpose.

All the more astonishing then is the next verse. The called

128

and empowered one, the one drawn to God's eternal purpose from the womb, slips into the mode of the lament, complaining bitterly that all his efforts have been in vain. Suffering, complaining Jeremiah comes to mind (cf. also Ps. 31:22; 66:17). God's task of saving the world is invested not in superhumans but in normal, faltering flesh and blood, a comforting thought indeed for faithful but fallible servants of all epochs. The Servant of Isaiah 49 found this comfort and reassurance as well. All worldly evidence notwithstanding,

> yet surely my cause is with the LORD,
> and my reward with my God.
> (Isa. 49:4*b*)

The word translated "cause" here is the word normally translated "justice" in Second Isaiah. (Cf. 40:27, where the word here translated by the NRSV as "my cause" is translated "my right.") As mentioned in relation to 42:1–4, *mišpāṭ* is the order of compassionate justice that God has created and upon which the wholeness of the universe depends. The world to which the Servant is called to bring justice-engendering words may be in turmoil, and this may lead to doubts whether anything is being accomplished. But the Servant, as one called to a purpose not his own but belonging to the sovereign of the universe, can be confident that the just order that will one day prevail against all opposing forces is already established in his own life, for his is a life relying solely on God. Or, as verse 5 concludes, "My God has become my strength."

For the human servant called to serve the world-embracing purposes of God, one of the chief temptations is to scale back the assignment to human dimensions. Elijah, having encountered the ruthless opposition of Jezebel, fled to a cave in the wilderness, and complained,

> I have been very zealous for the LORD, the God of hosts; for the Israelites have forsaken your covenant, thrown down your altars, and killed your prophets with the sword. I alone am left, and they are seeking my life, to take it away. (I Kings 19:10)

Jeremiah at the bottom of a cistern, Jesus hanging on a cross, and the apostle Paul in his afflicted body were similarly tempted. But at such moments God answers complaint with a renewal of the commission and even an enlarging of its compass. (The dialogue between Jesus and Peter in John 21:18–21

129

is related. Three times Jesus has repeated his commission to Peter to "feed/tend my sheep." He goes on to describe the violent manner of death that lay before Peter, and then restates the commission with the words, "Follow me.") The Servant in this passage is told by the Lord that restoration of battered Israel is "too light a thing." The entire world is to become his territory!

> I will give you as a light to the nations,
> that my salvation may reach to the end of the earth.
> (Isa. 49:6)

The *universalism* of Second Isaiah has been the subject of much debate. Some commentators insist that it derives less from biblical thought than from modern imagination. Others accept passages such as 42:1–4 and 49:6 at face value and recognize a universal dimension. Two considerations can contribute to a proper understanding of this aspect of Second Isaiah's message. The first concerns evidence of a lively debate within the Jewish community during the exilic and Second Temple period on the topic of Israel's relation to the nations. Isaiah 56:1–8 and 66:18–21, for example, advance a direct challenge to Deuteronomic legislation excluding outsiders from participation in the cult (cf. Deut. 23:3). The attitude toward foreigners in the books of Ruth and Jonah, when contrasted with that found in Ezra and Nehemiah, seems to reflect the same lively debate (cf. Ezra 9—10 and Nehemiah 13).

The second consideration stems from the inseparability of creation and redemption in the thought world of Second Isaiah. Since the compass of God's redemptive activity is the entire created world and its scope is the restoration of all that exists to wholeness, the nations are included in God's plan. The fact that books such as Ezra and Nehemiah reflect instances when leaders within the Jewish community emphasized that aspect of divine purpose that focused on the restoration of "the survivors of Israel" should not detract from the universal breadth of Second Isaiah's vision.

The differences that characterize divergent biblical traditions attest to the grounding of Scripture in real-life situations. Second Isaiah's expansive vision must be understood within his setting even as the narrower focus of Ezra and Nehemiah must be understood within theirs. Different issues were at stake in each. Together, such diversity contributes to a richer theologi-

130

cal understanding than could be gained through forceful efforts at harmonization.

It is important to realize that the issues faced by communities of faith during different periods of biblical history were as complex as corresponding issues are today. This will help us to understand that the meaning of Scripture for our time arises precisely out of its dialectical richness. For example, it is clear that there are times when faith communities are challenged to envision their responsibilities on a global or even cosmic scale, whereas at other times adversity leads to the more immediate need to preserve religious identity in the face of threatened extermination.

In the vast majority of cases, it is safe to say that contemporary communities of faith in North America have no excuse to retreat into narrow self-preoccupation when they compare their own prosperity and international influence with world hunger and ecological crisis. They need to recapture the vision of the Creator-Redeemer whose purpose embraces the vastness of the universe and then translate that vision into bold new initiatives that challenge all areas of human knowledge. A narrower focus would be "too light a thing" to be worthy of a servant endowed with such resources and opportunities. The same could not be said of persecuted enclaves of Jews and Christians in Nazi Germany, for whom perhaps the appropriate word would be the one overheard earlier by the prophet in the divine assembly: "Comfort, O comfort my people." And there are in our own day as well countless religious communities that live under similar conditions of persecution. For each situation God's word is specific.

Verses 7–13 amplify the message of the second Servant Song in verses 1–6 in the way that 42:5–8 amplified the first Servant Song in 42:1–4. It may be that a disciple of Second Isaiah here adds comment to what were perceived to be especially poignant aspects of the prophet's message in the somewhat later setting. For example, verse 7 may reflect a desire to relate the Servant's globe-spanning commission as described in verse 6 to the response of the kings described in 52:15. It is also possible that it was the prophet who added such additional thoughts. In any case, they grow very naturally out of the themes and concerns of the prophet of the exile.

131

Verse 7 thus presents a divine word giving explicit expression to the paradox that has run throughout the previous six verses: The lowly, fallible, entirely human Servant upon whom the powerful of the earth look with contempt is one before whom those same rulers will bow down. How can that be? The answer given is straightforward: It is "because of the LORD, . . . who has chosen you."

The mystery of the Servant is hidden in the purposes of the Holy God. There is nothing noteworthy about this people to those judging by conventional criteria such as earthly power and military acumen. For them, it is nonsense to think that a powerful God would choose as an ally a weakling whose only "weapon" is the utterance of the mouth. We encounter here the truth of the mysterious confession in 45:15a: "Truly, you are a God who hides himself." "Stumbling block to Jews and foolishness to Gentiles, but to those who are the called, both Jews and Greeks, . . . the power of God and the wisdom of God," the apostle Paul said of another Servant at a later point in history (I Cor. 1:23–24). It is a matter of perspective, Paul explained in a subsequent letter to the Corinthians:

> From now on, therefore, we regard no one from a human point of view; even though we once knew Christ from a human point of view, we know him no longer in that way. (II Cor. 5:16)

In fact, there was nothing about Israel that should call for special notice. The Deuteronomist put it this way:

> It was not because you were more numerous than any other people that the LORD set his heart on you and chose you—for you were the fewest of all peoples. It was because the LORD loved you and kept the oath that he swore to your ancestors. (Deut. 7:7–8)

It all comes down to perspective, to the restoration of vision, and that can come only from the same one who chose the unremarkable to accomplish remarkable things, only through the word of the Holy One of Israel. Later we shall see how the paradox of verse 7 receives much more extensive treatment in the fourth Servant Song.

"I have kept you and given you as a covenant to the people." Verse 8, with this exact repetition of the phrase in 42:6, introduces a description of the Servant's task in concrete terms that recall the similar description in 42:7. There is nothing theoretical about the Servant's assignment. It involves restoration of confiscated property, release of political prisoners, and

132

provision for their needs as they travel back to their homes. And all of that is patterned after Yahweh's care for the Hebrews as they fled from the Pharaoh toward the heritage that God had given them. Since the provider of the new generation of exiles remains the same one who guided the early tribes through the wilderness, this section appropriately ends with a hymn in which earth and heavens are invited to join in praising the Lord who shows compassion on "his suffering ones."

Isaiah 49:14–26
Answer to a Lament

In Isaiah 40:9, Zion/Jerusalem was personified as a "herald of good tidings" with instructions to announce the arrival of God who, both as victorious warrior and as gentle shepherd, brings deliverance to the exiled people. In 49:14, Zion appears again. This time, however, she is not personified as the "herald of good tidings" announcing the arrival of God but as a mother, bereaved and barren, lamenting God's absence! Her bitter complaints, which resurface in verses 21 and 24, give a glimpse of a situation in which the prophet's earlier promises of deliverance from bondage and return to the homeland hit the contradictory realities of a world in which ruthless tyrants refuse to release their captives.

Following the lament in verse 14, Zion is addressed by God in a long refutation (vv. 15–26) of her complaint built upon assurances that the long-awaited release is soon to occur. The passion that permeates that long address gives the modern reader a sense of the intensity of the crisis faced by the prophet. The political and military structures that had ended the community's life as a free nation held fast. Those who followed Yahweh were still scattered in lands far removed from Zion. Was this not evidence enough that God had forsaken this people?

The nature of the images and the intensity of feeling that permeate God's reply to Zion in verses 15–26 reinforce the sense that a very sensitive topic has been broached by her complaint. First, appropriate as a response to Zion portrayed as a mourning mother, the charge that God has forgotten Zion is

133

compared to the absurdity of imagining a mother forgetting her infant (v. 15). But the appeal goes beyond reference to God's compassionate nature. Announcement is made of intense building activity and of waves of exiles returning home. But where are they to be seen? Even a cursory glance indicated that the worldly potentates still maintained control. "Lift up your eyes and see!" Zion is told. As in the case of the paradox of the Servant discussed in the previous passage, the dispute between complaining Zion and God comes down to eyesight or, perhaps better, insight. More than a cursory glance is required. Zion is challenged to see with the eyes of one who is tutored by faith to trust not the politics of tyrannic power but the politics of divine justice and mercy. The power of the Babylonians, as the power of the Assyrians and the Egyptians before them, was only temporary power, delegated for a purpose by God. In keeping with the passionate rhetoric of the passage, God places God's own word on the line by promising that, rather than grieving, Zion would soon be dressed like a bride, with her children adorning her like jewels! In the same spirit, she is addressed in 52:1:

> Awake, awake,
>> put on your strength, O Zion!
> Put on your beautiful garments,
>> O Jerusalem. . . .

Soon she will compare her former desolation with the bustling activity of returnees filling her towns and cities and remark in astonishment, "Where then have these come from?" (49:21).

Another divine word in verses 22–23 explains the origin of the change in fortune that Zion was about to experience. The true sovereign would reorder social structures in such a way that rulers would serve as guardians and nurses of Zion's returning sons and daughters. To illustrate the total neutralization of their power, a conventional ancient Near Eastern image of submission to a higher authority is given, the licking of dust before the feet of the king (v. 23a). Of course, their submission is intended not to redound to Zion's own glory but to reveal the central fact of her life: "Then you will know that I am the LORD." Far from being opposed to Zion's well-being, however, God's glorification is the basis for Israel's hope even in the face of continued adversity: "Those who wait for me shall not be put to shame" (v. 23b).

134

Acknowledgment of God's sovereignty and God's faithfulness to the captives of Zion, however, was not to be limited to Israel. Once the violent oppressors had been removed and God's order of justice had been restored, all borders would become obsolete:

> Then all flesh shall know
>> that I am the LORD your Savior,
>> and your Redeemer, the Mighty One of Jacob.
>>> (Isa. 49:26*b*)

Isaiah 49:14–26 is an important passage in the corpus of Second Isaiah's sayings. It corrects some overly simplistic notions. Our image of this prophet sometimes moves in the direction of a pampering optimist, speaking to his audience words of comfort and salvation free from the travail of human anguish. Zion, bitterly complaining and filled with doubt, moves our image in the direction of genuine realism.

Another stereotype that we may carry pictures a prophet who promotes a God who is in perfect control, engineering events and human feelings in a trajectory that is free from challenge. This passage places against that passionless prime mover a God enmeshed in the travail of human anguish, a God pleading, arguing, refuting complaints that could jeopardize a plan for creation's healing.

In this passage we find a God struggling for the human heart at the center of life. It is not a God unacquainted with human emotion but a God moved with maternal feelings and committed more to the deliverance of those in bondage than to the maintenance of a heroic image. The God encountered here is one passionately opposed to injustice, deeply committed to righting wrongs, captured by love for his creation and drawn into the agony of involvement. The God encountered here is one we can picture in the streets of our crime-infested cities, in nations exploited for the resources they can supply to affluent societies, in wards consigned to persons lost to their delusions. But this is not just a God humanized and thus recognizable in our experiences but a God confident that mercy and justice will prevail, a God assuring servants of humanity that "those who wait for me shall not be put to shame" and certain that one day "all flesh shall know."

135

Isaiah 50:1–3
Encounter with the Truth

Self-deception is a bitter enemy of wholesome relationships. And it is the most illusive of life's evils with which to cope. In marriage, for example, it leads one partner to assert that the fault lies exclusively with the other. An impenetrable wall is constructed that silences honest communication. Self-deception allows the one to wallow in self-pity while the other languishes in despair. A relationship dies, bringing the happiness of two human beings with it.

The pattern of blaming everyone but self for difficulties is found not only on the level of interpersonal relations but on all other levels as well. One religious group asserts that the *fact* that God is entirely on its side proves the depravity of its opponent. Negotiations break down between contending nations when eyes are blinded by ideological nationalism to the actual issues.

With so much practice in the realm of broken human relations upon which to draw, it is no wonder that human beings jeopardize their relationship with God through the vice of self-deception. Such was the case in ancient Israel. Viewing the precarious juncture at which the exilic community was standing, Second Isaiah realized that now more than ever it was important that this people candidly face the facts of its situation. They were fugitives in a distant land as the result of repudiating God's gift of a homeland by claiming their own efforts as the source of their abundance. Their beautiful temple had been leveled to the ground because they had tainted worship with self-adulation. But more than allowing their relationship with God to be healed through admitting their faults, they valued preserving their pride by defending themselves against any blame.

It is not hard to reconstruct the background of 50:1–3. It is in the form of a trial in which Yahweh responds to the charges that the people have raised against their God: "Yahweh has broken the covenant promises by casting us off, selling us to our enemies!" Here is the ultimate in self-pity. The heavens themselves are against us. We are the saddest among all martyrs. How can anything be expected of a people so grossly neglected, so poorly esteemed? The sentiment was caught well by the psalmist:

> You have sold your people for a trifle,
> demanding no high price for them.
> (Ps. 44:12)

To allow a people to persist in such self-deception is to condemn them to their own self-destruction. All of their energy becomes directed toward finding further occasions for hurling blame. Lies become the norm, banishing confrontation with the true reasons for their plight and nullifying the possibility of regaining health.

The courtroom is the right place for such a case. It does not guarantee success, but it removes self-deceivers from the structures that support their lies and it exposes them to honest questioning. The Judge calls for exhibits, harsh reminders of their real situation. Bring in the divorce papers, let us examine the bill of sale. Has the break come as the result of my negligence? Or are other causes revealed by the evidence? Clear evidence is produced:

> Because of your sins you were sold,
> and for your transgressions your mother was put away.
> (Isa. 50:1)

God is not denying the historical facts underlying their charges. In fact they have lost the land that God had promised to the descendants of Abraham. In fact the freedom God had purchased for them when they were slaves in Egypt had been lost to the bondage in which they were now held in Babylon. The destruction of Jerusalem, the loss of their homes, and the humiliation of living in the territory of idols were undeniable facts of history. More than that, God concedes, it was God "who gave up Jacob to the spoiler, and Israel to the robbers" (42:24). That is a severe confession. But then again, the God of Hebrew Scripture is not dedicated to avoiding offense at all costs but to dispelling the delusions that imprison human beings: "I the LORD speak the truth, I declare what is right" (45:19).

Isaiah 42:24–25 casts valuable light on the trial passage here in chapter 50, for it too confronts the people of Israel with the bare facts of their tragic situation. First, it removes the evasive

137

tactic of those who would preserve the image of an indulgent patron God by attributing disaster to other divine forces. No, *the Lord did it!* Second, it takes away all pretenses for blaming others, whether they be foreign peoples, the fates, or a negligent God. No, *it was the people's sin that caused it!* Third, and of most poignant interest for the present trial, it indicates that even the extreme disciplinary measures taken by God in destroying nation and cult had failed to shock this people into honest confrontation with the truth of its situation, a people that still "did not understand; . . . did not take it to heart" (42:25).

The comfort offered by self-deception is hard to let go. Spouses, children, nations, civilizations, and—dreadful prospect—possibly even our entire planet, find the benefits of shrugging off blame onto others more attractive than facing harsh life-giving truths. Lies have become ingrained, have become lifestyle, habit, much like gambling or substance abuse becomes habitual. Every possible defense mechanism is used to avoid the fact that the blame rests on self, and hence as well the responsibility for the situation.

This trial comes close to the heart of the prophetic soul. How can one reach a people seemingly hell-bent on their own destruction? Life, wholeness, and happiness can come only through fellowship with God. Accept life in fellowship with God! But here is a people, all too typical, that believes it can have life and persist in self-indulgence that impoverishes others, in special privilege that oppresses fellow citizens, in worship practices that reinforce pride and prejudice. How does one drive home to their consciousness the fundamental fact that wickedness and life-giving fellowship with God are mutually exclusive?

Reference to the God who turns the heavens into deep darkness may seem like a weird answer. Indeed, it has become traditional in critical scholarship to assert that the conclusion to this trial has been lost. Claus Westermann, after citing Karl Budde for support, is typical in arguing that "we should expect v. 2 to be followed by an utterance of the kind proclaiming Israel's release. . . . The presupposition is that the final part of 50.1ff. fell out" (p. 225). We fear that an overhasty application of modern definitions of prophetic genres once again has hindered sensitivity to the inspired rhetoric of biblical prophecy.

In earlier oracles Second Isaiah has applied the traditional arguments in the effort to break through the stubborn self-deception of the people. He has built upon the indictments of his prophetic predecessors by elaborating on the connections between crimes and divine punishment. But the prophet of "the new thing" is not confined to traditional language. This time he hears God delivering a different kind of refutation of the people's charges. We might imagine Second Isaiah reasoning thus as God's new word comes to him:

> So they claim that my power has declined with the rise of the mighty empires of the Assyrians, the Egyptians, the Babylonians, and the Persians. So they quake before the stories of the victories of the gods Assur, Amun Re, Marduk, and Ahura Mazda. So they marvel at the cosmogonic myths recited by pagan priests and the signs read out of the heavens by the astrologers. Then let them hear who the true Creator really is.

It does not seem off the mark to hear some exasperation in Yahweh's rebuttal. Edmund Wilson captured a characteristic of good literary technique in the title of a collection of essays he edited, *The Shock of Recognition.* The prophets were masters of the art of shocking listeners into recognition. Israel, after the interpretations of the 587 B.C.E. disaster given by Jeremiah and Ezekiel, still "did not understand; . . . did not take it to heart" (42:25). Maybe they will listen to some unembellished Job-like talk about power, not just the kind of power that lifts up and casts down kings and nations, but the kind that is able with a word to "dry up the sea, . . . make the rivers a desert, . . . clothe the heavens with blackness, . . . make sackcloth their covering" (50:2*b*–3). Giving the appearance of something quite other than the inept intrusion of a later editor, the conclusion to this trial uncovers the depths of divine and prophetic passion as it struggles to save a people from the gridlock of self-deception.

It would be a somber litany that would recount the self-deceptions that hold modern human beings in bondage. We are preoccupied with efforts to blame others for the restlessness of our troubled sleep, for the pain of our broken relationships, for the emptiness of our lives from real meaning. Walls of self-defense are often strong enough to last a lifetime. And they imprison their victims, assuring spiritual death long before the heart stops beating.

139

What chance is there to break through the lies that hold life-giving truth at bay? What chance that honest encounter with the facts of our lives might lead to admitting that we need help, help that might restore us by freeing us from the need to defend ourselves, help that comes through confessing, "Because of our sins we were sold."

Second Isaiah reminds us that God never gives up in the effort to reach us, to call us back to a confrontation with our real selves. It would take poetic imagination to describe the modern versions of encounter with the God who can "dry up the sea" and "clothe the heavens with blackness." For some it might be the God who shows the emptiness of material possessions in the death of a loved one. For others it might be the God who calls mortal flesh back to truth through the Associated Press photograph of a starving child. In any case, what is involved is raw encounter with truth, with Truth, with the TRUTH that banishes all lies and self-deception and places one naked before the question of life's essential meaning.

Isaiah 50:4–11
The Teacher Who Is Taught

Second Isaiah's innovativeness in drawing upon traditional genres is again apparent in the third Servant Song (50:4–9). The Servant's references to suffering at the hands of opponents who struck him, pulled out his beard, insulted him and spit upon him echo the complaints of individual lament psalms. But they have been absorbed into the Servant's description of his task in such a way as to give them a new significance.

The empowerment of the Servant, which in 42:1 stemmed from God's gift of God's spirit, is here related to the divine word which he is authorized to speak (cf. 49:2). That empowerment in turn allows the Servant to accept the hostility his message evokes with the quiet confidence that the final victory lies with those who are faithful to God. In fact, he is able to challenge his adversaries to present their case in court, for he knows that the Judge who will hand down the decision is the very one who "morning by morning" speaks to him with words of instruction and encouragement.

140

The abuse and shame heaped upon the Servant loses its power over him, thanks to his knowledge that "he who vindicates me is near." This is not to say that the one faithful to God's command escapes moments of doubt. For Jeremiah, whose biography seems to have inspired important aspects of Second Isaiah's portrait of the Servant, the path to confidence in God's care was strewn with bitter questioning and times of deep despair (e.g., Jer. 20:7–12). But an important dimension of the suffering of the faithful Servant comes into focus both in Jeremiah's case and here: Through personal suffering there steadily grows the capacity to uplift a whole community that has been driven close to spiritual defeat by the fierce blows of history. It is one of the mysteries of life that those with the greatest ability to encourage the distraught are often people who, far from being exempt from suffering, discover special gifts of empathy and empowerment precisely in their own valleys of personal suffering.

But suffering qua suffering is not enough to enable the Servant "to sustain the weary with a word." The *word* in question here is defined very specifically. It is a word that comes through God's grace:

> The Lord GOD helps me;
> therefore I have not been disgraced.
> (Isa. 50:7)

The Book of Job gives full expression to the kind of word that the well-intentioned often bring to those in pain or bereavement. It is an empty word that further undercuts confidence and hope by implying blame or exacerbating the contrast between the lucky winners in life and themselves. The only word that can instill hope is the one that cuts through the dread inflicted by ruthless oppressors by exposing their wickedness and cruelty to the justice and compassion of the power that will prevail. Through intimate communion with that power the Servant can give the afflicted a twofold word of promise: their *a*. tormentors will "wear out like a garment" and "the One who *b*. brings victory is near."

As in the case of the first two Servant Songs, so too here a word of commentary has been added. The elaboration in 50: 10–11 is of particular note because it adumbrates a theme developed by the disciples of Second Isaiah whose words are collected in chapters 56—66, namely, the tragic division of the Jewish community into two contending parties caused by diverging responses to the prophetic word. It is possible that

141

verses 10 and 11 were added by those who announced that God blessed a group addressed as "my servants" at the same time that he cursed a second group addressed as "but you . . ." (cf. 65:13–15). For the same sort of dualism characterizes the contrast between the God-fearer who, like the Servant, trusts the Lord even in the time of trial and the "kindlers of fire" who may revel now but are destined for judgment. Also common to these verses and to Third Isaiah is a gloomy pessimism. In 50:10, the pious "walks in darkness and has no light"; in 59:9, "we wait for light, and lo! there is darkness; and for brightness, but we walk in gloom."

This addendum to the third Servant Song is a harsh word, but its realism cannot be denied. The Song proper spoke of the abuse suffered by the Servant. It also spoke of his hope for vindication. But how might the deliverance of the Servant come in a world filled with enemies of justice? Sadly but inevitably, justice is restored by removing injustice, and where that cannot occur through human repentance and conversion the only remaining recourse is divine judgment. It is not possible to give a general description of the divine judgment that will be pronounced against unrelenting wickedness. The third Song uses metaphors: "All of them will wear out like a garment; the moth will eat them up" (50:9). The addendum announced that they would "lie down in torment." Above all, the essential point cannot be mistaken. The world that God created and in which God is present as Redeemer is not an amoral order. It is built on a structure of justice assuring that the righteous will be vindicated and the community will be healed. In this process of reclaiming the world for God's righteousness, distinctions between good and evil and between vindication and judgment would be lost only at the cost of the final victory going to chaos.

Isaiah 51:1—52:12
The Taught Teacher's Lesson

In interpreting the richly poetic words of Second Isaiah, one often finds it difficult to resolve with any degree of certainty the basic literary and form-critical questions, such as: Where do divisions lie between separate sayings? Who brought them together into their present order? Within what settings were they originally spoken or written? and finally, Which verses, if any, stem from disciples of Second Isaiah? Within such a corpus of writings a rigid approach to the literary history of the text can dull the reader's sensitivity to the depths of meaning present. Specifically in the case of 51:1—52:12 it seems that understanding can be enhanced by a rather flexible attitude toward questions of structure and unit divisions.

When Claus Westermann applies traditional form-critical criteria to the analysis of these thirty-five verses, he finds a half dozen separate units and fragments (pp. 232–52). Even someone who is less steeped in critical methodology than the famous German commentator may respond to the poetic beauty and power of sections like 51:9–11 and 52:7–10 with the sense that one is encountering literary gems originally composed separately by the prophet-poet and then later embedded into his longer composition.

When, on the other hand, one shifts focus and reads 51:1—52:12 as a whole, its compositional intricacy gives an equally powerful sense of structural and thematic unity running from beginning to end. This is evident, for example, in the following stylistic features: In verses 1, 4, 7, and 21 of chapter 51, the Lord through the prophet introduces important lessons to the people regarding the imminent deliverance with the imperative "Listen." Folded into these imperatives is a set of four double imperatives calling those addressed to action: "Awake, awake," "Rouse yourself, rouse yourself," "Awake, awake," "Depart, depart" (51:9; 51:17; 52:1; and 52:11).

In the first case, the one addressed is Yahweh, who is thereby called to saving action on Jerusalem/Zion's behalf. In the following three cases, those addressed by the imperatives are Jerusalem, Zion, and finally the exiles, who are commanded to form a procession back to Zion. Inextricably tied to this intricate literary architecture is a thematic unity that unfolds dramatically: After having been admonished to listen and having received instruction in the form of fundamental lessons from its past, Israel first hears God summoned to saving action and then itself similarly summoned to imitate God through an incisive response on its own part leading up to a festive return to Zion.

Within the larger Second Isaiah corpus, there is something climactic about this long composition. It reaches back to the

143

major themes of earlier sections of Second Isaiah and weaves them into an elegant recapitulation. The connections are scarcely accidental. For example, the instructions found in the first half are intimately connected to the central theme of the Servant Song in 50:4–9, in which the Lord equips the Servant with the skills of a teacher enabling him "to sustain the weary with a word." Who are "the weary" to whom the Servant is sent with God's instructions in 51:1—52:12? Are they not the very ones addressed in the present composition as "you that pursue righteousness/seek the LORD" (51:1), "my people/nation" (51:4), "you who know righteousness/have my teaching in your hearts" (51:7), and "you who are wounded/drunk, but not with wine" (51:21)? The plausibility of this suggestion grows in the light of 51:7, where those "who have my teaching in your hearts" are instructed, "Do not fear the reproach of others, and do not be dismayed when they revile you," a lesson drawn directly from the personal experience of the Servant:

> I gave my back to those who struck me,
>> and my cheeks to those who pulled out the beard;
> I did not hide my face
>> from insult and spitting.
>
> (Isa. 50:6)

Finally, suffering Servant and suffering people are promised the same vindication vis-à-vis the ruthless adversaries: "All of them will wear out like a garment; the moth will eat them up," the Servant is promised in 50:9, a promise that is echoed in 51:8: "For the moth will eat them up like a garment."

Given this clear evidence that 50:4–9 introduces the Teacher and chapter 51 recites his lesson to the people, one could next ask whether the entire section 50:1—52:12 (with the possible omission of 50:10–11) comprises an original composition. Or did the third Servant Song inspire the lesson as its sequel? These are the kinds of literary questions that seem as impossible to answer definitively as they seem inconsequential for an understanding of the essential message. What is patently clear is that both the Servant Song and the lesson stem from Second Isaiah, and whether they were both written at the same time or sequentially does not alter the fact that together they now present a unified message.

With what message does the Lord equip the Servant teacher "to sustain the weary with a word"? First, the prophet who based the case for Yahweh being the only true God upon the evidence of history directs the attention of his audience to their past, more specifically, to their ancestral roots. Already in the story of Abraham and Sarah they would find a cardinal lesson, that their life as a people rests solely on God's grace (51:1–2). Did they feel like a helpless minority in a strange land? They were reminded of the one who became many. Did they wistfully compare memories of a beautiful lost homeland to life in arid refugee camps? They were invited to contrast desert and Eden and then thrill to thoughts of the renewal of Zion that was imminent (51:3). Section one of the lesson thus strikes an upbeat chord of "joy and gladness" over what the Lord was doing.

The second section (51:4–6) suggests that together with the third Servant Song the first also may have been in the mind of the prophet as he composed this lesson. The circle of those addressed has been widened from those "that pursue righteousness/seek the LORD" to "my people/nation." And the commission they receive is the one the Servant received in 42:1–9, to extend God's justice/light/teaching to the nations.

An envelope is created around the daunting commission to the nations by the return in the third section (51:7–8) to a word of encouragement to the "righteous," those who "have my teaching in your hearts." The whole nation has not rallied behind the Servant's task. In fact, it is a people riven, a community in which many abuse the faithful with reproach and reviling. The refrain that also ended the previous section (51:6) echoes here with a deepened meaning:

> but my deliverance will be forever,
> and my salvation to all generations.
> (Isa. 51:8)

Audacious promises that God's justice would be established among the nations and that persecution of the faithful would be ended were no doubt met with considerable skepticism. Doubt is answered in the fourth section (51:9–16) with a reply that bristles with the raw power of mythopoeic imagery. It is hard to imagine a more poignant reminder to a wavering people that neither the cause of world justice nor their own safety rested upon human self-help projects but solely upon the power that created the universe by repelling the forces of chaos, called 145 Israel forth from bondage to peoplehood, and even now was preparing to return the exiled community to Zion.

Isaiah 51:9–11 is a poetic gem embedded in its larger context. Like the first section, it directs the attention of the audience backward, this time all the way back to the "days of old," that is, the primordial age vastly antedating even the time of Abraham and Sarah. Those quaking before the might of emperors are summoned to witness the beginning of time with its conflict between the two forces to which all forces are finally reducible, chaos embodied in Rahab or the dragon and the arm of the Lord. Rhapsodically, Second Isaiah calls out to the power that in the birthing of the universe created the possibility of life and beauty: "Awake, awake, put on strength, O arm of the LORD!" (v. 9). In that power alone resided hope for a community now assailed anew by the dread specter of chaos. Here was the only weapon of any help to those against whom the most deadly weapons of human destruction had been directed. In holy defiance of all earthly power, the powerless audaciously celebrate the might of God before whom all that resisted the will of God would be vanquished like the dragon!

In his hymns, frequently Second Isaiah draws upon two elements of lament, namely, complaint and praise. Complaint has included reminders to God of events in the past when God had acted incisively on behalf of his creatures. The element of complaint is introduced here with the question: "Was it not you who...?" Implication: "Where *are* you *now?*" The repetition of that question elicits memory of the two most important moments in Israel's history: creation of the universe through the defeat of primordial chaos and creation of a people through the defeat of political tyranny. Creation and exodus, these are the moments to which the faithful are to return in moments of crisis and doubt, trusting that the God who was faithful to order and justice in the past has not changed holy resolve. The blending of myth and history in this portrait of the Creator-Redeemer has the effect of evoking a sense of awesome majesty combined with tender loving care. It is an effect similar to the one produced in 40:10–11 through the blending of images of powerful Divine Warrior and gentle Shepherd. With this twofold lesson and the vivid imagery it has evoked, the prophet is prepared to move to a third moment in Israel's history.

The third moment lies in the future, but it is implicit already in the paradigmatic events of the past. Deliverance from exile *shall* occur. God has *not* changed! God *will* act as God acted in creation and the exodus! God's power *is* sufficient to

146

defeat the pernicious forces of chaos! God's love reaches out to the people even in their bondage, even *most emphatically* in their bondage!

The powerful lesson of this recapitulation of history in three verses is immediately applied to the present situation of the exilic community (51:12–16). Their problem is that they now live in the fear of tyrants and the dread of oppressors; they have no control over their own destiny.

Consistent with the first verse of his call (40:1), Second Isaiah realizes that the principal word he is commissioned to bring to this anxious community is a word of divine *comfort.* The comfort he brings is not a facile, well-intentioned human word of sympathy but a powerful assurance that verses 12 and 13 contrast the earthly oppressor "who fades like grass" with the Creator of the heavens and the earth. Here too echoes from the call narrative are unmistakable (especially 40:6–8). The challenge he brings is this: "Do not forget, remember!" Remember that the one who determines the future is the God simultaneously creating the universe and loving his creatures, at once "stretching out the heavens . . . and saying to Zion, 'You are my people' " (51:16).

The lesson introduced by an appeal to the arm of God and depicting the might of the Creator-Redeemer is followed by two complementary lessons that seek to elicit a fitting human response, a response that renounces despair as the bondage that keeps the tyrant in power and instead embraces God's deliverance as a celebration of the faith community's partnership in the new creation.

Earlier we noted that in contrast to chapters 40—48, where the community was most commonly addressed with the synonymous pair Jacob/Israel, chapters 49—55 favor the pair Zion/Jerusalem. The prophet has created a tight relationship between the final two lessons addressed to the community by drawing on the latter parallelism: 51:17 begins, "Rouse yourself, rouse yourself! Stand up, O *Jerusalem* "; 52:1 is introduced with, "Awake, awake, put on your strength, O *Zion!*" Both depict the Holy City as a mother of the children of Israel. They also indicate that the cry of the people out of their bondage to Yahweh has been answered and now comes full circle; the people are to rouse themselves from their helpless stupor and awaken to the freedom they have received from God to join in the drama of restoration.

147

INTERPRETATION

The word to Jerusalem addresses the mother in her bereavement. The image used to describe the tragic loss she has suffered is one that was widely used by the exilic community to portray God's judgment (Jer. 25:15, 17, 28; 49:12; Ezek. 23:33; Ps. 75:8; Lam. 4:21). Recipients of the cup of God's wrath were both the foreign nations and Israel, reflecting the universal character of divine justice.

The way this image is developed in 51:17–23 vividly depicts the historical juncture at which the exilic community had arrived. It was from God's hand that Jerusalem had received "the cup of his wrath" (51:17). The result was "devastation and destruction, famine and sword" (51:19). But now a new word comes to the forsaken mother from "your God who pleads the cause of his people" (51:22). He has taken the dreaded cup from her hand and is about to place it into the hands of those who have tormented her.

The sequel addressed to Zion summons her to awaken to the new reality that was depicted symbolically in 51:3 and now is to be celebrated as having dawned upon her. The fact that the same imperatives, "Awake, awake, put on strength," are directed to her as were to the "arm of the LORD" in 51:9 suggests that Zion is to act with the same vigor and resolve as did the Lord in the divine initiating activity. Her release has been accomplished by God, but that miracle in turn becomes a reality as she responds in joyous assent and allows the strength of God to become her strength to act. She is to cast off her bonds, dress in festal garments, and reclaim her birthright as a free and holy city.

Zion stands ready, expectant, dressed for the celebration of her release from bondage. But there are two more movements in the drama the Teacher wishes to describe before concluding his lesson.

The first comes in 52:7–10, beginning with a jubilant shout from the prophet:

> How beautiful upon the mountains
> are the feet of the messenger who announces peace,
> who brings good news,
> who announces salvation,
> who says to Zion, "Your God reigns."
>
> (Isa. 52:7)

To those sublime words one commentator replied, "How strange this mention of feet, one of the ugliest parts of the human body." Wrong! Human feet in fact are not only beautiful but remarkable. Think for example of the bare feet of a Nigerian Olympian sprinter! But the point regarding the messenger's feet seems to be a different one than a lesson in podiatric aesthetics. Considering the geography and customs of the Near East, we can assume that the messenger's feet, after the long journey over the mountains, were not only dusty but very callused and perhaps bleeding. To those feet the witness exclaims, "How beautiful!" For these are feet that bring words that thrill the heart longing for just this announcement, "Your God reigns." It is like the old man peering into the still-sparkling eyes of his ninety-year-old wife, eyes bordered by wrinkles enfolding the wisdom of a thousand revelations, and exclaiming, "How beautiful!" It is like the loving husband stroking the stomach of the mother of his children, gently tracing the stretch marks that memorialize her maternal labors, and exclaiming, "How beautiful!" Yes, indeed, how beautiful these feet bruised on behalf of the blessed mission of proclaiming the coming of salvation!

Who is the messenger, coming with lightning speed, to announce, "Your God reigns"? Likely it is one of the divine messengers commissioned by God in 40:1–2, "Comfort, O comfort my people. . . . Speak tenderly to Jerusalem." For the sentinels who observe this remarkable event respond, "The LORD has comforted his people, he has redeemed Jerusalem" (52:9).

What precisely is this event which is described in 52:8 as "the return of the LORD to Zion"? Second Isaiah is drawing on a pattern that was very familiar to his audience, it being found in the mythology of all ancient Near Eastern cultures. Responding to an attack on the divine realm by ferocious agents of chaos, the warrior God goes forth into battle. After a fierce struggle that threatens to cause the collapse of the divine habitation into primordial formlessness, the warrior God slays monster Chaos, restores order to the life of the gods, and then with the carcass of the slain beast demonstrates consummate artistic skill in fashioning the universe. The mythic drama culminates with watchmen announcing the Warrior's return and with everyone joining in a festival of rejoicing and celebration of the restoration of celestial harmony.

149

As not infrequently in the Bible, we here find echoes of this mythic drama. In 51:9–10 the battle against the chaos monster

Rahab was described. In verses 51:17 and 52:1 Jerusalem/Zion was summoned to rouse herself and prepare herself for a celebration of victory by clothing herself in beautiful garments. The celebration itself breaks forth in 52:7–10 with the announcement to Zion that the victorious God has returned to the capital city. True to the universal scope of the ancient pattern, the victory is witnessed by all nations, for the restoration thereby accomplished affects the ends of the earth (52:10).

With consummate dramatic skill, though, Second Isaiah adds one culminating word in 52:11–12. In the mythic pattern, the celebration of the Warrior's return to his city would have been the end of the drama. King and people would have been at rest in their own land. In returning to Zion, however, Yahweh is returning to a city still in exile! The drama must move one further step toward its denouement. The people must march back to their homeland. Climatically, one last imperative is sounded: "Depart, depart!" The procession is about to begin that will end Zion's mourning. Led by the Lord, it is a holy procession, calling for rites of purification (cf. 51:11). For the pilgrims bear the temple vessels Nebuchadnezzar had taken from the Jerusalem temple and for whose return Cyrus recently had granted permission. It is a procession, moreover, that outstrips even the original birth experience of Israel, the exodus from Egypt.

> For you shall not go out in haste,
> and you shall not go in flight;
> for the LORD will go before you,
> and the God of Israel will be your rear guard.
> (Isa. 52:12)

With these words the long composition ends in celebration of the very heart of Second Isaiah's message, the announcement of the return of the Lord to the midst of the people. All else pales to insignificance before the reality of Immanuel, God with us. Other themes pass in and out of the prophet's story, themes concerning Israel's suffering in exile and its complaints, concerning the Babylonian oppressors and their gods, concerning the rise of mighty empires and their fall. All such themes are gathered up finally into the sole reality upon which all that is dear and worthwhile rests: "Your God reigns. . . . The LORD will go before you."

Thus concludes the Teacher's eloquent lesson delivered to

150

a community tottering between despair and hope. It is a timely lesson, in that it reminded a searching people of crucial moments in time that define the meaning of all time, moments that give orientation to those tempted to fall prey to lethargy by placing them in the presence of the source of all meaning. They are reminded of the moment of creation, the mysterious origin of all that is in God's incisive move against chaos. They are reminded of the moment of the awakening of destiny, the mysterious stirring of hope in the faithful response of one ancestral couple. They are reminded of the moment of deliverance, the mysterious birth of a nation in divine deliverance from political bondage. And they are reminded of restoration, the return of the God without whom they are lost.

Such moments define the meaning of all human life. To forget them jeopardizes our viability as creative individuals, constructive communities, and responsible members of the family of the nations. Amidst this lesson in remembering, the prophet issues the warning: "You have forgotten the LORD, your Maker. . . . You fear continually all day long" (51:13). Loss of memory, forgetting the moments that remind us of our origin in grace, implies loss of everything, of identity, of meaning, of destiny. The "sound and the fury" of the oppressor replaces God as the molder of our consciousness. Despair banishes hope. Chaos engulfs God's order of justice.

It is not to be so among God's people, says the Teacher. Awake, awake, he calls out to God. Awake, awake, he calls out to Zion. A faithful people will be drawn into God's redemptive activity of banishing chaos and creating the new order of blessing. And the Teacher's audience can be confident that the word thus proclaimed is dependable, for it originates not with the human spokesman but with the one who "morning by morning wakens—wakens my ear to listen as those who are taught" (50:4). Second Isaiah is not a clever poet but a faithful messenger who passes on the word of the Creator-Redeemer, the one who promises,

> for a teaching will go out from me,
>   and my justice for a light to the peoples.
>   (Isa. 51:4)

For communities of faith, the significance of that teaching 151 was not limited to the time of the exilic prophet. To listen to the words of the messenger, to remember the moments of God's saving action, and to awake to the new order of blessing that God has created, these are activities whose validity remains undiminished to our own day. They are activities through which God still seeks to restore sight to human beings in order that they may distinguish between earthly treasures that "will wear out like a garment" and God's gift of salvation that "will be forever" (51:6).

One might ask: Is the prophet's word dependable? Is there substance to the images of the wilderness becoming like Eden and the desert like the garden of the Lord? Did not the exilic community pass from hardship in Babylon to renewed hardship in their own land?

It has been the belief of faith communities through the ages that the word of promise spoken by God through the prophets is dependable and that indeed God's "salvation has gone out" and God's "arms will rule the peoples" (51:5). For in the midst of the hardships of historical existence the faith community experiences the transformation of despair and brokenness into faith and hope. This transformation occurs not by the faithful being elevated above hardship but right in the midst of life as they become agents of God's grace and witness how the broken "shall obtain joy and gladness, and sorrow and sighing shall flee away" (51:11).

Second Isaiah witnessed the reduction to dust of all the human institutions and achievements upon which the Jewish community had placed its trust. Gone was the dazzling temple, the imposing Davidic dynasty, the awesome armies, the life of culture and luxury. Where others found reason to despair, however, this prophet recognized the gracious activity of God removing penultimate loyalties from the consciousness of the people as preparation for receiving the only eternal reality, the word of God. Upon this reality they could rebuild their broken lives!

The poignancy and validity of that word is as clear today as it was on the day in which the prophet first uttered it:

> I, I am he who comforts you;
>> why then are you afraid of a mere mortal who must die,
>> a human being who fades like grass?
> You have forgotten the LORD, your Maker,
>> who stretched out the heavens
>> and laid the foundations of the earth.
> You fear continually all day long

because of the fury of the oppressor,
who is bent on destruction.
But where is the fury of the oppressor?
The oppressed shall speedily be released;
    they shall not die and go down to the Pit,
    nor shall they lack bread.

(Isa. 51:12–14)

This word of comfort abides as the priceless treasure of all persons of faith today, no matter what circumstances surround them, for it draws them into communion with the source of all life and blessing. It also abides as their commission, for through grace they grow in the awareness of human life coming to fulfillment through participation in God's redemptive activity through which all that is broken is embraced in healing love.

Apart from the eyes of faith, the wilderness remains as threatening as ever, the desert as dry and forbidding. But for those "that pursue righteousness," "that seek the LORD," the wilderness is like Eden, the desert like the garden of the Lord, for from the perspective of faith they see not oppressors and victims living under the domain of evil but a world graciously undergoing transformation into compassion and justice. The assurance that this envisioned transformation is not an illusion but the only true reality rests not on their own wisdom but on the good news delivered from God through the messenger: "Your God reigns."

Isaiah 52:13—53:12
The Power of the Powerless Servant

The fourth Servant Song (52:13—53:12), like any fine poem, places images before the reader that elicit deep reflection without providing answers to every problem of interpretation. From the time of early Jewish and Christian interpretation down to the present, commentary on this Song has thus provoked much debate. Not infrequently, as in the case of writers as diverse in time and perspective as Don Isaac Abarbanel in the fifteenth century and Claus Westermann in our own day, a single author will acknowledge various interpretive possibilities.

153

At the outset it is wise to establish whatever objective markers can be identified. The first has to do with form, namely, the Song's affinities with thanksgiving psalms such as Psalms 30 and 54, in which the psalmist recalls adverse circumstances, whether of a personal or national nature, and then offers thanks for deliverance. While the author of our passage clearly has drawn upon this genre, the adaptation is undertaken with great freedom, as seen especially in the fact that whereas the thanksgiving psalms are written in the first person, this passage begins and ends with divine speech and in between presents a third-person voice that describes the suffering of the Servant. Visible in this adaptation is the theological perspective that permeates Second Isaiah. What is occurring in the experience of the Servant bears significance that extends far beyond the life of the Servant. The divine oracle that frames the composition indicates that the events of the Servant's life are episodes in God's providential care for the whole world.

The second noteworthy mark is that this Song has important connections both with the other three Servant Songs and with the other allusions to the Servant in Second Isaiah. This is not a magic key to interpretation, however, since the picture of the Servant given in those other passages varies. At times we encounter what seems to be an individual with a divine commission to serve his people. At other times the Servant is Israel appointed as God's agent in relation to the other nations. Finally, there are instances in which the Servant appears to be a specific subdivision within Israel called into God's service on behalf of the rest of the nation or of the wider world.

Attempts to push conclusions further by appeal to evidence outside the Second Isaiah corpus have led to useless speculations. For example, while it is helpful to note that the suffering of the Servant in chapter 53 bears resemblance to experiences of prophets such as Elijah and Jeremiah, little has been gained by efforts to *identify* the Servant with either of these figures or with the countless other individuals or groups that have been suggested. As we turn to the passage itself for the primary clues to its meaning, we must be satisfied with two modest background conclusions: (1) The author utilizes aspects of the thanksgiving psalm. (2) The author writes with awareness both of the other instances of the Servant motif in Isaiah 40—55 and of the long history of suffering among the prophets of Yahweh.

Beginning with the framework formed by 52:13–15 and 53:12, we observe a paradox that is central to the meaning of

154

N.B.

this Song. The final divine announcement is that the Servant will prosper, but the path that leads to that exaltation is the path of a suffering unto death for the sake of sinners that was so terrible that it caused observers to be appalled. Yet the reason that nations and their kings are startled into wonder is not just, or even primarily, the severity of the suffering; it is the unprecedented nature, the absolute novelty of what they are seeing that drives them to silence. In this most unlikely of all places, among helpless exiled Jews, and more specifically in the presence of the most lowly of their kind, nations and kings encounter the awesome power that upholds the universe and determines the destiny of peoples. Before such a spectacle they are made speechless. This theme was encountered earlier at the conclusion of the second Servant Song in chapter 49:

> Kings shall see and stand up,
>   princes, and they shall prostrate themselves,
> because of the LORD, who is faithful,
>   the Holy One of Israel, who has chosen you.
>   (Isa. 49:7*b*)

The irony is sharpened and suspense heightened as the poem next moves to describe the Servant who thus startles and astonishes the powerful of the world. This description, in 53:1–11, is given in the first-person plural, which raises the question of the identity of the group observing the Servant and making the remarkable confession that through his suffering God has forgiven their sins and made them whole. The reference to kings and nations in the preceding verses has suggested to some that it is the nations of the world that speak here, a suggestion that is not unthinkable in a thought world that envisioned the Servant actively doing God's work

> until he has established justice in the earth;
>   and the coastlands wait for his teaching.
>   (Isa. 42:4)

In 49:6*b*, God had said to the Servant,

> I will give you as a light to the nations,
>   that my salvation may reach to the end of the earth.

Along with the majority of Jewish and Christian commentators, however, it seems more accurate to recognize in those describing the Servant the voice of the Jewish community. Demonstration of the plausibility of this interpretation requires

155

a brief look at the situation of the Jewish exiles in the mid-sixth century B.C.E.

The exile was a time of profound spiritual searching on the part of the Jewish community. The institutions and customs that constituted the heart of its identity had been destroyed by a ruthless foreign power. The Book of Lamentations gives voice to Israel's sickness of soul and grief as it probes the intractable question of how it was possible for the people of God to be scattered and destroyed like some loathsome object.

The answer that emerged out of Second Isaiah's inspired reflection was one that had been cultivated among the prophets over the long and troubled history of the monarchy. Israel had refused to uphold the terms of its covenant relationship with God by insisting on disobeying the commandments and turning to other deities. Should such blatant sin and apostasy be left unpunished, the moral structure of the world would collapse into chaos (42:23–25). *Mišpāṭ*, the universal order of divine justice, required redress. What is more, as undeniably bitter as was Israel's plight, it was the only recourse open to a God who sought to return a straying people to the covenant of grace through repentance, that is to say, by reawakening within human beings a desire for God's righteous and saving presence.

The exile, then, was a time of profound spiritual searching. Out of adversity arose leaders who dared to claim that God's mercy was being manifested even in the recent calamity and to invite the nation to reclaim their inheritance as God's children. The participants in this spiritual quest included prophets, priests, and laity. The disciples of Jeremiah were called to reflect on their master's concept of a new covenant, in which God's will was written on the human heart (Jer. 31:31–34). Ezekiel and his followers dreamed dreams of a new heart replacing the heart of stone that had led the people away from God (Ezek. 36:26) and of dry bones being filled with the spirit of life (Ezek. 37:1–14). Levitical priests reflected on the Day of Atonement and God's gift of the sacrificial blood, mysterious in its divinely given power to wash away the sins of the people (Lev. 16:11–19; 17:10–14).

Isaiah 53 is Second Isaiah's contribution to this spiritual quest for an answer to the question of how the tragic pattern of sin and punishment could be broken and replaced by the wholeness that accompanies a hearty embrace of God's compassion and righteousness. It revolves around the notion of a Servant of the Lord whose surrender to God's will was so total that he took the consequences of the sin of the community upon himself, even though he was innocent of any wrong. This of course is the stuff of martyrdom, which can be moving but totally ineffective in relation to the human plight unless accompanied by one critically significant dimension: "Yet it was the will of the LORD to crush him with pain" (53:10). The Servant is not acting alone. The Servant is serving God's purpose. Not tragic fate, but obedience to the Lord motivates the Servant to place no limits on self-giving love.

But what sort of divine logic is it that leads to such a plan, placing an innocent human being as an "offering for sin" in order to atone for those caught in the web of deadly self-assertion? Christians are conditioned by substitutionary theories of the atonement originating in the Middle Ages to think in abstract mathematical terms when answering this question. The result is to impose anachronistically on pre-Christian Scripture views that cannot be justified on the basis of sound exegetical method. While the history of biblical interpretation is a valuable resource for interpretive insight, the unique voice of the text in its ancient setting must never be silenced by later theological developments. Within the interplay of original message, subsequent appropriations of the text by later generations of believers, and contemporary reflections on Scripture arises the possibility of a clearer understanding of the prophetic message that can refine and deepen our understanding of later Jewish and Christian writings, such as those dealing with the role of Judaism in relation to the Gentile world or those reflecting on the meaning of the life and death of Jesus.

The crux of the matter for our author is the central tragedy of Israel's history: the refusal of the people to obey God's will that has led to a web of sin that degrades not only the life of the offending generation but the life of their posterity as well. What could possibly break this pattern of stubborn persistence in sin and consequent calamity? Although priests have performed the atoning sacrifices year after year and prophets have preached repentance and threatened punishment day in and day out, the pattern persists unchanged. The tone of the fourth Servant Song is urgent, passionate, even desperate. It aims to arrest the attention of the listeners by introducing something so startling that it causes nations and kings to shut their mouths. It presents an alternative to the pattern of crime and commensurate punishment of the guilty party, an alternative so new that it has never been heard or even thought of. Human beings are driven to the limits of their imaginative powers by being obliged to contemplate a shuttering divine decision. Since the many have proven incapable of denouncing their tragic sinfulness, and since the sacrifice of animals has not proven capable of atoning for their sin, God has taken an innocent human being, allowed the punishment deserved by the many to fall upon him in what is admittedly a "perversion of justice," and in this startling manner restored the people to righteousness and wholeness.

This audacious alternative is shaped by considerations vastly different from detached divine arithmetic. The heaping up of words to designate pain and suffering, disgrace and sorrow, as well as the startling confession that this "perversion of justice" is "the will of the LORD," signifies a daring plunge into the heart and mind of a God who suffers so intensely with the people as to lead to a course of action that breaks all conventions of justice. In accompaniment with the recasting of the genre of the thanksgiving oracle, we witness here a recasting of the tradition of atoning sacrifice with the stakes raised astonishingly from animal bearing sin to human becoming offering. What is more, the person described is not just anyone, but the one closest to the heart of God, the kind, gentle, and obedient Servant of the Lord.

When the question of the theological meaning of an enigmatic text such as the fourth Servant Song is raised, it is a common tendency to limit possibilities to the following two alternatives: (1) A "historical" meaning is sought based on antecedents, that is, traditions that can be assumed to have been available to the original author; for example, since the idea of individual resurrection is not attested during the time of Second Isaiah, the Servant's being rewarded after pouring himself out to death must be taken metaphorically as referring to the restoration of the nation after the exile. (2) A "spiritual" meaning is sought by appeal to divine revelation; for example, although the idea of resurrection was not current in the time of Second Isaiah, God now reveals through the prophet that the Servant will be raised as a reward for his obedience. This dichotomy is unbiblical, for it breaks asunder what the faith of Israel struggled to hold together in the face of constant assault by the mythological thought of antiquity, namely, history and revelation. It was in the midst of their historical experiences that the

158

faithful discerned God's presence and will. Israel found the spiritual meaning of their existence not apart from the stuff of their everyday experience but in the course of it. This historical perspective, on the other hand, neither set a limit on what was possible, based on something equivalent to Ernst Troeltsch's analogical principle, nor dulled eschatological imagination. History, understood as the arena of the creative, saving activity of God, was dynamic in its capacity to awaken new dimensions of understanding within the faith community. Second Isaiah bore witness to this open view when he reported God's words to the exiles: "I am about to do a new thing" (43:19).

The fourth Servant Song carries the sense of anticipation to new heights:

> For that which had not been told them they shall see,
>   and that which they had not heard they shall
>   contemplate.
>
> (Isa. 52:15)

The prophet whose honest confrontation with life enabled him to describe the peril engulfing a people that repeatedly had repudiated God's grace (42:23–25) was equally capable of recognizing the advent of hope where others saw "no form or majesty that we should look at him, nothing in his appearance that we should desire him" (53:2). Here we meet revelation in the biblical sense, that is to say, not as a mechanical process detached from life, but as a vital aspect of a life so given to divine purpose as to recognize in everyday human experience the mysterious ways of the God compelled by love to recapture the hearts of the lost.

What was it that this faithful follower saw as God's new saving initiative? It assumed the form of a Servant, one appealing to the hearts of the lost neither through irresistible attractiveness nor overwhelming power but through a devotion to God that was so complete that concern for personal comfort and gain was eclipsed by the desire to serve. Oneness with divine purpose in such a case rendered conventional standards of evaluation obsolete, standards that declare that it is not right for the innocent to suffer and that unearned punishment constituted a perversion of justice. The Servant did not submit to affliction through pathetic resignation but as a bold choice to participate with God in an act aimed at breaking the stranglehold that sin had maintained for countless ages

159

over the human family. Accordingly, in his death-defying commitment he does not lose his life but redefines the nature of life as light that breaks through darkness, as forgiveness that destroys the bondage of sin and death, and as knowledge that makes many righteous.

In 53:11*b*–12 the divine discourse that introduced the Song now brings it to a conclusion. It stresses an essential point that runs against the grain of human reason: In the life of a lowly and despised human being, one appearing to be the antithesis of the glamorous ones admired by the world, *God* has been present atoning for the sin of the people.

The background of the audience in the sacrificial systems of antiquity, however, almost assured a misunderstanding. The sacrificial animal, whether sent by Babylonian priests into enemy territory or offered up by the sons of Aaron on the Day of Atonement, had no power over the circumstances of its fate. The simile in 53:7 could in fact reinforce the sense that, like the lamb led to slaughter, the Servant was a victim of a sacral decision over which he had no control. The divine word in the conclusion declares that the simile must not be pressed in the direction of identifying the consciousness of the Servant with the passivity of the sacrificial lamb. The active verb in the first half of verse 12*b* makes the point emphatically: "because he poured out himself to death." The force of the following verb is similar, for as Claus Westermann has noted, it should be translated as a reflexive rather than a passive: "and let himself be numbered with transgressors" (p. 268). In other words, the Servant was not a pawn in the hands of an arbitrary god but one who had committed himself freely to a deliberate course of action. Not a victim of circumstances, not a pathetic casualty in the ruthless atrocities that have always been a part of human existence, but one who willingly and obediently followed the vision of God's order of righteousness in defiance of all worldly wisdom and all human cowardice. Such was the Servant who chose to make his life an instrument of God's healing.

The portrait of the Servant thus banishes the dichotomy that religious traditions have often constructed between divine intent and human response. God's will is done where a human being regardless of his or her standing in the eyes of the powerful, finds the highest expression of human dignity in expressing solidarity with fellow human beings through a love that acknowledges no bounds because its source is in God.

160

A portion of the story.

Only after the obedience unto death of the Servant is fully appreciated can one understand the significance of the final point, the reward given by God to the Servant. For only against the background of that obedience can one see that it is not a private divine favor that is at issue but an affirmation of the moral structure of the universe (Westermann, p. 268). Although the death of an innocent, righteous one had pushed the question of morality to the breaking point ("by a perversion of justice he was taken away"), a higher structure of thought than human sensibility is revealed: By bearing the sin of others and pouring himself out to death, the Servant has become the human vehicle through whom those others are healed. Within the context of this higher morality it becomes entirely fitting that the Servant is rewarded by God with seeing his own vindication and reward. But not only the Servant sees this final validation of the moral order that God has created. The first half of the framework of the Song, with its portrait of kings standing speechless before the Servant, indicates that through this suffering human being nations and their leaders will come to see the alternative power of God that brings peace and harmony to all. At this point the first Song offers helpful commentary on the last:

> He will not grow faint or be crushed
> until he has established justice in the earth;
> and the coastlands wait for his teaching.
> (Isa. 42:4)

The portrait of the Servant who finds identity and fulfillment in God's service is pivotal in a larger context than Second Isaiah. It stands at the center of the biblical theme of the election of individual, clan, or nation for a specific divine purpose. It brings to mind the eighth-century prophet whose life served as the crystallization point for the entire tradition-building process culminating in the canonical Book of Isaiah. Having experienced the cleansing of God's seraph in his call, Isaiah responded not by lingering in transcendental meditation but in obedient service: "Here am I; send me!" (Isa. 6:8). It recalls the very raison d'être of the people of Israel as expressed in Moses' demand to the Pharaoh: "Let my people go, that they may *serve* me in the wilderness" (Exod. 7:16). The people of God as Servant of the Lord is a people given to obedient service. At those times when it lost its way through preoccupation with self, God

161

provided faithful servants who reminded them of the message they were in the world to proclaim: The true self is found when it is given to others, even when that givenness implies obedience unto death. For amidst all the uncertainties of life, one reality abides, the reality of God's presence.

> If I ascend to heaven, you are there;
>   if I make my bed in Sheol, you are there.
> If I take the wings of the morning
>   and settle at the farthest limits of the sea,
> even there your hand shall lead me,
>   and your right hand shall hold me fast.
>   (Ps. 139:8–10)

The life of the people of God is life in the Presence, and from that fact alone comes the desire to obey and the strength to endure.

The pivotal position of the fourth Servant Song is also seen by looking beyond the exile. A period of crisis for the Jewish community equal in horror to the Babylonian conquest and exile was the time of Selucid rule in the second century B.C.E. Facing martyrdom as the cost of faithfulness to the God of Israel, masses succumbed to the blandishments of the conqueror: "He [Antiochus IV Epiphanes] shall seduce with intrigue those who violate the covenant; but the people who are loyal to their God shall stand firm and take action" (Dan. 11:32). The action taken by the faithful is described by the author of the second half of Daniel with the use of a term borrowed from the fourth Servant Song: *The wise* among the people shall give understanding to many" (Dan. 11:33). The participle that is here translated "the wise" corresponds to the verb in Isaiah 52:13 translated in the NRSV as "my servant *shall prosper.*" The savants who prepared the first Greek and Latin translations, as well as later translators such as Martin Luther, gave clearer expression to the connection made by the author of Daniel to Isaiah 52 when they translated the verb as "will act wisely" instead of "will prosper." At any rate, it is clear that the persecuted community described by Daniel found in the Servant of the fourth Song a model for those seeking to be steadfast to the covenant in times of extreme trial. Those who imitate the Servant by obedience even unto death will "give understanding to many," that is to say, will correct the vision of their weaker compatriots, thereby enabling them to reclaim the path of righteousness that alone leads to blessedness.

162

At a still later period of foreign domination, this time under the Romans, certain Jews, seeking to understand the religious significance of the recent life, death, and resurrection of Jesus of Nazareth, once again looked to the fourth Servant Song for guidance. In that Song they found a key to interpretation. The figure of a Servant of God, who, although innocent himself, would willingly accept God's commission to give his life as an atoning sacrifice for his people, seemed to them to be fulfilled in Jesus.

Also during the early Roman period the Pharisees, who were gaining ascendancy as leaders of the majority of religious Jews, were developing another dimension of the Servant image, namely, the one identifying the faithful Jewish community as the Servant. Although a messianic interpretation, which variously saw in Isaiah 53 reference to one who would restore the scattered Jewish people to their homeland or who would atone for their sins through his suffering, is found in sources ranging from the Isaiah Targum to the thirteenth-century commentator Ramban (Rabbi Moshe ben Nachman), the more prevalent view among the rabbis was the collective one. And it was one that played an especially important role during times of persecution. Rashi, during the eleventh century, lived in a world in which crusaders massacred Jews in the Rhineland on their journey to the Holy Land. Such atrocities notwithstanding, he still maintained that Israel's suffering was for the atonement of the nations! (Driver and Neubauer, p. 38.) In the same period, in Spain rather than France, Ibn Ezra sees in the description of the Servant's suffering reference to the oppression endured by the Jews of his time, oppression that the nations would one day acknowledge, to their shame, as unjust (Friedländer, pp. 239–42).

One of the reasons why Jewish interpretation tended to favor the collective interpretation was no doubt the christological use to which the fourth Servant Song was put by Christians from New Testament times on. One of the most vivid early examples of this christological use is found in Acts 8, where Philip responds to the Ethiopian eunuch's question about the meaning of Isaiah 53:7–8 by using the text as a starting point for presenting the Christian understanding of Jesus as Messiah. First Peter 2:22–25 gives an explicit christological interpretation of the fourth Song. After citing Isaiah 53:9*b*, it goes on to describe Jesus' death in terms of vicarious atonement: "He him-

163

self bore our sins in his body on the cross, so that, free from sins, we might live for righteousness; by his wounds you have been healed" (I Peter 2:24).

As a part of his discussion of the proper behavior of slaves toward their masters, I Peter uses Isaiah 53 to stress the virtue of humility in the face of adversity. This moralizing interpretation was to grow in popularity among Christian writers. Clement of Alexandria, for example, employs Isaiah 53 as part of his admonition to suffering Christians in Rome to humble themselves as the Lord Jesus Christ had humbled himself (*I Clement* 16:1–14; Richardson, pp. 50–51).

Especially interesting are cases where the divergent interpretations offered by Jews and Christians become the object of discussion. In *Contra Celsum,* for example, Origen in the third century engaged the objection put forward by Jewish interpreters that the idea of a defeated messiah was an offense by appealing to the Song in Isaiah 53. Jesus' suffering was something he accepted of his own free will out of the desire to fulfill his mission of redeeming sinners. The debate between Celsus and Justin revolved in large part around the same issues that engage scholars in modern commentaries, especially the question of whether the biblical texts lend stronger support to the individual or the collective interpretation.

Which, then, is the "correct" interpretation? This question must be approached with an understanding of the kind of literature with which we are dealing in the Servant Songs. We are not dealing with biography in a strict literal sense. We are dealing, rather, with poetic language, which through symbols, metaphors, and similes reveals something important about God's will and the nature of the one/those who seek faithfully to obey God's will.

The roots of the divergence between individual and collective interpretations lie in the Isaian text itself. The fact that at times Second Isaiah describes the Servant as Israel, or a remnant of Israel, and at other times as an individual seems incontestable. Is this a case of blatant inconsistency that simply discredits the prophetic message?

This question hinges on our understanding of the two offices that Second Isaiah describes in relation to God's purpose, the office of messiah and the office of servant.

164

The books of Haggai and Zechariah suggest that the popular piety of the time looked for a divinely appointed messiah (i.e., *anointed one*) from the royal house of David as the agent of God's saving activity. The Israel of the future would resemble the Israel of the Davidic and Solomonic era.

The vision of Second Isaiah differs in important respects from this popular view. First, the *political* restoration of Israel was to come not through the activity of an indigenous hero but through the agency of a pagan king, a Persian called Cyrus. The special covenant that, according to tradition, God had established with the Davidic house (e.g., II Samuel 7) therefore could be extended to the entire nation (Isa. 55:3). This revision of expectations is in itself very significant. The prophets long had criticized the tendency among Israel's kings to lead the nation astray through preoccupation with their own military conquests and the resulting worldly splendor. The boasting of Israel's kings would be eliminated in the new act through which God would liberate the Jews from their bondage in Babylon, for the agent whom God was choosing as messiah for the release of the exiles was not a Davidide, was not a Jew, was not even a Yahweh worshiper! Surely this must have been a stinging blow to the nationalistic pride that many Jews felt in relation to the Davidic dynasty and to the lofty hopes they still associated with the exiled King Jehoiachin (II Kings 25:27–30) and the prince Zerubbabel (Hag. 2:23).

This relativization of the authority of Israel's monarchy effected by the announcement that Cyrus had been appointed God's messiah is one aspect of the prophet's daring revision of Israel's theological traditions. Israel's primary purpose could not be defined in terms of royal splendor. Indeed, the reclaiming of true destiny could result only if idolatrous nationalism were banished. Israel's true calling was the one announced already to Abraham, to be a blessing to the nations. That calling, no longer simply identifiable with the traditional messiah-king of the royal house of David, would have to be carried by another figure. Thus it was that Israel's role in God's purpose came to be depicted by Second Isaiah through the rich symbolism of the Servant.

The Servant whom one encounters in Second Isaiah's poetry dramatically challenges worldly understandings of power. The Servant does not accomplish God's purpose through force but through gentleness (Isa. 42:1–4). The Servant is acquainted with suffering and abuse (Isa. 50:4–7). In fact, it is through the Servant's humiliation and suffering that God accomplishes the redemption of God's people from bondage to sin (Isaiah 53).

Even that act, though, is preliminary. Israel's redemption prepares the way for God's salvation to reach the ends of the earth. For by being restored to spiritual wholeness Israel becomes the fitting instrument through which God can teach the *tôrāh* to all nations as a reliable basis for universal peace. The Servant Songs of Second Isaiah thus complete the picture in the second chapter of Isaiah of the nations streaming to Zion to learn God's ways as the basis for an alternative to war. God has now appointed the teacher who will instruct the nations in this path to universal harmony. That teacher is the Servant.

Against this background, we return to the question that has vexed scholars for ages: Is the Servant an individual or a people? To make this the central focus of the study of the Servant Songs seems fruitless, and it easily degenerates into Jewish-Christian polemic. The central point is, rather, the redefinition of power that occurs in the Songs. The power that can annul the wages of sin and restore human beings and their communities to health is not the power that worldly potentates wield. It is, rather, the power with which God has endowed the Servant, the power to place God's will over selfish desire and thereby to become an instrument of God's healing. Can an individual, through faith and obedience, become such an instrument of God's will? Yes, and the hearts of God's people naturally yearn for the Servant who will be drawn completely into the will of God. Can a community become such an instrument of God's will? Yes, and it is the hope of all who trust in God's providence that one day God's people will allow God's compassionate justice to be written upon their hearts. Finally, then, is one of these views more faithful to the Servant Songs than the other? The answer would seem to be this: Both arise quite naturally out of the biblical text.

If one understands the Servant Songs in this manner, one comes to appreciate the history of interpretation that has emerged within Christianity as well as the interpretation that has unfolded over the course of Jewish religious history. One comes to see how the message of the Servant has been incorporated by righteous Israel throughout the many periods of its history in which oppression, rather than extinguishing its witness to God's *tôrāh,* has been viewed as a part of God's redemptive plan. Thus Rashi, in the midst of persecution, comments on Isaiah 53:6: "All we like sheep have gone astray: it is now revealed how all the Gentiles have erred. Yet the Lord let Himself be entreated by him . . . and propitiated for the iniquity of us all, in that He refrained from destroying His world" (Driver and Neubauer, p. 38).

Appreciation of this communal interpretation need not threaten the spiritual meaning many people of faith find in the life of the one whom early followers came to acknowledge as the Messiah. For the Christian, from ancient times to the present, Christ is God's Servant, for he gave himself fully to God's purpose by obeying God's will and thus becoming an instrument of the transforming power of compassionate justice. Indeed, it was Christ's obedience that enabled him, even when worldly powers sought to kill him, to pray, "Not my will but yours be done" (Luke 22:42).

Appreciation of both the individual and the communal traditions of interpretation goes beyond superficial toleration of those who differ. It leads Jews and Christians to recognize in the voice of the other an invitation to a fuller understanding of God's redemptive purpose in the world. Christians, when they look back upon their past, face both faithful applications of the gospel as well as grossly perverted ones. Alongside examples of individuals and communities modeling themselves after the one who lived so intimately in the presence of the loving God that he prayed for his persecutors and died for the redemption of all human beings we see a distorted picture of a Christ triumphantly destroying Jews, Muslims, and Christians who do not get it right. In the light of pogroms and holocausts, the Christian needs to hear the messages of Rashi and Ibn Ezra, so as to recognize the witness of Israel through the ages to God's justice and to allow this to become an opportunity to repent. By accepting the testimony of Judaism to the universality of God's justice, Christians can add to their rejoicing over the redemption that was initiated by God's act in Christ the yearning for the complete healing of all creation as described by the apostle Paul in Romans 8. When this happens, Christians will no longer be threatened by the question of the Jew, If the Messiah has come, where is the messianic reign of peace and justice? They will, rather, be moved by this question to pray all the more fervently, "Thy kingdom come. Thy will be done, on earth as it is in heaven." In this way they can be cleansed of the trium-

167

phalism and attending history of lies that claims that with Christ all has been finished, that all that has happened to Jews since that time has been due to their unfaithfulness, that those who suffer today do so only because of their own infidelity.

Jews of course must speak for themselves in the dialogue in which Christians and Jews share their views on the meaning of the Servant Songs. We only can hope that the kinds of deep insights that have arisen already in the writings of Martin Buber, David Flusser, and P. E. Lapide will continue as Jews and Christians continue to yearn for the redemption of God's creation. We do disservice to the bonds that unite us, therefore, when we see individual and communal interpretations of the Servant as mutually exclusive. Although Justin Martyr can hardly be held up as the patron saint of Jewish-Christian relations, he perhaps can point the way beyond the impasse when he observes that the fourth Servant Song describes two phases in Jesus' mission: one in the past and one yet awaited. Christians, like Jews, can rejoice in what God has done even as they await the fulfillment of God's redemption. The differences should not be ignored, but neither should they be exaggerated to the point that the lessons each tradition has to share with the other are lost.

The deeper understanding of essential relationships to which the Servant Songs and their subsequent history of interpretations invite us is particularly relevant today. In the Middle East peace agreements between Israelis and Egyptians and between Israelis and Palestinians have broken an impasse that many had accepted as permanent. The idolatry of nationalism that militated against peace in the Eastern Mediterranean was transcended through the courage and patience of negotiators on both sides of the table. At the same time, however, narrow fundamentalist appropriations of Christian, Muslim, and Jewish tradition threaten to undo the peace process by tying God's will exclusively to sectarian ideology. Within the Christian version of this sinister tendency, a central role is played by the picture of a triumphalistic Christ who rejoices over the destruction of all who do not adhere to the explicit fundamentalistic beliefs of the protagonist group.

In relation to both ideological messianism and nationalistic idolatry the Servant of Second Isaiah stands as a chastening corrective. For here Jews, Christians, Muslims, and people of other faiths as well, can glimpse a power that does not magnify

168

one person or group at the expense of others but sees the wholeness of each person and nation as essential to the wholeness of all others. The Servant can thus stand as an invitation to transcend hostilities on the basis of an alternative to war, namely, on the basis of a peace from which all will benefit. What better grounds for global understanding can be found than the qualities of the Servant, the qualities of gentleness, compassion, justice, and the willingness to suffer for the sake of the healing of the entire human family? The alternative power of the Servant empowers the friends of peace to rebuke the power of military force, for it enables them to speak confidently of the superiority of gentle patience over aggression, of understanding over self-assertion, and of love over hate.

Isaiah 54:1–17
The Wrath and Love of God

Buckminster Fuller introduced a new word into the realm of architecture, *tensegrity.* It described the integration into one structure of dissimilar elements. The result was thus neither the kind of homogeneity that results from the replication of the same form nor the kind of chaos that arises where dissimilar forms are haphazardly thrown together. Rather, a lively whole was created with inner tensions integrated into a larger harmony.

Tensegrity describes well the structure of Isaiah 54. It juxtaposes what at first seem to be dissonant themes. For example, in verse 1 a hymn is opened with a call to a barren woman to sing praises. In verse 4 comfort is extended to one suffering disgrace as a widow. By the end of the chapter, however, it is clear that a sense of coherence has emerged out of the seeming contradictions.

The metaphors of childlessness, bereavement, widowhood, and divorce that the prophet uses to describe the background of those who are being addressed strike the reader with a powerful poignancy. Anyone who has suffered personal loss in life immediately identifies on a profound level with the victims of such devastating disappointments. The same empathy may not be extended as readily, however, to the God who in the name

169

of the prophet invites the suffering ones to burst out with praise and rejoicing. On what basis can the desolate be convinced that their trials will end in blessings worthy of such exuberant praise?

The passionate tone of chapter 54 indicates clearly that the outrageousness of inviting the bereaved to "burst into song and shout" is not taken lightly. The composition invites the reader to engage in rigorous soul searching. Rather than offering facile promises, it penetrates the frightening realm of divine absence. God confesses, "For a brief moment I abandoned you. . . . In overflowing wrath for a moment I hid my face from you" (54:7a–8a).

The moral outrage that the listener experiences in being confronted with metaphors of barrenness and divorce takes an astonishing turn when the metaphors lead to God as the source: "I abandoned you. . . . I hid my face from you." Suddenly the invitation to allow bereavement to be transformed into the joy of praise becomes something very different from facile wishful thinking. Listeners are obliged to delve into the depths of the issue to wrestle with none less than the divine purposer. God is not exculpated from the tragedy of bereavement and forsakenness. God is identified as the cause of the tragedy on the basis of direct testimony.

The historical background of this tensive passage is the destruction of Jerusalem by the Babylonians and the ensuing exile. This is not the first time that Second Isaiah has addressed the disturbing concept of God as the cause of destruction to temple and land. In 42:24–25, God is named as the one "who gave up Jacob to the spoiler," who "poured upon him the heat of his anger and the fury of war."

If God is the one who has brought on the catastrophe rather than some dark and evil agent, how can there be hope for release? If it were some wicked human being or even some pernicious demon that had brought this shame upon them, there could be hope that their God could regain the upper hand in the conflict and save them. But what could reverse their destiny if God was the cause of the calamity?

This is the terrifying form that theodicy takes in a monotheistic religion. Within that framework, when one penetrates to the deepest level, there can be only one answer to the question of how shame and desolation might be transformed into restoration and blessing. The transformation must originate with God.

170

God's intentions lie at the heart of the matter. For this reason, verses 7 and 8 are pivotal within the overall structure of chapter 54. There God describes the change in divine intention that provides the keystone for the structure of tensive relations within the composition:

> For a brief moment I abandoned you,
>   but with great compassion I will gather you.
> In overflowing wrath for a moment
>   I hid my face from you,
> but with everlasting love I will have compassion on you,
>   says the LORD, your Redeemer.
>
> (Isa. 54:7–8)

These verses, located at the heart of the chapter, thus explain the apparent contradictions that first leap out at the hearer or reader. The barren woman in verse 1, all appearances notwithstanding, has good reason to sing with joy. God has promised that her desolation will be transformed into blessing. Of course, the effect of the message depends on its persuasiveness. The warrants to which the prophet appeals are thus important. What evidence can he marshal that lend credibility to the claim that God will bless the chastened nation?

The prophet turns, as on other occasions, to the religious traditions of the people. So you have difficulty with the notion of the barren one rejoicing? Hear God's promise: "The children of the desolate woman will be more than the children of her that is married" (v. 1*b*). Now that has a familiar ring! It recalls the rejoicing of ancestress Hannah: "The barren has borne seven, but she who has many children is forlorn" (I Sam. 2:5*b*). The God who was able to bless the barren matriarch of old surely is able to do so again.

To add further warrant to the case, the prophet assures the people of increase of descendants by using language echoing the promise that God made to Abraham and repeated to the other patriarchs and matriarchs of old (vv. 2–3). The promise of restoration is presented accordingly as something very different from a novel concept. It is a renewal of God's original intention for this people. It is the desolation and destruction that represent a deviation from Israel's true destiny. Israel is to think of itself as a people of promise.

Barrenness is followed by another powerful metaphor for desolation in verse 4. The person experiencing the shame and disgrace of *widowhood* is promised a change of fortune. This

171

INTERPRETATION

time the promise is grounded on a very daring claim. The one
abandoned by her husband (v. 6) receives a far more dependable husband, "for your Maker is your husband, . . . the Holy
One of Israel is your Redeemer." The "redeemer" in Hebrew
society was the brother, or next eligible kinsman, of the de-
ceased husband who married the widow, thus maintaining the
security of her household. Here too the listener would have
been aware of echoes from the past, recalling Hosea's description of Yahweh as Israel's true husband and stories of faithful
redeemers like Boaz. The language of verses 7 and 8 also brings
to mind Hosea's moving description of the tension between
wrath and compassion in the heart of Yahweh, and the ultimate
victory of compassion (Hosea 11).

The prophet seems to anticipate the further doubting of the
people: "But how can we be sure that God's wrath has been
overcome by everlasting love?" Again he turns to tradition, this
time to the story of Noah. This parallel to Israel's experience is
apt. Although through war rather than flood, the effect of recent events has been comparable: The nation has suffered great
loss. But will not such calamity just continue to repeat itself?
The prophet recalls a story from the past describing God's solemn commitment not to repeat total devastation. The Noah
story becomes the basis for a remarkable oath:

> For the mountains may depart
>   and the hills be removed,
> but my steadfast love shall not depart from you,
>   and my covenant of peace shall not be removed,
>   says the LORD, who has compassion on you.
> (Isa. 54:10)

The overall effect of the prophet's proclamation of salvation
is powerful. God's words of assurance are filled with passion.
Added to this personal testimony is the line of witnesses the
prophet presents from Israel's past to testify on behalf of the
redeeming God. Noah and Abraham are summoned as reminders that God's love is stronger than divine wrath. God's assurance in verse 10, "My steadfast love shall not depart from you,"
recalls the God praised in connection with the exodus, "In your
steadfast love you led the people whom you redeemed" (Exod.
15:13). The epithet "Yahweh, who has compassion on you"
echoes Israel's earliest laws protecting the "poor among you":
"If your neighbor cries out to me, I will listen, for I am compas-

172

sionate" (Exod. 22:27). The theological challenge raised by chapter 54 is formidable, for it bears on the central confession of biblical faith, namely, that God guides all of history according to God's redemptive purpose. This passage constructs a reply that is commensurate with that challenge.

The final third of the chapter supplements what precedes. Verses 11–12 picture God's preparation of Zion for the return of the faithful people. The restoration of God's people is not a fuzzy abstraction. As stated so clearly by a later visionary architect, "The home of God is among mortals" (Rev. 21:3). The covenant people will sing their praises within a real-life context, a city adorned and protected by God.

The key to social integrity and shared prosperity will also be safeguarded: The children will be taught by the Lord, thereby establishing righteousness as the nation's defense against the powers of destruction. It is important to note that it is not the winners of the earth, those blessed with vast wealth and power, who receive the promise of peace and blessing. "This is the heritage of the servants of the LORD" (54:17), that is, the blessing coming to the kinsfolk of the barren, the desolate, and the forsaken with whom the chapter began. It is the "afflicted one, storm-tossed, and not comforted" (54:11) who is to be the recipient of the blessings set in motion already at the beginning of Second Isaiah's career when he heard the God of compassion instructing the heavenly council, "Comfort, O comfort my people."

In connection with 54:12–13 we noted above that the promise of restoration being proclaimed to the exiles in the midst of their desolation represented less a change in divine purpose than a renewal of the future that God had intended for Israel from the beginning. In other words, *sub specie aeternitatis,* calamity was a serious deviation from the proper course of history. From the perspective of human beings, however, calamity was all too real, so real that it threatened to rob many exiles of both their faith and their ability to sing hymns of praise (cf. Psalm 137).

We have already shown how the prophet in this chapter has refused to take the facile route out of the dilemma by blaming some evil agent independent of God's sovereignty. Courageously he traced calamity to its source in divine decision: God had abandoned Israel. What makes this courage even more remarkable is the fact that he records God's confession of hav-

173

ing abandoned Israel immediately after provoking the moral indignity of the people against the man who casts off the wife of his youth. Is God not just as reprehensible?

Second Isaiah has a clear answer to that question, but it is not developed in this chapter. Here the prophet's focus remains riveted on the momentous turning point at which Israel stands, one that will put exile and destruction behind and righteousness and prosperity ahead of it. The answer is implied, however, in the allusion to the story of Noah. The waters that destroyed the inhabitants of the earth, unlike the waters of the flood stories in ancient Mesopotamia, were not due to feuds among the gods or divine caprice but were sent as a judgment on the great wickedness of humankind (Gen. 6:5–9). So too the destruction of the Babylonian armies was not the result of God's whimsy but an expression of divine judgment upon Israel's sin (Isa. 42:24–25).

This explanation itself, however, makes many modern readers recoil. Can one trust the great compassion and the everlasting love of one who confesses, "For a brief moment I abandoned you. . . . In overflowing wrath for a moment I hid my face from you"? This question haunts the consciousness of those living in the shadow of Auschwitz and Dachau. It is one that can be answered only with the kind of careful reflection cultivated within the prophetic movement over its entire history.

The prophets, in effect, reply to the question of how a compassionate God could possibly inflict such judgments as humiliation and defeat before the enemy with reference to the alternative, namely, a world in which wickedness would go unpunished. That would be a world, in the words of Isaiah of Jerusalem, in which people, with impunity, "call evil good and good evil, put darkness for light and light for darkness, who put bitter for sweet and sweet for bitter" (Isa. 5:20). It would be a world filled with the boasting of those "who hide a plan too deep for the LORD, whose deeds are in the dark, and who say, 'Who sees us? Who knows us?' " (Isa. 29:15). All the prophets, diverse as they are in their backgrounds and emphases, agree on the basic fact that the moral structure of the universe would collapse if evil ceased to be punished.

174   To this understanding of the moral structure of the universe the prophets added a second theme, namely, that underlying God's judgment on Israel was always God's compassion seeking

to break through Israel's stubborn refusal to accept the blessings of life in God's "covenant of peace." The prophet whom we suspect set the tone that Second Isaiah picks up in this chapter, namely, Hosea, expresses this second theme with moving eloquence as he describes the inner struggle of God in the face of Israel's persistent refusal to return to God:

> How can I give you up, Ephraim?
>> How can I hand you over, O Israel?
> How can I make you like Admah?
>> How can I treat you like Zeboiim?
> My heart recoils within me;
>> my compassion grows warm and tender.
> I will not execute my fierce anger;
>> I will not again destroy Ephraim;
> for I am God and no mortal,
>> the Holy One in your midst,
>> and I will not come in wrath.
>
> (Hos. 11:8–9)

But could there not be a gentler way? we still ask. Hosea's daring glimpse into the heart of God indicates that this question causes God great distress. The story told by Jeff Musselman, star pitcher at Harvard College who in the late 1980s was catapulted into the limelight of Major League baseball when he signed a contract with the Toronto Blue Jays, may assist us as we struggle with this question today. No sooner had Musselman reached the pinnacle of which virtually every American boy at some point dreams than his career crashed into the wreckage of alcoholism. The emptiness and fear of inadequacy that he had felt like a knot in his stomach from the age of fourteen he had addressed with the bottle. Fortified with alcohol, he felt invincible. Numbed to the distress signals going off deep inside him, he drank his way from one pressured week to the next with a reckless bravado that threatened everyone around him, especially his wife. After one drunken escapade, she announced to him that she could travel no farther with him along this treacherous road, that she did not want him back. Suddenly the lies he had been living, his denial of alcoholism, his trust in his booze-induced sense of invincibility, his belief in his ability to control his destiny, were all stripped away by the voice at the other end of the phone. He admitted his defeat, his helplessness, and he reached out for help. And he found help, in an athletic counselor who had sought for years to awaken him to

175

his addiction as well as in family and friends, and ultimately in God.

Why could God not have chosen a gentler way to bring him to the truth? According to Musselman, fear, pride, insecurity, youthful bravado, all sorts of walls resisted gentler acts. Only a blow so crushing as to lead him utterly to despair of his ability to save himself was able to break the lie that held him in a grip that was sure to lead him to a premature death. Only at the end of his own resources could he open himself to the One capable of filling the void that was destroying him.

Reflecting on the mystery of human suffering as it relates to divine purpose must never lead to self-confident pronouncements on the benefits of the suffering of others. We must grieve over human pain and tragedy, whether individual or collective. We must work tirelessly to alleviate human suffering wherever it is encountered. What careful reflection properly does, however, is to bring us, on the basis of both personal experience and the stories of others, to the awareness of the power of evil and the tenacity of the defenses that human beings construct to resist confronting the truth of human bondage in its many forms. Classical Judaism and Christianity have never been glib in attributing punishing acts to God. For example, in puzzling over such acts, Martin Luther referred to God's alien acts or to God's left hand, that is to say, to tactics dedicated to God's ultimate salvific purposes but due to human resistance to grace necessitating moves that seem to contradict God's nature. The Jewish community of Second Isaiah's time was brought back to God's covenant of peace through the devastating stroke of national calamity and the experience that even in exile God was present. Jeff Musselman was restored to spiritual health and physical healing by the crushing blow of personal defeat and the strong love of his wife through which God was active. People of faith through the ages have recognized God's presence even in God's absence and have been aware of the deep sorrow experienced by the compassionate God driven by human stubbornness to acts of severe mercy.

Isaiah 55:1–13
The Word of God Stands

Chapter 55 brings the message of Second Isaiah to a fitting conclusion. Several of the main themes of the prophet's message are woven into a composition that bursts with excitement as suggested already on a grammatical level by the heaping up of interjections and imperatives.

First an unusual invitation is extended. The list of those to be included is not limited to people of social standing, not even to people of sufficient means to come properly attired. The only requirement is hunger and thirst. The previous chapter has prepared us to hear this as more than a gratuitous statement. The echo of the Song of Hannah, recognizable in the call to the barren, desolate, and abandoned in 54:1–6, and its reiteration in the Magnificat remind us of the banquet scene where God "has filled the hungry with good things, and sent the rich away empty" (Luke 1:53).

Is this some sort of conspiracy against the wealthy, a proletariat death wish against those who possess what they themselves desire? Hardly. It is a reminder that those who disdainfully refuse to come to a banquet open to all, and who turn instead to the more elegant company of the few enjoying special privilege, belong to those who "spend [their] money for that which is not bread, and [their] labor for that which does not satisfy" (Isa. 55:2).

In antiquity, banqueting was arranged to celebrate the completion of a new temple, and properly so, for upon the temple rested the hopes for prosperity of the whole land. This custom developed in Scripture into the notion of a final (eschatological) banquet celebrating the New Jerusalem, the dawn of God's universal reign of righteous compassion that would be a blessing to all lands. Jesus captured the essence of this banquet in the parable of the wedding feast (Matt. 22:1–10). The invited guests had more important business to which to attend. So the invitation list was revised: "Go . . . into the main streets, and invite everyone you find to the wedding banquet." There it is, stated plainly and simply: The most precious gift of all, the gift

177

of life in God's presence, is *free*. All that can exclude you is your insisting that there are places you would rather be. Why would anyone ever decide thus? Because you want to determine the menu. You want to be in control of the company you keep. *(Mrs. Peters may be there, she's the single mother. Joe, who's been on welfare for years, may come. Martha, she's the one who stays in the shelter, she might arrive.* But don't you understand, Yahweh is going to be there. *Yeah, but I heard you say that anyone could attend!* Jesus may join the wedding feast! *It's probably some kind of trick.)*

At first reading, the promise in 55:3–5 may seem to have little connection with the invitation in the first two verses. But there is a common thread. We recall that the unique feature of the invitation was that it was open to all. The following verses turn to the theme of the covenant that unites Israel with its God. According to the monarchical tradition, it was a covenant mediated by the king based on the *special* relationship that God had established with the Davidic house (see II Samuel 7). But that tradition had been thrown into crisis by the Babylonian conquest of Judah, for the royal family in Jerusalem had been disgraced along with the population in general. This crisis is reflected in Psalm 89, a royal psalm first celebrating God's eternal covenant with David and then, in what is likely an appendix necessitated by the contradictory events of 587 B.C.E., lamenting how God had "renounced the covenant with your servant" (Ps. 89:39). The burning question left by the calamity was this: "Lord, where is your steadfast love of old, which by your faithfulness you swore to David?" (Ps. 89:49).

One tradition, coming to expression in the prophetic books of Haggai and Zechariah, responded to this question with the announcement that God would raise up from the house of David a new king (Zech. 3:8). Specifically, the object of their prophecy was Zerubbabel, grandson of King Jehoiachin (Zech. 4:8–10). Haggai ascribed to him the royal title of "servant" and added God's promise: "I will set you as a signet ring; for I have chosen you" (Hag. 2:23*b*, New American Bible).

For Second Isaiah, the calamitous events of the early sixth century B.C.E. seemed to discredit the traditional way of regarding the covenant between God and the Davidic house as the channel through which divine blessing entered the nation. Not only had national defeat and shame punished the nation for its godlessness; it had placed before the people the challenge to perceive the new ways in which God was acting to fulfill divine purpose (Isa. 43:18–19). We have already noted the audacity of Second Isaiah's ascription to Cyrus of the title earlier associated with the Davidic king, "messiah," and the novel way in which the prophet recast the figure of the Servant within the context of God's salvific plan.

But what of the contents of the covenant made with David, the promises of blessing, security, and peace? These promises, encapsulated in the phrase translated in the NRSV as "my stead-fast, sure love for David" (55:3*b*), were essential to Israel's well-being. Without God's beneficence, the Jewish people would be scattered and lost among the nations of the world. From the time of Abraham, through the age of Moses, and over the entire period of the monarchy, it was on the basis of the promises of the covenant that a remnant of the faithful preserved the light of God's righteousness.

In the name of the same God who invited *all* to the ban-quet, Second Isaiah announced that God's plan had not been defeated by the ruin of the royal house of David but rather that the everlasting covenant was now to be expanded beyond the privileged elite to embrace the entire community of those obe-dient to God's word. The connection with the Servant Songs is evident here, for the covenant people "shall call nations that you do not know" (55:5*a*). The vocation of being "a witness to the peoples" assigned to David would now pass to the entire community of those faithful to God.

In these concluding sections of the literary legacy that he leaves behind for posterity, it is clear that Second Isaiah has the situation of his audience vividly in mind. One of the reasons that this prophetic message has retained its relevancy through the ages is no doubt this pastoral concern. The message speaks to the heart with honesty and clarity. It is infused with a directness born of deep caring and empathy. What is more, the situation addressed is in essential respects one that persists for those who read Scripture today. The words of Second Isaiah remain lively and poignant.

In commenting on chapter 40 we observed that the situa-tion addressed was one that revolved around twin doubts, the first relating to God's power to save, the second concerned about God's will to save. Maybe there were forces in the uni-verse that were mightier than Yahweh, some pondered. As the inhabitants of Ur earlier had concluded that the destruction of

179

their city and their patron deity's temple evidenced that deity's decline, so also many Jews were turning away from Yahweh in search of a more powerful alliance. Or was Yahweh's attention turned elsewhere, so as to lead to neglect of this small group, engulfed as it was by the mighty empires of the world?

Second Isaiah has already made a strong case for God's power and God's abiding love for Israel. Now he turns in verses 6–9 to the essential point: He calls out to the people to "seek the LORD." The plight in which they find themselves traces not to weakness or inattention on God's part. The blessing of the covenant of peace awaits them like an open door. Instead, they have chosen death, that is to say, they are preoccupied with wicked ways and selfish thoughts that cut them off from communion with the source of life. The prophet therefore urges them to "return to the LORD, that he may have mercy . . . , for [God] will abundantly pardon" (55:7).

In the next generation, the disciples of Second Isaiah would find it necessary to renew that plea:

> See, the LORD's hand is not too short to save,
>   nor his ear too dull to hear.
> Rather, your iniquities have been barriers
>   between you and your God,
> and your sins have hidden his face from you
>   so that he does not hear.
>
>   (Isa. 59:1–2)

In spiritual life as in personal, it is humbling to admit that the fault lies on our side of the relationship. It is comforting to blame the other. So human beings invoke logic: If God possessed sufficient power and concern, Jerusalem would not have been destroyed by pagans and we would not be exiles in a foreign land. At this point, Second Isaiah seems to sigh. His intricate argument about God's wrath being a necessary response to the persistence of sin and God's judgment being subservient ultimately to God's mercy has been lost to those still straining to maintain their pride. "Your logic simply is incapable of grasping the truth, and you will continue to stumble in the darkness of your self-imposed doom unless you grasp in faith the higher truth proclaimed through the prophets," Second Isaiah in effect says. Or more expressly:

180

> For my thoughts are not your thoughts.
>   nor are your ways my ways, says the LORD.

> For as the heavens are higher than the earth,
>   so are my ways higher than your ways
>   and my thoughts than your thoughts.
> (Isa. 55:8–9)

With these words the prophet reaches beyond the imperatives "seek" and "return" by glimpsing the disposition of the heart. Unless human beings cast aside their pride and smug confidence in their rationalizing defense of their position, unless they assume a posture of awe before the Creator of the universe, they will not get the point that opens up to them the covenant of peace, the point that it is all free for those who confess the inadequacy of their own solutions and therefore desire God's thoughts and God's ways.

One senses that Second Isaiah, after protracted disputations with the exiles and polemics against foreign idols, in these closing words finds rest in the sublime beauty of God's presence. The image in verses 10–11 is suffused with quiet confidence in the triumph of God's righteousness and the trustworthiness of God's promises. Human beings do not produce the rain and snow. It descends upon the earth apart from human effort, producing grain and food:

> So shall my word be that goes out from my mouth;
>   it shall not return to me empty,
> but it shall accomplish that which I purpose,
>   and succeed in the thing for which I sent it.
> (Isa. 55:11)

The sense that the prophet is arriving at a point of repose, task accomplished and day finished, is reinforced by the inclusio completed here by the reference to the word going forth from the mouth of God. For in the call narrative at the beginning of Second Isaiah, the prophet moved from despairing over the grasslike inconstancy of human beings to the dependability of the one central reality that endures:

> The grass withers, the flower fades;
>   but the word of our God will stand forever.
> (Isa. 40:8)

Faithfully, Second Isaiah has delivered that awesome word to despairing human beings, motivated by the belief that upon God's word alone could their personal and corporate lives be reconstructed. At the end of his labors he, like the Servant

181

receiving his reward (53:12), delights in the truth of the word of God:

> It shall not return to me empty,
> but it shall accomplish that which I purpose,
> and succeed in the thing for which I sent it.
> (Isa. 55:11)

The Servant and the Word play closely related roles in relation to God's will in Second Isaiah: "Through him [i.e., the Servant] the will of the LORD shall prosper" *(yiṣlaḥ)* (53:10); "[My word] shall . . . succeed *(hiṣlîaḥ)* in the thing for which I sent it" (55:11).

The description of the word of God in the call narrative was followed by an announcement of God's coming to the people: "Here is your God." Drama also rounds off Second Isaiah's message, as in verses 12–13 the prophet announces the festive procession of the freed exiles as they return to their home in joy and in peace. It is a fitting conclusion, for ultimately salvation is God's accomplishment, to which human beings need only open their hearts with rejoicing and their voices with song. In the festive celebration, humanity is joined by nature, for everything in creation is brought to wholeness by the Redeemer. The transformation into glory of all that the Lord has created provides the proper milieu for the abiding presence of the God of glory. Perhaps the most sublime commentary on the biblical theme of God's return to the renewed creation is the one written by John of Patmos:

> See, the home of God is among mortals.
> He will dwell with them as their God;
> they will be his peoples,
> and God himself will be with them;
> he will wipe every tear from their eyes.
> Death will be no more;
> morning and crying and pain will be no more,
> for the first things have passed away.
> (Rev. 21:3–4)

In Second Isaiah's depiction of the procession to Zion (see also Isa. 35:8–10), as well as in John's vision of the New Jerusalem, we see the completion of the work assigned by God to the heavenly assembly:

182

> Comfort, O comfort my people,
> says your God.

> Speak tenderly to Jerusalem,
>> and cry to her
> that she has served her term,
>> that her penalty is paid,
> that she has received from the LORD's hand
>> double for all her sins.
>
> (Isa. 40:1–2)

Once the new creation has been brought to its God-intended fullness, "it shall be to the LORD for a memorial," Second Isaiah adds (55:13*b*). Then it is that not only the prophet but reality in its totality will be gathered to the purpose for which all was created, giving glory to the only one worthy of praise, the Holy One of Israel.

PART TWO

Third Isaiah

ISAIAH 56—66

Overview

Historical Setting

In the 540s B.C.E., Second Isaiah had announced to the Jewish exiles in Babylon God's intention to bring about their release from captivity and their return to Zion. He had even specified that King Cyrus of Persia was the one whom God had chosen for this purpose.

In 538 B.C.E., Cyrus issued an edict allowing the Jews to return to their homeland and to rebuild their temple. The deliverance prophesied by Second Isaiah seemed to be unfolding. Clearly it was a time of high expectations for those close to the prophet.

Although only part of the exiled community chose to leave Babylon for the uncertainties of repatriation, they carried with them plans for rebuilding Zion and restoring their customs and institutions. Under the leadership of Sheshbazzar—likely one of King Jehoiachin's sons whom Cyrus had named governor—they laid the foundation of the temple in Jerusalem (Ezra 5:14–16). But then the situation began to deteriorate.

The first chapter of the Book of Haggai, written in 520 B.C.E., describes the plight of a community ravaged by drought, crop failure, hunger, and inflation. Haggai was very specific in his analysis of the situation. The troubles afflicting the people were all attributable to one cause: While they had busied themselves with sundry projects, the key to the entire restoration project had fallen into neglect, namely, the rebuilding of the temple. In other words, the deplorable conditions in the land testified to the fact that God was punishing them for failing to

185

build God's house. Haggai therefore admonished them to commence with the construction, adding the promise that if they obeyed, their ill fortunes immediately would be transformed into unprecedented prosperity.

The major portion of Isaiah 56—66 arose against the background of the severe hardships that prevailed in the time between Sheshbazzar's unsuccessful early attempt to rebuild the temple and its completion under Zerubbabel in 515 B.C.E. These eleven chapters complement the bleak picture painted by the prophet Haggai. They describe bitter emnity between rival groups in Judah. They make reference to civil and religious leaders who looked only after personal gain and to a court system riddled with corruption. They reflect a low level of community morale and a vindictive spirit that excluded the other nations of the world from any participation in God's plan save destruction. The contrast in tone between chapters 40—55 and chapters 56—66 is thus enormous.

The Relation of Literary Character to Social Setting

The writings that arose out of this situation and then were added to the Book of Isaiah are quite complex. Unlike Second Isaiah, this body of material is not homogeneous either in style or in theme. Most scholars agree that one must reckon with multiple authorship. The change in mood and message from one section to the next also suggests major changes in the underlying historical situation and social conditions. In a broad sense, however, a distinct line of continuity is discernible. The pattern that emerges from a careful reading of the eleven chapters is one of increasing inner-community conflict and worsening social and economic conditions. The contrast between Second Isaiah and Third Isaiah is both fascinating to the student of social change and challenging to those looking to Scripture for spiritual guidance.

"Comfort, O comfort my people." With those words Second Isaiah had introduced sixteen chapters that constitute one of the most beautiful parts of the entire Bible. "And they shall go out and look at the dead bodies of the people who have rebelled against me; for their worm shall not die, their fire shall not be quenched, and they shall be an abhorrence to all flesh" (66:24).

Thus ends the section of Scripture called Third Isaiah. As we turn from Second Isaiah to these eleven chapters, we must be prepared for some sobering reflection.

The Worldview of Third Isaiah

The central theme and mood of Second Isaiah is expressed by the divine announcement in 43:19, "I am about to do a new thing." As a suitable contrast, we can approach the world of Third Isaiah accompanied by the words of Ps. 139:8*b*: "If I make my bed in Sheol, you are there."

Those who returned to Zion sadly did not experience the fulfillment of Second Isaiah's brilliant promises of prosperity and peace and joy. "I will turn the darkness before them into light," God had announced through Second Isaiah (42:16*b*), thus fulfilling a wonderful promise found in the eighth-century Isaiah: "The people who walked in darkness have seen a great light" (9:2*a*). "We wait for light, and lo! there is darkness; and for brightness, but we walk in gloom," the people lament in Third Isaiah (59:9*b*). What happened to the brilliant promise of light proclaimed to the exiles by Second Isaiah? Are we dealing with failed prophecy? Is Second Isaiah's taunting of the gods of the other nations coming back to haunt Israel: "Tell us what is to come hereafter, that we may know that you are gods" (41:23*a*)?

The answer to that question depends on how one understands biblical prophecy. Is its intended function that of providing knowledge of events before they happen? Statements such as that quoted above from chapter 41 could suggest as much. Even when one moves from the quoting of isolated passages to the major themes underlying Second Isaiah's prophecy, one finds frequent reference to God's plan for the world and vivid descriptions of what God was about to do on Israel's behalf.

There is no mistaking the fact that the prophets were explicit in both the threats and the promises they pronounced in God's name. It is misleading, however, to identify the truth of those pronouncements with a mechanistic unfolding of the details contained within the threats and promises, for this is to trivialize the office of the prophet. The prophets did not locate the essence of their calling in proving clairvoyant abilities but in fostering obedience to God's covenant among the people. They were, to be sure, remarkably sensitive readers of human

187

events. Their understanding of righteousness and wickedness and their clear convictions regarding the consequences of both enabled them to translate God's will into the particulars of their nation's history within the wider context of world events. But as the Book of Jonah illustrates so poignantly, the fundamental purpose underlying their activity was not to prove their skill as prognosticators of future happenings but to bring about repentance. If their threat of judgment, however specific in detail, failed to materialize because it had led the people to return to God in obedience, it had fulfilled its purpose. Of this lesson the prophet Jonah was a notable, if reluctant, pupil.

Against this understanding of biblical prophecy, how are we to understand the fate of Second Isaiah's message? Here apparently we have an instance of promises not being fulfilled, not at least in the specific manner pictured by the prophet.

Looking at Second Isaiah's career within its concrete historical setting, we are able to glimpse the intention and function underlying the message in chapters 40—55. Here we see the prophet addressing a people, severely chastened by bitter experiences and profound loss, giving up hope for the future. What was at stake? Nothing less than the witness to the world of God's righteousness for which Israel had been called since the time of Abraham. God's chief witness was in the process of being assimilated to the nations, representing a regression to the time when, as described so imaginatively by Jewish haggadah, Abram worked for his father in his idol shop in Ur on the Euphrates.

Second Isaiah entered this bleak situation with a message that was so bright and filled with hope that it broke the exiles out of the bondage of their hopelessness. God had not forsaken Israel but had punished them so as to make them more fit to extend the witness of God's reign far beyond their own borders to the ends of the earth. God had not abandoned God's plan for creation but was even now active to restore all that had fallen and to heal all that had become broken. The message of Second Isaiah does not constitute a scientific prediction of future events; rather, it is a visionary description of God's plan for creation and of the part that faithful Israel was to play in that plan. Second Isaiah, to be sure, does not hesitate to apply the broad vision to specific world events: Cyrus, as he transformed the balance of power among the nations of the then-known world, was fulfilling God's purpose by repatriating Israel

188

(among various displaced peoples) and thus restoring them to the place from which they could renew their service to God and God's creation. Second Isaiah was not reluctant to address Jewish institutions either: The leadership role of the Davidic king would be taken up by the faithful community, while the Servant of the Lord would be God's chosen instrument for the atonement of the people.

We return to the question, Is Second Isaiah an instance of failed prophecy? The answer is yes if one equates the function of prophecy with prediction in the strict sense. A level highway was not miraculously constructed over the wilderness between Mesopotamia and Judah. Trees of the field did not clap their hands, and thorns were not all replaced by cypresses. All those who strove against Israel did not disappear. The Judean wilderness did not turn into a pool of water. However, the people were enabled to return under the royal edict of Cyrus. They were able to begin the rebuilding of their fallen cities. But did the Servant persevere until he had established justice in the earth, as Second Isaiah claimed he would?

We begin to sense the complexity and richness of the prophet's vision. It is rich in metaphors, laced with historical detail, and spiritually challenging, all at the same time. And the effects that it had on the people addressed were equally complex.

There is little doubt that Second Isaiah's message played a key role in mobilizing those who set out on the difficult journey back to the Jewish homeland. The metaphors of divine protection along the way surely encouraged and sustained them. They were able to draw parallels between their experience and that of the Hebrew slaves escaping bondage in Egypt. Nor is it likely that they took all of the metaphors concerning clapping trees and leveled mountains literally! The point they got was the essential one: God was present in their travels and hence they could muster the courage to undertake the dangerous journey back home.

Did all darkness turn to light? No. But the brilliant salvation promises do not exhaust the content of Second Isaiah's message either. This prophet's assessment of the Jewish community combines lofty expectations of what it can accomplish when faithful to God with realistic awareness of its shortcomings. Promise is thus interlaced with God's accusation that the Servant is blind, the people stinting in their offerings, the nation persistent in its iniquity. The tension between promise and

189

accusation, moreover, is neither accidental nor incidental. It is completely in harmony with Second Isaiah's view of God's activity: God commissions real human individuals and communities to the task of redeeming the lost and renewing the fallen. Thus it is that the same Servant who complains, "I have labored in vain, I have spent my strength for nothing and vanity" (49:4), is the one whom God commissions as "a light to the nations" (49:6).

We grasp Second Isaiah's prophecy aright when we recognize its dynamic witness to the creative, redemptive activity of God that occurs within the real stuff of human experience and world history. The word that God pronounces and that the prophet proclaims, the word taking form both in judgment and in promise, accomplishes its purpose by reshaping the thoughts of people, driving them to abandon their self-reliance, to repent of their wickedness, and to accept God's will as their own. Although the effect of God's word spoken by Second Isaiah did not take the form of immediate paradise on earth, but instead must be seen as a sort of leaven within the ambiguities of Israel's ongoing history, it is possible to discern very specific ways in which it accomplished what God purposed. It was instrumental in freeing the people from the self-imposed bondage of futility that kept them in exile, it was effective in encouraging them to begin the rebuilding process that would reestablish the Jewish homeland, it was spiritually powerful in directing the attention of human beings to the release from sin and restoration unto wholeness that was the most miraculous of all God's gifts and the one that set the foundation for all that they were called to do.

One of the surest marks of the truth of Second Isaiah's prophecy was precisely that it did not unfold mechanistically as a force that suspended human involvement. Instead, it came as an efficacious divine word that drew a people back onto a historical pilgrimage that was not limited to one generation but reached out over the ages. Its powerful images of sacrifice, healing, and redemption renewed the creative process that sustained the witness of the Jewish community to God's righteousness through the ages down to the present time and that helped the followers of Jesus of Nazareth to understand the significance of what they were experiencing within the context of God's purpose.

To understand Second Isaiah on a sufficiently deep theological level is to recognize a rare classic of biblical faith. Audaciously it presents God's word as a dynamic, destiny-shaping presence in the midst of history. Its scope is cosmic, its outreach embraces all nations. It utilizes the language most appropriate for such a vision of God's creative, redemptive purpose, the language of poetry, replete with metaphors and mythical allusions. To force such a poetic vision into the narrow confines of literalistic interpretation is to mute its boundary- and epoch-transcending voice. Proper interpretation recognizes both the specific historical conditions the prophetic word originally addressed and the way in which it transcends its original place and time to help shape the community of faith in subsequent ages down to the present.

The uniqueness of the poetic vision created by Second Isaiah is evidenced even in its place within the transmission history of the biblical writings. Contrast other prophetic corpora contemporary with it, such as Jeremiah or Ezekiel. Both of those books bear the marks of repeated editorial revisions. They were, in effect, more embedded in the day-to-day experiences of the community. This seemed to provide ample cleavages for ongoing reworking of the message. In contrast, Second Isaiah was preserved virtually intact, testimony to its being regarded from the beginning as something like a spiritual gem to be preserved in its original form as a source of inspiration for subsequent generations.

Third Isaiah, in turn, indicates how later generations related that gem to changed circumstances, sometimes through the use of paraphrase, sometimes allusion, sometimes revision. In all cases, the responses were nonintrusive, taking shape finally as a postscript to Second Isaiah, elaborating on the exilic prophet's central themes and applying them to a new setting.

While the writings in Third Isaiah were nonintrusive in terms of literary structure—being placed as a separate block on the end of the Isaiah corpus—they nonetheless betray a deep level of engagement with Second Isaiah's message. In fact, they give the appearance of an ongoing dialogue, with changes in the nature of the engagement reflecting the changes in the social and political conditions being experienced by the returnees as they sought to reestablish themselves in their Jewish homeland.

At the earliest stage of that dialogue, likely arising shortly after the exiles had returned, the message closely resembles that of Second Isaiah both in form and in content. Thus 57:14–

191

19, introduced with the repetition of an imperative and following an even meter much in the style of Second Isaiah, develops the twin themes of a way for the returning of people and of the healing and comfort that God intends for them. Chapters 60—62 are also replete with themes familiar from Second Isaiah, such as the announcement of the return of God's glory, the ingathering of the dispersed sons and daughters of Israel, the restoration of Jerusalem, and the participation of the nations in rebuilding Zion and praising God.

In other passages of Third Isaiah, themes of inner-community conflict and bitter vindictiveness begin to qualify the mood of promise and hope that prevailed in Second Isaiah. Harsh accusations are hurled by one segment of the community against another. God's judgment is summoned against the nations. The light of Second Isaiah seems to have turned to gloom. The universal vision of salvation narrows down to rigid sectarianism. Herein lies the theological challenge: Can God's word be found in the dissonance between the major sections of the Book of Isaiah and in the acrimonious conflict between fighting factions within the Jewish community that come to expression in Isaiah 56—66?

Above we offered one half of what we believe to be an answer to these questions when we portrayed Second Isaiah as a vision of God's purpose formulated in the language of poetry. The second half of the answer will arise in the course of our commentary on chapters 56—66, where we will find the word of God entering the harsh realities of human struggle and suffering. The vision of God's purpose is not lost, but its applicability to a situation that seems hostile to God's peace becomes problematic. For those who might have interpreted Second Isaiah's vision as implying that they would experience quick and painless transition to peace and prosperity, the experiences of the 530s and 520s B.C.E. raised the harsh questions of God's relation to injustice and social unrest. The temptation to draw Second Isaiah into a facile understanding of biblical faith is thus repudiated by the hard-hitting polemics of Third Isaiah. These two parts of Isaiah in their unity are essential as background to an understanding of God's presence that can meet the challenges facing those who seek to fathom the complexities of contemporary life from the perspective of a biblically informed faith. "Comfort, O comfort my people" must be kept in tension with "After all this, will you restrain yourself, O LORD? Will you keep silent, and punish us so severely?" (64:12).

Isaiah 56:1-8
The God Who Gathers the Outcasts

Isaiah 56:1-8 forms a fitting link between Second Isaiah and Third Isaiah. At the heart of Second Isaiah's proclamation was the promise that God was about to accomplish *deliverance* and *salvation* for the exiled community (cf. 46:13; 51:5, 6, 8). The prophet also placed major emphasis on *justice,* that is, the universal order created by God and revealed to Israel that was to become, through servant Israel's witness, the basis for peace among all nations. The themes of deliverance, salvation, and justice all reappear in the first two verses of Third Isaiah. Those addressed first are admonished to maintain justice and to do righteousness. They are then informed of the reason they should act thus, namely, because God's salvation is soon to come, and God's deliverance is about to be revealed. The word for *deliverance* in verse 1*b* is the same Hebrew word translated *righteousness* in the previous half verse. There is thus a play on the Hebrew word *ṣĕdāqāh,* for it is both the mighty act of God and the upright way of life that is the appropriate human response.

The first verse of the third major section of the Book of Isaiah thus seems to give a summary of the message of the prophet of the exile. But there is a subtle shift in emphasis from an announcement of what God is about to do to an admonition concentrating on what the community is to do. Reference to God's act is placed in a motive clause that functions in relation to the admonition. We thus are given a glimpse into a community deeply concerned with right action. This initial impression will be corroborated by what follows in the next eleven chapters. We are dealing with a community fearful of losing the promise because of the *un*righteous behavior of many of its members!

Verse 2 goes a step farther in defining righteous behavior by specifically referring to *keeping the Sabbath.* The exilic and

193

the Persian periods were both times in which assimilation threatened the promises of blessing and salvation. It is not surprising that Sabbath observance became a critically important emblem of Jewish identity. Those who faithfully keep the Sabbath distinguish themselves as members of the people of Israel.

Membership remains the subject in the rest of this passage. But the way in which it is treated takes an astonishing turn in verses 3–7. Presented is a decision in the area of *tôrāh*, that is, sacral law. We are accustomed to thinking of such clarifications as belonging to the legal sections of the Bible found in the first five books, the so-called Books of Moses, or the Pentateuch. In the late prophetic period, however, prophets did not hesitate to utter a legal decision in the name of Yahweh. Or, as in the case of Haggai 2:10–14, the prophet engages in halachic discussion with priests.

Here at the beginning of Third Isaiah a divine decree is presented that alters the law regarding two classes of people: males whose sexual organs are damaged and foreigners. In Deuteronomy 23, the case is straightforward: "No one whose testicles are crushed or whose penis is cut off shall be admitted to the assembly of the LORD" (Deut. 23:1). "No Ammonite or Moabite shall be admitted to the assembly of the LORD" (Deut. 23:3).

Both laws are congruous with sacral customs in early Israel. If sacrificial animals were to be without blemish, it is understandable that those officiating in the sacrificial cult should be free of blemishes. And given the hostilities suffered by Israel at the hands of the Ammonites and the Moabites, exclusion of such foreigners is also understandable.

What is astonishing is the contestation of laws embedded in the Torah, since the five Books of Moses were well on their way to becoming normative in the Jewish community by the time of Third Isaiah. What principles are visible within 56:1–8 that serve as warrants for such a notable challenge to standing customs?

The eunuchs who will be given a place in the house of the Lord, that is to say, in the temple, are those who "keep my sabbaths," "choose the things that please me," and "hold fast my covenant" (v. 4). Obedience and covenant fidelity, especially in relation to Sabbath observance, are such decisive issues that they are capable of overriding ritual considerations such as bodily defects.

194

As for the foreigners, the qualifying characteristics are again those of keeping Sabbath and holding fast to the covenant. The fear of those not born within the Jewish community that they will be rejected is addressed head-on:

> Do not let the foreigner joined to the LORD say,
> "The LORD will surely separate me from his people."
>
> (Isa. 56:3)

On the basis of Mosaic law, that fear was well founded, as we noted above. But as emphatic as was the exclusion in the Deuteronomic law ("even to the tenth generation"), so emphatic is the inclusion here: "Their burnt offerings and their sacrifices will be accepted on my altar" (v. 7). Foreigners will serve as the Lord's "servants" ministering as priests in the temple (v. 6). Second Isaiah's universalism is thus picked up and developed in a daring new direction: "for my house shall be called a house of prayer for all peoples" (v. 7). This passage seems to reflect the same expansive vision that is expressed in the Book of Malachi, a writing that also comes from the early restoration period: "For from the rising of the sun to its setting my name is great among the nations, and in every place incense is offered to my name, and a pure offering; for my name is great among the nations, says the LORD of hosts" (Mal. 1:11). In this case, the background is a condemnation of the offerings of the officiating Zadokite priests, who are accused of corruption. The Book of Malachi places hope instead on a recovery of the "covenant with Levi." What seems apparent is that both Isaiah 56:1–8 and Malachi had their origin in the wider circle of Levitical priests who, although long forced to the periphery by the Zadokites, were finding their voice anew as protagonists of an expansive vision of faith that drew upon the universalism of Second Isaiah.

The passage concludes with a theme that both echoes Second Isaiah (45:22–23; 49:6; 54:4–5) and makes a connection with the first major section of the Book of Isaiah (11:11–12). The God who "gathers the outcasts of Israel," that is, who through Cyrus enabled the exiles to return, will continue the redemptive process: "I will gather others to them besides those already gathered" (56:8).

Anticipating certain aspects of the discussion that follows, we shall now make several suggestions regarding the background of 56:1–8. We have noted several echoes of themes that were prominent in Second Isaiah, most notably those describ-

195

ing God's imminent salvation and the gathering of outcasts to Zion. We have also noted, however, that the promise has been tied to admonitions to "maintain justice" and to "do righteousness." Our first suggestion is that we are glimpsing a situation in which the promises of Second Isaiah have come into question, with the result that the followers of Second Isaiah are reflecting on the reasons for the delay and finding them in the *un*righteousness of many of their compatriots. Several oracles that follow will give vivid illustration of the wickedness that they observe around them.

In spite of their bleak assessment of the situation, however, they maintain a breadth of vision that comports with the universalism coming to expression in some of Second Isaiah's pronouncements. Their vision, at the same time, itself implies a sharp rebuke of the leaders of their community, namely, the Zadokites, for the claim that God would include foreigners in the priesthood ran directly counter to the Zadokite position.

Earlier we suggested that unlike Isaiah 40—55, chapters 56—66 cannot be attributed to a single author. Multiple voices are heard, voices forming a chorus taking cues from Second Isaiah, to be sure, but at the same time differing in certain respects.

Isaiah 56:1-8 is one half of a literary framework that encloses Third Isaiah, the other half being found in 66:18-23 (supplemented in 66:17 and 24 with additions by a rather cantankerous editor). In the second half of the framework, God also promises God's coming "to gather all nations" and the return of "all your kindred from all the nations," from whom God would choose some to serve "as priests and as Levites." And, as in 56:7 God announced, "My house shall be called a house of prayer for all peoples," in 66:23 God says, "All flesh shall come to worship before me."

Second Isaiah had its own framework, with chapter 40 portraying God's word which, while all else withers and fades, "will stand forever" and with chapter 55 depicting that same word going forth from God's mouth and not returning empty but accomplishing its divine purpose (55:11). We can admire the effort of the disciple of Second Isaiah who, having gathered a body of prophetic messages both more diverse than the Second Isaiah corpus and more disturbing, nevertheless was able to draw it together within a framework that lifted up the central underlying theme, namely, the faithfulness of God to God's

196

promises. Thanks to that disciple, we are able to recognize in Second Isaiah and Third Isaiah two very different prophetic collections that nonetheless are unified around one vision of divine providence. Both in turn thus form fitting additions to the writings of the eighth-century Isaiah, the prophet who was the first in a line of outstanding prophets to describe the sovereignty of God over all of the created world.

In creating that overarching theological framework, however, was the disciple actually drawing forth conclusions implicit in the material or imposing a false sense of unity on material that was much more chaotic? This question cannot be answered before closer examination of the material in Third Isaiah. Dissonant themes are undeniably present there. Do they all point to the God who gathers those who are scattered and delivers those who maintain justice? Or has the disciple engaged in a tour de force that cannot be defended by detailed study of the specific passages contained in Isaiah 56—66? These are questions that we bring to the body of writings found in the last major section of the Book of Isaiah.

Isaiah 56:9—57:13
All Have Turned to Their Own Way

With 56:9—57:13 we take leave of the theological overview of the framework and enter into the midst of the conflicts of a struggling community. The passage is replete with strong emotions, ranging from somber lament to accusations steeped in bitter irony.

At the outset the beasts of the field are summoned to come to devour. We can picture the carcasses of newly slaughtered animals scattered over the field as the lions and the hyenas move in for the feast. But we ask, who are the victims of the predators? Ezekiel 39:17–20 fills in the background of the bloody scene. There the princes of the earth, depicted as domestic animals, fall prey to wild animals. In both texts, we have a grim picture of divine judgment on those who exercise their governing power with wickedness and cruelty. 197

The judgment motif of beasts feasting on human flesh is applied in the Third Isaiah passage to an inner-community situation. It is used to pronounce divine punishment on the leaders of the community, variously called watchmen, shepherds, and perhaps also seers (in 56:10 reading *hōzîm*, "seers," rather than *hōzîm*, "dreaming," as does the NRSV). Rather than looking after the best interests of the people, they simply pursue their own gain. They are inattentive to the duties of their offices, preoccupied instead with greedy pursuits and high living. They closely resemble the false shepherds described by Ezekiel: "My sheep have become food for all the wild animals, since there was no shepherd; . . . the shepherds have fed themselves, and have not fed my sheep" (Ezek. 34:8).

Creating the sharpest possible contrast, the passage shifts in 57:1–2 to lament the righteous and the devout who perish without so much as passing notice from the callous onlookers. Whereas those who amass the pleasures of unjust gain are the objects of biting words of judgment, the innocent dead are promised rest and peace.

This brief requiem, however, does not extend its rest and peace to the soul of the prophet. With lightning force, the prophet lashes out against the wicked in 57:3–13*a*. The attack is introduced with the phrase, "But as for you *(wĕ 'attem)."* By the time we have completed our study of Third Isaiah, this phrase will become quite familiar (57:3; 65:11, 13[3×], 14). It is a stylistic feature of an oracle form invented by Third Isaiah to address a new community situation. Up to the Persian period, the prophets of Israel addressed the community as a whole when they pronounced words in God's name. The pronouncement was most commonly a word of judgment for sin, although at times it was a promise of salvation. Third Isaiah introduced the hybrid "salvation-judgment oracle." It reflected a situation of deep division within the Jewish community. Simultaneously, in the same oracle, one group received promise of salvation, while the other was indicted and sentenced to divine judgment.

The prophet has called forth judgment on the community's leaders, lamented the death of the innocent and promised them peace, and now in direct address turns to a scathing indictment of a group accused of sins so heinous as to lead to God's decision to abandon them to their idols.

The polemical nature of the extended indictment places obstacles in the path of the interpreter seeking to determine the actual nature of the practices being attacked. It opens with a plural address. The accused are described as children of an

198

adulterer and a whore who carry on the promiscuous ways of their parents. What are those ways? They "burn with lust among the oaks, under every green tree" (57:5). These are stock phrases used in prophetic tradition to attack syncretism, especially the blending of Yahwistic with Baalistic practices of Canaanite religion (e.g., Jer. 2:20; 3:6, 13; 17:2; Ezek. 6:13; II Kings 16:4). There can be no doubt that large numbers of the population were lured into the fertility rites of local Baal shrines, even as many of the exiles were attracted to the worship of Marduk and some contemporaries of Jeremiah renounced Yahweh in favor of the Queen of Heaven, that is, the Assyrian deity Ishtar. For those who followed the popular tendency of identifying patron god with land and nation, there was much reason to move away from Yahweh toward gods like Baal and Marduk and Ishtar. Did not Yahweh fail to protect Israel from Babylon and the Babylonian pantheon? In contrast, did not the fertility gods prove their vitality with every harvest?

The description becomes even more grim as the indictment moves on to child sacrifice. Again, this passage is not alone in its accusation (cf. Jer. 7:31; 32:35; Lev. 18:21; 20:2–4; II Kings 23:10). As in the case of individuals, so too with communities: when they become lost in the desperate search for security, grisly results often follow. Although the use of stereotypical language does not facilitate reconstruction of exact detail, it is clear that the prophet is describing a chaotic situation in which people, in their drift away from the God of compassionate justice, are indiscriminately attaching themselves to degrading cults that promise immediate satisfaction free of moral obligations.

In 57:6–13 the form of address switches from plural to singular. A female prostitute is addressed, her sexual activities described, her professional zeal condemned to futility. Whom does she represent? The image of her preparing the chief accouterment of her trade, her bed, may contain a clue, since the Hebrew for bed *(miškāb)* may here be a thinly veiled cipher for temple *(miškān)*. From 66:1–4 it is clear that chapters 56—66 of Isaiah stem from a group that have no faith in the temple rebuilding program of the dominant priestly party, the Zadokites. God's purpose has been missed by those who would ensure prosperity by reconstituting the temple cult of preexilic times. The one who grasped God's purpose aright was "the humble and contrite in spirit, who trembles at my word"

199

(66:2b). The bitter irony contained in equating temple with whore's bed seems to arise from the conviction that the temple builders, far from leading the people back to the true God, are merely abetting the syncretizing tendencies of the populace. This is not an edifice chosen by God. It is another instance, in the long history of prophetic critique, of cult missing the point by worshiping not Creator but creature. The sentence in 57: 11–13 is totally in harmony with classical Hebrew prophecy:

> Whom did you dread and fear
>   so that you lied,
> and did not remember me
>   or give me a thought?
> Have I not kept silent and closed my eyes,
>   and so you do not fear me?
> I will concede your righteousness and your works,
>   but they will not help you.
> When you cry out, let your collection of idols deliver you!
>   The wind will carry them off,
>   a breath will take them away.
>
>   (Isa. 57:11–13a)

No matter how great the zeal and fervent the effort, all human activities are in vain if they do not originate in loving obedience to the one true God. The prophet, in a conceit that may be a bit excessive to our taste, has pointed to the futility of misdirected passion. Although fueled by unbounded commitment to the restoration of religious practices, the reform movement of the Zadokites is no better than the machinations of the whore, for it has failed to grasp the essence of true religion in justice and compassion.

Only a hint is dropped on the end of the polemical passage that the faithful have not disappeared completely from the land:

> But whoever takes refuge in me shall possess the land
>   and inherit my holy mountain.
>
>   (Isa. 57:13b)

Land and place of worship will not be lost to the deserters forever. Hope breaks through like a slender shaft of light in thick darkness. Although sorely threatened, that light has not been entirely extinguished. Of the struggle between light and darkness, we shall hear more in what follows, for it is a dominant image in Third Isaiah.

Each age must struggle with its own threats to wholeness.

In one age it is the fertility cult of Baal with its cultivation of self-indulgence free from moral integrity and responsibility. In another it is nationalistic pride that blinds a people to the humanity of other nations. Unbridled materialism, globe-trotting imperialism, technological arrogance—many are the forms of idolatry that tempt human communities. The language of fertility worship, strange in our ears at first, takes on a stinging relevance when we recognize its ability to mask our own idolatries, flirtation with power that threatens human life, wealth that impoverishes, sexual indulgence that degrades. For our age the prophetic word still pronounces judgment. Every human project that turns in upon itself will lead to nothing but despair. There is only one refuge, one source of wholeness, one promise of individual integrity and communal health. Any culture's most urgent task is to locate that refuge.

Isaiah 57:14–21
God Is with the Humble and Contrite

This unit, 57:14–21, gives a vivid example of the lively nature of prophetic tradition. Its metric structure and its message both suggest that the passage derives from a period somewhat earlier than 56:9—57:13. Its parallel bicola resemble Second Isaiah's style. It also addresses the people as a whole, thus suggesting a period before the sharp split into the righteous and the wicked reflected in the previous passage. As in Isaiah 42:24–25, God here confesses that God has punished them because of their stubborn persistence in sin. Also like Second Isaiah, this passage promises that the age of punishment has ended and that God will comfort the people and lead them.

Together with chapters 60—62, then, we have here words from disciples of Second Isaiah, or what could be called the Third Isaiah group, words proclaimed shortly after the return in 538 B.C.E. of the first wave of exiles from Babylon. It was a time when enthusiasm was at a high level for full restoration to security and prosperity in the homeland. These words echo Second Isaiah's majestic proclamation of a processional way back to Zion in chapter 40: "Prepare the way of the LORD." In keeping with the common tendency found throughout Scripture of reapplying metaphors to new situations, the message assumed an extended meaning once the people had completed their journey across the wilderness back to Judah. Words originally directed to God's angelic helpers charged with overseeing the return of the exiles were now redirected to the people themselves. It has become *their* turn to join in the drama. "Build up, build up, prepare the way" has become a call to join in restoring just social structures and forms of worship worthy of the God "whose name is Holy." "Remove every obstruction from my people's way" has become an admonition to cleanse the land of the apostasy and sin that had led to God's anger and punishment.

The passage identifies those designated to join the heavenly messengers in serving God's purpose, namely, the "contrite and humble in spirit." Unlike those whose stubborn rebelliousness had brought on the calamity (42:25), this group was to prepare the place of God's return to dwell among the people. The importance of the circle of the contrite and humble is thus manifest, for they, more than any holy ground or sacred building, were to become the entry point for the only One able to bring back blessing and healing to a land devastated and forsaken.

Consider now the tradents who have preserved the various words of the Third Isaiah circle, some spoken early in the restoration period and reflecting an optimistic attitude, others spoken later and reflecting bitter controversy with rival circles. Among their collected materials they have a hard-hitting proclamation of judgment on the religious leaders directing the rebuilding of the temple who solicit support through a policy of accommodation that relaxes traditional ethical standards (56:9—57:13). On the end of that hard-hitting message we find a brief reference to those who had remained faithful in the face of oppression, those taking refuge in the Lord (57:13*b*). In gathering together the prophetic heritage left in their care, would it not be appropriate to conclude the present unit with a fuller description of the heirs to God's promises? Would not an earlier word, one echoing Second Isaiah's promise of God's returning with healing and comfort, form a fitting conclusion? Thus we can imagine they came to a felicitious decision. Isaiah 57:14–19 reveals God's presence even in the bleakness of bitter inner-community struggle. Second Isaiah's original promise of a cessation of warfare and of healing and comfort to those chastened by hardship and bereavement is reaffirmed. God identifies

202

those who will be recipients of divine grace with names with which they can readily identify, "contrite and humble in spirit." Although assailed once again by the enemies of God's righteous rule, the faithful are assured that the broad universal vision of Second Isaiah remains valid:

> Peace, peace, to the far and the near, says the LORD;
> and I will heal them.
>
> (Isa. 57:19)

Out of the depths of the inner-community conflict arose yet another comment, lacking any of the poetic qualities of the preceding verses. Isaiah 57:20–21 sharpens the distinction created by the cleavage of religious conflict. Lest anyone should be led to think that God's comfort and healing would extend to the entire people, a word found in Second Isaiah (48:22) is elaborated into the dark simile of the restless and tossing sea.

Vividly, then, 57:14–21 illustrates the nature of prophetic proclamation. It does not present God's word as abstract, timeless proposition. God's word is address. It speaks to specific situations and particular persons. But neither is God's word whimsical. It reveals God's faithfulness through all the flux of human experience and historical change. Judgment on human rebellion will be followed by forgiveness of the contrite and comfort of the humble in spirit. Human understanding can never fully comprehend God's ways, and hence the messages of judgment and promise must be repeated in relation to new situations. As in Second Isaiah, so among the disciples continuity and change form a necessary dialectic in the relationship between the living God and the human community.

The dynamic quality of biblical faith is threatened by efforts to translate prophetic pronouncement into timeless truth. God's faithfulness is unchanging, but God's relationship with God's people is responsive to human response. Fitting interpretation of Scripture will always be sensitive to context. The faith of the contemporary reader is enriched not by a collection of timeless truths but by the living witness of ancestors in the faith to the God who never ceases to address the hearts of those whom God has created. It is through study of all the episodes in the long history of God's initiatives and human responses that we find both our understanding of the nature of the loving God enriched and the image of God in ourselves restored to wholeness. Precisely because of the liveliness of God's word in Scrip-

203

ture, the potential for individual and communal spiritual
growth that it holds is inexhaustible.

Isaiah 58:1–14
Your Own Interests, or the Interests of God?

Chapter 58 is a classic example of prophetic tradition in the
Bible. Here the fidelity of the Third Isaiah circle to the central
themes of justice and proper worship developed by Amos,
Hosea, Isaiah, and Jeremiah comes to clear expression.

Once again those themes are shaped in relation to the
specific issues of the early restoration period. The polemic is
directed against a group described as self-righteous and meticu-
lous in religious observances. Its members engage in theological
study, seek out divine oracles, engage in cultic rites, and fast.
But, according to the prophetic voice in this passage, it is all a
sham, mere external motions, hypocritical acts that fail to meet
the test of genuine religion. Their faith is faith in the subjunc-
tive mood,

> as if they were a nation that practiced righteousness
> and did not forsake the ordinance of their God.
> (Isa. 58:2*b*)

Earlier (see Overview) we observed the central importance
of the concept of *mišpāṭ* (above translated "ordinance") in the
thought of Second Isaiah, as the order of compassionate justice
God has created and upon which the wholeness of the universe
depends. The problem is not that the people are unreligious.
That would be easy to condemn. No, they are hyper correct in
their religious observances and delighted to exhibit their piety,
but in their very exercise of religion they miss the essential
point, God's order of compassionate justice. They are thus indicted in the prophetic word for "their rebellion" and "their
sins." How can that be?

204

> Look, you serve your own interest on your fast day,
> and oppress all your workers.
> (Isa. 58:3)

These religionists have memorized all the conventional forms of religion such as "to bow down the head like a bulrush, and to lie in sackcloth and ashes" (58:5). God remains unimpressed: "Will you call this a fast, a day acceptable to the LORD?" What is a true fast? It is "a day acceptable to the LORD." What such a day entails is clear. It is described in 61:1–3, a passage repeated in Jesus' reading from the Isaiah scroll in the synagogue in Nazareth (Luke 4:16–21). It is the Jubilee, the time in which God's *mišpāṭ*, or order of compassionate justice, is restored. It is the time of healing, of remission of debts, of release from slavery, of return to one's confiscated property. This passage thus locates God's central concern in the exercise of justice and the practice of compassion. Without these, all the pious motions of religion are mere "as ifs."

The severity of the prophetic attack on self-serving, dehumanizing religion is matched by the grandeur of the description of the fast that is pleasing to God. The fact that it takes the form of a series of rhetorical questions spoken in the divine first person adds to the beauty of the passage:

> Is not this the fast that I choose:
>   to loose the bonds of injustice,
>   to undo the thongs of the yoke,
> to let the oppressed go free,
>   and to break every yoke?
> Is it not to share your bread with the hungry,
>   and bring the homeless poor into your house;
> when you see the naked, to cover them,
>   and not to hide yourself from your own kin?
>   (Isa. 58:6–7)

In a community where those who regarded themselves as the most religious had converted religion into private acts of study and ritual, thereby leaving the entire realm of social relations and commerce under the dominion of ruthless, self-serving exploitation, the prophet reaffirms the classical understanding of Yahwism that grew out of the experience of God's liberating slaves from their bondage, feeding them in the wilderness, and giving them a homeland of their own. It is a rigorously moral understanding that places the one who would be true to God on the side of the same ones whom God reached out to help and empower, those suffering injustice at the hands of authorities, those imprisoned for acts of conscience, those denied their fair share of the land's produce, those denied housing and proper clothing, those turned away even by their own relatives. The appeal is an impassioned one to the heart of the community. It is a plea to reclaim authentic humanity by replacing cold, calculating self-interest with acts of loving-kindness that restore genuine communal solidarity.

The community-building effects of such a return to true personhood are stated in terms beloved by the entire Isaiah tradition, namely, light, healing, and restoration (vv. 8, 10–11). What is more, persons who have thus experienced the restoration of human community find that they have simultaneously become reconciled with God. Healing encompasses all aspects of their existence. The barriers that their cold-heartedness toward their fellow human beings had constructed have dissolved. In contrast to those who complained bitterly, amidst their fasting, that God did not hear them, those who have directed their attention to the needs of their neighbors in need find that God is present with them (v. 9).

This leads to the final motif of the chapter, namely, proper religious observance. The prophet has not attacked the practices of the self-righteous in order to dismiss religious rites categorically. Much to the contrary, the prophet has sought to purge false religion from the land in order to restore true religion. Acts of loving kindness toward the neighbor do not exhaust the life of faith. They culminate in worship. The life of compassionate justice comes to its most sublime expression by taking delight in the Lord (v. 14). This completes the all-encompassing harmony characterized by God's order of justice and mercy. Even as they live true to the image of God in their day-to-day life by imitating God's acts of loving-kindness and giving expression to authentic community through mutual caring, God's people celebrate the origin of all life in life's source through worship, by honoring God in a special way on the Sabbath (cf. 56:6–7). The inseparability of worship from the life of justice and compassion thus is reaffirmed and held up as the only reliable foundation for a people trying to rebuild a nation after a period of calamity. Reconciled with God and embodying God's shalom, the nation would find its ability restored to go about the specific tasks confronting it in the 530s and 520s B.C.E.:

> Your ancient ruins shall be rebuilt;
> you shall raise up the foundations of many generations;

you shall be called the repairer of the breach,
  the restorer of streets to live in.
(Isa. 58:12)

The integration of the prophet's spirituality and social consciousness thus takes shape in relation to the specific circumstances of his time. A nation must be rebuilt upon a foundation that is both consistently moral and deeply spiritual if the calamities of the past are not to be repeated. No aspect of the nation's life therefore escapes prophetic scrutiny. For every aspect of life is within the domain of God's concern.

Few passages in Third Isaiah reach across the centuries with as much power as this chapter. It requires no fancy interpretive ploys. Its message addresses the heart as passionately today as it did in the sixth century B.C.E. One cannot read these fourteen verses without the sense of having been addressed by God, without having heard a divine word that is at once severe in its attack on the perversity of self-preoccupation and assuring in its invitation to return to authentic personhood. Like Micah 6:6–8 and Matthew 25:31–46, Isaiah 58 states God's will with a clarity that wins the assent of all that is true within us and then goes on to evoke our deepest sense of joy with the invitation to delight in the Lord through worship purified by loving-kindness.

Isaiah 59:1–21
Mercy That Requires Repentance

Songs of lamentation are well attested in the Hebrew Bible, especially from the decades following the destruction of Jerusalem by the Babylonians in 586 B.C.E. The frankness with which the people of Israel addressed their God in times of adversity bespeaks their understanding of the divine-human relationship as authentic and open to unadorned honesty. Out of the ruins of national calamity the faithful raised their complaint to God:

Why have you forgotten us completely?
Why have you forsaken us these many days?
(Lam. 5:20)

The lament could take on a scolding tone, casting blame and even accusing God of ignoring their entreaties:

207

> Though I call and cry for help,
> he shuts out my prayer.
> (Lam. 3:8)

> You have wrapped yourself with anger and pursued us,
> killing without pity;
> you have wrapped yourself with a cloud
> so that no prayer can pass through.
> (Lam. 3:43–44)

In the faith of ancient Israel, such lamentation was an expression of true piety, for it was an aspect of the community's longing for God's pardon and for the restoration of God's grace. It was accompanied by soul searching to uncover the turpitude within the nation that had given rise to God's righteous wrath. Balancing complaint is thus confession of sin:

> The LORD is in the right,
> for I have rebelled against his word.
> (Lam. 1:18)

Most important, both complaint and confession occur within the context of an affirmation of God's grace:

> Although [the LORD] causes grief, he will have compassion
> according to the abundance of his steadfast love;
> for he does not willingly afflict or grieve anyone.
> (Lam. 3:32–33)

Isaiah 59 opens with reference to a lament heard within the community of those who had returned from exile and were attempting to rebuild viable institutional and social structures. As the Book of Haggai indicates, the last third of the sixth century B.C.E. was characterized not by the brilliant restoration envisioned by Second Isaiah but by economic adversity and religious laxity. Increasingly, complaints were being heard that God had failed to deliver on the earlier promises and was showing indifference to the prayers of the people. Here the prophet addresses the specific accusations that God was deaf to the entreaties of those in need and powerless to save the people that cried to heaven out of their distress.

Both of these themes are familiar ones in the communal laments found in the Bible. Within the context of the life of a faithful, suffering community such as comes to expression in the Book of Lamentations and the Psalter, the complaints that God had failed to hear and to act upon were integral parts of genuine piety. In this passage, however, the prophet argues that they are something quite different, not an expression of true faith at all but of a distorted misuse of prayer and supplication. What, then, is the difference between the complaints found in the Book of Lamentations and the complaints alluded to here?

Those raising their complaints to God in this case, according to the prophet, are perverting true lamentation into a blasphemous coverup for their own sin. Unaccompanied by repentance and a longing for God's grace, their accusations are a mockery of true piety. The reason God has not answered is not that God has become indifferent to human suffering. God's failure to save them from their plight has one cause, the barriers they have created between themselves and God through their persistence in a life of violence and oppression (v. 2). For God to be present with such a company would be for God to become an accomplice in all of the dehumanizing acts that characterize their degraded lifestyle.

Can we be more specific in describing the lives of those denounced in this prophetic speech? Clearly, the prophet is drawing many of the charges from the stock phrases of earlier tradition. In Isaiah 1:15, the eighth-century prophet announced that God would hide his eyes from and refuse to listen to those praying to him, because their "hands are full of blood." The prophet echoes that accusation in 59:3. Similarly, the charges of iniquity, lying, and violence are formulated in conventional terms. What is more, verses 5 and 6 develop metaphors intended for shock effect more than descriptive accuracy.

To conclude from this rhetorical style, however, that the prophet is blindly hurling accusations out of vindictive fury rather than the desire to address a specific situation in the life of the nation would be a mistake. The rhetoric is rather indicative of the enormity of the tragedy that the prophet sees unfolding. After all, it was only a matter of two or three decades earlier that Second Isaiah had used many of the same metaphors in a brilliant announcement:

> I will lead the blind
>> by a road they do not know,
> by paths they have not known
>> I will guide them.
> I will turn the darkness before them into light,
>> the rough places into level ground.
>
> (Isa. 42:16)

209

Here too we find traditional formulations laced with poetic imagery, but the announcement of Second Isaiah related to a specific situation, the exile, and promised restoration in the Jewish homeland and a rebuilding there of a righteous and faithful community. In Isaiah 59 a prophet arising within the same stream of prophecy and nurtured by the same vision of the return of a chastened and obedient people to a new era of divine favor witnesses not that vision's fulfillment but the undoing of God's plan through the disdainful disregard for God's will that was sweeping across the land. Reference to lying, wickedness, shedding innocent blood, and running to do evil are not empty generalities. They describe the disintegration of social order as people embrace deceit and brutality to promote their own power and wealth at the expense of others. The prophet witnesses the era of peace announced by Second Isaiah being turned upon its head: "There is no justice in their paths. . . . We wait for light, and lo! there is darkness. . . . We grope like the blind" (59:8–10).

Closer attention to the language of the indictments allows one to glimpse facets of the social disintegration that the prophet was observing. Consider the following:

> No one brings suit justly,
>   no one goes to law honestly;
> they rely on empty pleas, they speak lies,
>   conceiving mischief and begetting iniquity.
>   (Isa. 59:4)

> Justice is turned back,
>   and righteousness stands at a distance;
> for truth stumbles in the public square,
>   and uprightness cannot enter.
> Truth is lacking,
>   and whoever turns from evil is despoiled.
>   (Isa. 59:14–15)

An equitable judicial system is a sine qua non of any civilized society. If there is to be civil order, there must be due recourse for those suffering violation of their basic rights. In the nation described by this prophet, every semblance of judicial integrity has collapsed. The de facto rules of public trial have become lying and bribing, with the inevitable result that "truth stumbles in the public square." Rewards go not to the honest person seeking to contribute to society but to those seeking to rob it for their own gain. In fact, anyone who would repent of such cor-

210

ruption and seek to live honestly and uprightly is assured of falling prey to hoodlums (v. 15).

How does one who is filled with bitter sadness over this ruin of the nation and with deep disappointment over the unraveling of a restoration plan that lay at the center of decades of prayer and dedication respond to the deplorable situation the prophet has just described? In a threefold manner.

First, in verses 9–11, the prophet sings out in imploring lamentation, genuine lamentation in contrast to the mockery of those who complain that God fails to hear them even as they pursue their corrupt schemes. The prophet cries out to God,

> We wait for justice, but there is none;
> for salvation, but it is far from us.
> (Isa. 59:11)

The second response, quite remarkably, is a confession of sin! But is it the prophet's responsibility to confess sin? Is he not the one sinned against? Should he not be urging confession upon those mired in sin rather than confessing personal culpability? We encounter here an astonishing phenomenon. Even in this hour, at the point in time when those whose "thoughts are thoughts of iniquity" (v. 7) are threatening the downfall of the nation, the prophet demonstrates communal solidarity by intoning the very acknowledgment of guilt that could open the ravaged community to divine pardon: "For our transgressions before you are many" (vv. 12–13). Sadly, though, such genuine confession is the farthest thing from the lips of his compatriots.

Hence the third response, one dark and foreboding, the response of a dreadful threat of divine judgment (vv. 15b–20). It seems as though the prophet is at wit's end. Indeed, the text indicates that God is too:

> [God] saw that there was no one,
> and was appalled that there was no one to intervene.
> (Isa. 59:16)

This is not as it should be! In God's covenant with Israel, God called the people into a partnership in which people and their God were to join in joyous cooperation toward the completion of a universe living in praise of God and enjoying the beneficence of a loving creator. "There was no one." Tragic conclusion! Dreadful end of the experiment in "you shall be my people and I shall be your God." "No one." Gone, the faithful people living true to a calling to be a "light to the nations."

211

We have difficulties with the grim portrait of God found in this third response of the prophet to truth fallen in the public square: God "saw that there was no one . . . so his own arm brought him victory . . . wrapped himself in fury as in a mantle . . . like a pent-up stream." We prefer images describing a God of endless patience, of untiring tender mercy.

Psychologically, it is quite possible to understand the prophet's description of harsh divine retributive action against those who drag the entire nation down to chaos. But perhaps we can go a step farther. Is not the divine wrath portrayed in verses 15b–19 also consistent with God's mercy?

The violent oppressors have not only persisted in sin, have not only threatened to bind the nation to the desolation it has known for fifty years, they have the audacity of claiming that they deserve God's attention and grace. What if the prophet were to describe to them a God of endless mercy, a God resorting never to judgment but ever extending pardon and blessing at every human behest? What sort of grace would the prophet then be giving to those not only reveling in a life of iniquity but imprisoning the entire nation in a curse? It would not be divine grace at all but pathetic, pampering, dishonest, groveling abdication of prophetic integrity. The prophet chooses instead the path of courageous, sincere, albeit severe, mercy. He, like Second Isaiah before him (40:10; 51:9–11), appeals to the ancient Near Eastern tradition of the Divine Warrior, which had been adapted to Jewish faith already by early Israel to portray God as the foe of chaos and evil and the champion of the alien and the oppressed.

> According to their deeds, so will he repay;
> wrath to his adversaries, requital to his enemies.
> (Isa. 59:18)

Perhaps even in this late hour such truthful custodianship of God's order of justice would effect repentance. If not, at least suffering under the ongoing oppression of ruthless oppressors would not be exacerbated by the bitter disappointment of witnessing their prophets turning into collaborators with the wicked.

Because the God of the prophet is not the patron of the powerful oppressor but rather the one who upholds justice by opposing the wicked, the final word can be a word of promise and hope to those who accept the invitation to return to the God of righteousness and mercy:

> And [God] will come to Zion as Redeemer,
>   to those in Jacob who turn from transgression.
>
>   (Isa. 59:20)

Although battered and shaken by the assaults of the ungodly, the moral order of the universe remains intact under the sovereignty of the Redeemer God. The third response of the prophet found in verses 15*b*–20 adumbrates a form of eschatological hope that would grow in popularity within the Jewish community in periods of distress and persecution to follow, the form commonly referred to as apocalyptic. We shall find further examples of its development in chapters 65 and 66. While standing in continuity with prophecy and preserving the prophetic tradition's central affirmation of God's final victory over all enemies of righteousness, it is marked by a change in emphasis. The classical prophets of the Bible, acting as witnesses to God's sovereignty and also as social reformers, religious critics, and advisers to kings, involved themselves in matters of state and society. With the conviction that all spheres of life belonged to God and were of concern to God, they labored to bring both individuals and institutions into conformity with God's order of justice. As is evident in the case of the eighth-century prophet Isaiah's relations with King Hezekiah, the prophets of Israel were able to exert considerable influence on the public sector. Never losing sight of the ideal state of universal peace and righteousness intended by God that transcended every temporal reality, they nevertheless engaged their generations with God's will as revealed in the Torah in the tireless effort to create a just and compassionate society.

Third Isaiah marks a turning point in the history of prophecy. Perhaps the disappointment with the delay in the promises announced by Second Isaiah coupled with the harsh opposition to their reform efforts raised by rival religious and civil leaders led to the shift. At any rate, emphasis began to turn from engagement with political and social structures to a longing for a more direct path to God's reign: "[God] saw that there was no one, . . . so his own arm brought him victory" (v. 16).

The apocalyptic emphasis on God's direct intervention to eradicate the forces of evil is not the most central biblical vision

213

of divine presence. Far more common is the vision of a mediated presence, God active in the righteous community, God represented by faithful prophets, God served by obedient leaders. Such was the emphasis that lay at the heart of Jesus' teaching, guided by his own petition, "Thy will be done, on earth as it is in heaven." Ever guiding the classical prophets and Jesus was the vision of that final day when all nations would acknowledge God's sovereignty, thereby introducing an era of universal peace. But the appropriate preparation for that day was found in the daily task of doing justice and loving kindness and walking humbly with God in the here and now.

This, however, is not to dismiss the more apocalyptic posture as unbiblical. Apocalyptic is a form of refuge for those threatened with spiritual defeat by unrelenting evil and suffering. Whether the intractability of the evil encountered takes the form of powerful foreign oppressors like the Antiochenes in the books of Daniel and Maccabees or the compatriots in Isaiah who act "as if they were a nation that practiced righteousness," it can batter the lives of those seeking to live in faithful obedience unto the point of despair. Precisely at that point, where there seems to be no earthly possibility of foreseeing the victory of righteousness over evil, the apocalyptic vision offers its defiant affirmation that, although "there was no one to intervene," the victory was still assured. Such defiance, by making possible perseverance in faith and steadfastness in obedience, certainly is consistent with the central themes of biblical religion. With uncompromising clarity, it makes the affirmation of God's universal sovereignty and the irreducibly transcendent nature of the destiny intended by God for all those created in the divine image. Moreover, it preserves the spiritual identity and vitality of communities of faith through periods of crisis, thereby enabling them to reengage the realities of this world when circumstances once again allow.

Not infrequently, scholars assess negatively the theological significance of late prophetic passages such as this one relative to earlier prophecy. Noted is the mixing of genres (e.g., the lament with the sermon), the use of conventional language (e.g., "your hands are defiled with blood"), the move from prophetic specificity to apocalyptic generality (e.g., v. 18). While no one can deny the power of Amos's realism or Isaiah's diplomacy, the unique theological perspective of Third Isaiah should not be lost either, for it is urgently relevant to our own world. Through social engineering, an economics of expediency, and an uncritical confidence in science and technology, we are invited to join in creating a foundation for society that has no need for transcendence. Talk of iniquities creating barriers between a people and God and sins hiding God's face from them is regarded as primitive superstition.

But what happens when a culture has no higher standard for justice than its own human standards, where definitions of right and wrong appeal to no norm other than current humanistic values? History teaches us that the door swings open to the victimization of those rendered expendable by prevailing definitions of human worth. Debates over medical experimentation, euthanasia, abortion, foreign intervention in human rights' struggles, and distribution of the earth's resources are driven by personal, partisan, or nationalist self-interest often barely informed by a critical-historical perspective. Religious, ethnic, and racial minorities, as well as indigenous peoples, the economically underprivileged, and the physically and mentally disabled, do not have extended to them an intrinsic equality based on a teaching such as creation in the image of God.

In arguing for the participation of prophetic voices in the formulation of the values upon which we base our personal and communal lives, we are not overlooking the implied complexity and dangers. David Koresh and Jim Jones were regarded as prophets by their followers. The community of faith that intends to add its voice to public debate must follow very stringent rules, including rigorous study of its beliefs and their sources, self-criticism and openness to criticism offered by other traditions, awareness of relevant scientific research, and a global consciousness. For this reason, ordination requirements that involve years of demanding study and field experience, institutional structures that embody the highest standards of fairness and professionalism, and community life that embodies the very values introduced for discussion into the public arena are all mandatory requirements of religious bodies.

Only communities of faith that observe such strict standards of self-regulation, criticism, and rigorous reflection will contribute to the preservation of a perspective that transcends personal, partisan, and national self-interest. By following such standards, the bishops of the Roman Catholic Church have produced pastoral letters on peace and economic justice that have lifted up the concepts of the irreducible dignity of every human being, the preferential option that a civilized society must extend to the poor, and the indefensibility of nuclear military strategies.

The role of the prophetic voice in a modern pluralistic society is necessarily different from that in a more homogeneous society such as that of ancient Israel. Within the context of the First Amendment tradition in the United States, for example, no one denomination can impose its particular view of transcendence on others. What each community of faith or ethical body must contribute if it is to live true to its responsibility as a group enjoying the benefits of civil order and security, however, is critically informed and reasonably presented insight into questions of value and the common good.

In the case of communities growing out of biblical tradition, the courage to speak with impartiality at times when popular opinion is being swayed by materialistic individualism, myopic expediency, racism, sexism, economic elitism, or nationalistic self-interest will be fostered by the prophetic tradition of which Isaiah 59 is a part, and especially by the central reality of the God of compassionate justice. Particularly difficult are confrontations with powerful lobbying groups that have a skillfully formulated religious rationale for programs of special privilege. In such encounters the stringent moral standards of the prophets must be normative; stated simply, no religious position can be deemed credible that violates the moral standards of universal human dignity and the accompanying ethical laws formulated in biblical torah.

Biblical faith demands a second response, based on the first response of testimony to universal ethical norms. The prophetic posture is not only a pulpit posture, it is a posture of advocacy, solidarity, and participation. The prophet goes to the perpetrators of the evil schemes that threaten the very foundation of a society and confesses with them corporate sin in the hope of bringing about a change of heart. The prophet renews the hope of the oppressed by announcing the presence of the Redeemer even at the point where all the forces of evil seem to rise up against them. The prophet discovers allies in the struggle for justice who prove their authenticity in the first instance not through lofty rhetoric but through concrete acts of courage and compassion.

216

Certainly in the face of statistics on crime, corruption, and violence that, when compared with other civilized societies, can suggest that the United States belongs to the category of lawless nations, we have reason to pray for a renewal of moral conscience and prophetic courage among its religious communities. For many who are impoverished, homeless, infirm, or growing up in neighborhoods devastated by drugs, crime, and public apathy, "justice is turned back" at the heart of the wealthiest nation in the world. Little wonder that people are flocking to sects that speak the rhetoric of apocalyptic, for many are living in situations in which they find "no one to intervene" on behalf of justice and decency.

Before renewal can come to mainstream denominations, they will have to rediscover the prophetic voice. "See, the LORD's hand is not too short to save, nor his ear too dull to hear. Rather, your iniquities have been barriers between you and your God, and your sins have hidden his face from you so that he does not hear" (vv. 1–2). If we in fact share the conviction of our spiritual ancestors that without God's grace a people cannot survive, we need to take to heart that precisely the kinds of injustice and cruelty that are condoned in our society are the kinds that have cut us off from God's presence and God's blessing. The last word spoken by the prophet in our midst will still be one that extends that presence and blessing to us, but we must be clear that it is a word not of pampering mercy but of authentic mercy demanding repentance:

> And [God] will come to Zion as Redeemer,
> to those in Jacob who turn from transgression,
> says the LORD
> (Isa. 59:20)

Isaiah 60:1–22
Peace Your Overseer and Righteousness Your Taskmaster

Chapter 59 culminated in an announcement: "And [God] will come to Zion as Redeemer." Chapters 60—62 follow up on that announcement with an elaborate description of the advent of the Redeemer and of the transformation of Zion that would result. The logic that led the final editors of Third Isaiah to place

217

these three chapters where they did is transparent. What also seems apparent is their intention to make chapters 60—62 the center around which the remaining parts of Isaiah 56—66 were arranged. The result is a literary structure that gives unity to an otherwise rather disparate collection of materials.

Looking behind the final canonical shape of the material to earlier stages in its literary history leads us to the conclusion that chapters 60—62, together with 57:14-18, originated at a point in the restoration period somewhat earlier than the other sections of Third Isaiah, perhaps not long after the arrival of the first wave of exiles in 538 B.C.E. In style, we find poetry closely resembling that of Second Isaiah. In theme, we find an announcement of salvation that renews Second Isaiah's promise to the exiles, with this subtle change: The proclamation now is given to a group that has already returned to the homeland and now awaits fulfillment of the glorious promises announced by Second Isaiah. Continuity with Second Isaiah's message is underscored by frequent quoting and paraphrasing of the words of that great prophet, examples of which may be seen in 60:4a (cf. 49:18a); 60:16b (cf. 49:26b); 61:1 (cf. 42:1); and 62:10 (cf. 40:3). At the same time, the fact that circumstances have changed for the Jewish community is reflected in the manner in which the earlier message is reinterpreted. Whereas in Second Isaiah the announcement of salvation was related to specific historical events and persons, especially the campaigns of Cyrus, in chapters 60—62 salvation is described in more general terms, quite detached from specific historical happenings. How is this shift to be explained?

These three chapters were addressed to an audience that consisted of people who had been moved by Second Isaiah's vision of God's deliverance to return to the Jewish homeland and those who had remained in the devastated land and now viewed the arrival of the exiles as a sign of God's favor. Both groups, therefore, were eagerly looking for signs that the divine promises proclaimed by the prophet of the exile had begun to unfold.

Already in the years immediately following Cyrus's edict of release, however, there were ominous signs that the path to national health and prosperity would not be as smooth as Second Isaiah's vision might have suggested. First attempts to rebuild the temple foundered amidst partisan strife and eco-

218

nomic uncertainty. The number of those returning from diaspora resembled more a trickle than a mighty stream. The grave doubts regarding God's power and fidelity to covenant promises that surfaced at a slightly later period, which we saw in the lament refuted by the prophet in chapter 59, were no doubt already gathering like dark clouds over the thinking of many. It is to this situation that God speaks through the prophet in chapters 60—62.

The prophetic promise that God would come to reestablish a nation living in righteousness and peace is restated here with exuberance and color. Its tone is in keeping with other religious literatures written in crisis situations with the intention of renewing the languishing spirits of a people. One can think, for example, of Hans Lilje's commentary on the Book of Revelation written during the Nazi period in Germany. Claus Westermann relates his personal experience of the deprivations suffered in the years after World War II to the picture in 60:4–9 of the wealth that the nations would bring to Judah and to the description in 60:17 of the substitution of base commodities for precious ones (Westermann, p. 362). Mindfulness of the harsh circumstances addressed by these three chapters corrects what can easily be the conclusion drawn from a facile reading, namely, that the school of Isaiah has lost the realism of its predecessors and has slipped into a dreamy utopianism. In our interpretation we shall seek to understand how these words functioned to strengthen hope and to equip a people to persist in their vocation as a nation with a divine commission in spite of conditions evoking questions concerning God's presence.

Chapter 60 opens with the announcement of light breaking forth in darkness as an image portraying God's saving entry into the brokenness of human bondage and suffering. It belongs to a thread that extends through the entire Isaiah corpus, beginning with First Isaiah's majestic "The people who walked in darkness have seen a great light" (9:2), continuing with Second Isaiah's proclamation of God's promise, "I will turn the darkness before them into light" (42:16), and extending to the introduction found in our present passage:

> Arise, shine; for your light has come,
>   and the glory of the Lord has risen upon you.
> For darkness shall cover the earth,
>   and thick darkness the peoples;

> but the LORD will arise upon you,
> and his glory will appear over you.
> (Isa. 60:1–2)

In the Gospel of Matthew, the Isaiah 9 passage is quoted by way of introducing Jesus' public proclamation: "Repent, for the kingdom of heaven has come near" (Matt. 4:12–17). And in the traditional lectionary, Isaiah 60:1–6 is the Old Testament reading for Epiphany. It is obvious that the prophet presented as the introduction to a composition that was intended to renew the hope of a wavering community an image timeless in its majesty and power. In our own day, patients who have experienced the phenomenon of return to life from clinical death have described a vision of brilliant light breaking into the darkness of death.

The other side of the image, darkness, carried a meaning for the Jewish community imprinted upon the consciousness by repeated hardship. Once again, after having their hopes lifted by the promise of restoration, they found themselves longing for the shaft of light that would pierce the gathering gloom and guide them toward a life of integrity and wholeness. The prophet announces the arrival of just that light: "Arise, shine; for your light has come" (v. 1). Affirmation that light will ultimately prevail in a situation so bleak as to threaten to extinguish the human spirit can be dismissed as utopian only by those who have not experienced the dark moment when all human resources have been exhausted. The figure of Job stands tall in the Bible as one of those who knew such a moment. From the deep darkness of his suffering he burst forth unexpectedly with a similar affirmation:

> For I know that my Redeemer lives,
> and that at the last he will stand upon the earth.
> (Job 19:25)

With similar holy defiance, hunted Christians in the catacombs maintained their lives of prayer and worship, black slaves in antebellum United States sang of Elijah's chariot swinging low to carry them to freedom, Jewish prisoners in concentration camps painted butterflies on the walls of their cells, Dutch Calvinists gathered in defiance of Nazi orders in memorial services honoring their martyrs, and Oscar Romero, with the sights of his assassins' rifles trained upon his heart, raised the host and thus offered both the bread of Christ and his own life as a sacrifice to God.

In verses 4–16 we find a depiction of caravans from distant nations traveling to Judah loaded with precious gifts and bearing those members of the Jewish community not yet returned to their homeland. Is its ascription to God of the sponsorship of contributions of flocks, silver, gold, frankincense, and various other commodities not a reduction of eschatology to crass materialism? Here too we must be sensitive to the context within which the words are being spoken, namely, a situation in which a people, shaken by uncertainty and adversity, are tempted to give up hope that quality life is any longer possible for them. A gathering still representing only a fraction of the scattered nation and lacking sufficient materials even to rebuild the temple are here given by the prophet a glimpse of the fullness of life they yet would enjoy when righteousness was reestablished in the land, thereby allowing God to dwell in their midst. The glimpse is described with all the earthiness expected of those smitten by deprivation and humiliation. But the spiritual meaning of their existence is not lost even amidst the extravagant imagery. Those who come bearing gifts do so in praise of God (v. 6), the flocks they bring become sacrifices offered up to the Lord (v. 7), and the timber from Lebanon is applied to rebuilding the temple (v. 13).

The prophet sees more than the restoration of a human community in the transformation to come. For this particular community exists for a purpose beyond its own pleasure; it exists "for the name of the LORD your God, and for the Holy One of Israel" (v. 9). The glory that will be restored to Israel will redound ultimately to the glory of God! A balance is thus achieved between the material side of restoration and the religious. The people's welfare is not seen apart from their praise of God; but neither is God's glory achieved apart from the glorification of God's people. This mutuality is intrinsic to the biblical understanding of the covenant relationship, as expressed beautifully in Psalm 126:

> When the LORD restored the fortunes of Zion,
>   we were like those who dream.
> Then our mouth was filled with laughter,
>   and our tongue with shouts of joy;
> then it was said among the nations,
>   "The LORD has done great things for them."
> The LORD has done great things for us,
>   and we rejoiced.

221

The apostle Paul also described the reciprocity inherent in the glory that was both God's nature and God's gift when he spoke of the hope of sharing the glory of God (Rom. 5:2) and even described how that glory would be extended beyond the children of God to embrace a redeemed creation (Rom. 8:18–25).

Verses 15–16 summarize in nutshell fashion the background, message, and underlying spiritual meaning of chapter 60. They address a people "forsaken and hated, with no one passing through." To this people is proclaimed God's promise: "I will make you majestic forever, a joy from age to age." The promise, however, goes beyond material prosperity to spiritual understanding, "And you shall know that I, the LORD, am your Savior and your Redeemer, the Mighty One of Jacob." This spiritual understanding is the possession that outstrips all others, for not only do all the others depend on it, but its reward, unlike the various material blessings promised, is eternal.

Verses 17–22 end the chapter with an expression of the shimmering idealism held defiantly against growing uncertainties regarding the ability of the community to control its own destiny. By the time these words were written, strife was beginning to arise in the community between the followers of Second Isaiah, with their universal vision of restoration, and the more pragmatic priests of the Zadokite line, who, on the basis of the restoration program outlined in Ezekiel 40—48, were seeking to reestablish structures of government under their own leadership. Guided less by political strategies than by holy yearning, the Third Isaiah group found its voice in a description of the blessed "City of God," thus adumbrating similar visions in Revelation 21 and in Augustine's *City of God.* Those receiving political appointments are Peace and Righteousness, the fortifications are called Salvation, the gates Praise. Within this city there will be no more violence or devastation, for the "people shall all be righteous." How and when will this city be established? The prophet refers the curious and the impatient audience to one agent and to a timetable beyond human ken: "I am the LORD; in its time I will accomplish it quickly."

The "when" question is perennially on the lips of the community faithfully waiting for injustice to cease, the power of the occupying armies to be broken, and racism and discrimination to end. It is an inevitable question, and the passion with which it is directed to God is often a measure of the purity of the hearts that ask it.

In Jesus' time the Pharisees kept alive the ancient promises of the redemption that God would finally accomplish for the suffering Jewish nation. The Roman occupation was a bitter reminder that the blessings of the covenant were being withheld from them. In their prayers they pleaded for God's coming, and in their hearts they yearned for the day when Messiah would inaugurate the kingdom of righteousness. According to Luke 17:20, some of them put the question straight to Jesus, when was the kingdom of God coming? Jesus' answer is interesting:

> The kingdom of God is not coming with things that can be observed; nor will they say, "Look, here it is!" or "There it is!" For, in fact, the kingdom of God is among you. (Luke 17:20–21)

Thus the people of God are left with two assurances in response to their longing for God's reign of justice and peace. The first assurance is that God remains with the faithful, even in their suffering, and guides them and all creation toward the era of *shalom.* The second assurance is that their faithfulness, amidst the trials of life, is not incidental but is a crucial part of the kingdom's coming. The kingdom of God is among them, among the servant people as they, through their acts of mercy and their witness to *tôrāh,* hasten the coming of God's order of justice.

Isaiah 61:1–11
A Prophet for the Lowly

Isaiah 61:1–3 takes a bold turn. By applying the words used to describe the Servant of the Lord in 42:1 to a new time and situation, some person or group here seems to be claiming inheritance of the office of that important figure in Second Isaiah's prophecy. We noted in commenting on the four Servant Songs the presence of considerable ambiguity regarding the figure of the Servant, both as to identity and whether reference was to an individual or a community. We concluded that the ambiguity was intentional and that the Servant was set forth as a model for both the individual and the commu-

223

nity that in faith and obedience accepted the calling to be agents of God's reign of compassionate righteousness. It seems entirely appropriate, therefore, that the sense of being called to the role of Servant should be experienced by a leader within the circle of Second Isaiah's disciples who desires to be used by the Lord as an instrument of reconciliation and healing and who passes that calling on to others in the community who are open to God's call.

This disciple, possibly facing challenges to authority and office, points to the only authority and status possessed by the Servant, that coming from the spirit of the Lord God. Since, however, any person can *claim* divine appointment, the more significant credential is perhaps contained in the description the Servant gives of the mission entailed, for it summarizes the heart of the Yahwistic vision of redemption. The identity of this Servant is inextricably tied up with commitment to God's will, a commitment to be present as an agent of God's mercy to the broken and the oppressed and as one announcing that after years of mourning the time had arrived in which God will restore the conditions of justice and peace that characterize God's reign.

While false prophets can claim divine authority, their deceit is unmasked by their commitment to self-gain. The prophet is validated as Servant of the Lord by being free from preoccupation with self. Power is not hoarded but is passed on to the community as a whole, enabling all members to join in the rebuilding of what had been destroyed:

> They shall build up the ancient ruins,
> they shall raise up the former devastations;
> they shall repair the ruined cities,
> the devastations of many generations.
> (Isa. 61:4)

In this verse we see the concrete form that the liberating work of God announced in verses 1–3 was to take. And concrete it is, for, ever since the exodus from Egypt, Israel's God had demonstrated deep concern for all dimensions of human life. A spiritually healthy community would be a community dwelling in a secure and productive land, and this involved brick and mortar. But always what is built in obedience to God goes beyond bricks and mortar. By placing God's justice and mercy at the heart of the rebuilding project, the Servant enables the commu-

224

nity to reach the highest purpose possible for any human group, "to display [God's] glory" (v. 3). Thus a people, long lost in its preoccupation with the false gods of greed and self-indulgence, finds the authentic life in praise of God.

After thus clarifying the transcendent purpose that was the talisman of Israel's existence, the prophet returns to a description of the restoration of the dignity of the people in their land (vv. 5–7). Those who had been humiliated by being deprived of temple and home and forced to serve foreign masters were to be served by the very ones who had subjugated them. This would enable them to assume the calling that more than any other manifested the character of this nation as one called into God's service. They would "be called priests of the LORD, . . . ministers of our God," thereby fulfilling God's promise to Moses on Mount Sinai:

> Now therefore, if you obey my voice and keep my covenant, you shall be my treasured possession out of all the peoples. Indeed, the whole earth is mine, but you shall be for me a priestly kingdom and a holy nation. (Exod. 19:5–6)

Israel's credentials for this high calling are not lacking. They were established in the strictest of all pedagogies, namely, suffering. The prophet echoes another theme of Second Isaiah, namely, that this people has suffered double for its sins. As we have seen in the prophet's refutation of the lament of some of the people in chapter 59, suffering does not necessarily lead to spiritual growth. It can lead to scapegoating *the other* as the cause, or even to blaming God. Only suffering that leads to repentance of sin and throwing self completely on God's mercy can redeem suffering by transforming it into an openness to God's healing power.

Is God then a whimsical power broker? Does God inflict shame and dishonor in double measure for a time and then suddenly decide to show mercy instead? In verse 8 a brief divine word answers such questioning by describing God's nature:

> For I the LORD love justice,
>   I hate robbery and wrongdoing;
> I will faithfully give them their recompense,
>   and I will make an everlasting covenant with them.

225

Neither whimsy nor blind fate guides the destiny of Israel, but the principle of justice. But not abstract justice, either, but

justice embodied in the living God, the advocate of the oppressed and the redeemer of those in bondage. The future of
those who have suffered at the hands of this world's tyrants is
in the hands of a personal sovereign who not only enacts laws
but *loves* justice, who not only decrees punishments for mis-
deeds but *hates* robbery and wrongdoing. Israel's future does
not depend on divine caprice but is guided by God's *faithful*
adherence to the covenant relationship. At this crucial moment
in history when a people, on the threshold of a new era of peace
wedded to justice, flirts with the notion of serving its own self-
interests, the prophet announces the steadfastness of the God
who even now desires to renew the covenant. God, the same
friend of justice who created from helpless slaves a kingdom of
priests, seeks still to preserve in the world a living testimony to
the only source of hope, that "all who see them shall acknowledge that they are a people whom the LORD has blessed" (v. 9).

The prophet, involved so intimately with those addressed
as to identify with Zion, the city of God, breaks forth in rejoicing
as the bride described by Second Isaiah (52:1). The wedding
that unites God and people in a covenant of faithfulness and
blessing is as good as accomplished, for such is the nature of God
to accomplish what has been promised as surely as "the earth
brings forth its shoots" (v. 11). The challenge confronting the
people thus is clear: Remain steadfast and the restoration of
peace and justice in the land is certain, for the God who remains
faithful to God's promises reigns.

Isaiah 62:1–12
A City Not Forsaken

More painful than captivity or losing one's way is the mental anguish caused by the thought that those able to help have
abandoned the search. A prisoner captured by the enemy, a
child separated from parents on a wilderness outing, a sailor lost
at sea—in each case dread sets in at the thought that the rescuer
has given up the search.

The exiles had endured the hardships of exile, had undertaken the risk of returning to a devastated land, had put shoulders to the task of rebuilding the ruins of their nation. All this

they endured through the assurances of Second Isaiah that God was present among them fulfilling the promises made through the prophets. But now evidence was mounting that the dawn of the new era of peace and justice was fading in the face of insurmountable obstacles. The resolve necessary to keep the restoration effort on track was being broken by a crescendo of doubts regarding the credibility of Israel's God. The God who had not prevented the Babylonians and their gods from destroying Jerusalem was still powerless to reestablish the security of the nation. Or perhaps God was indifferent, lacking in resolve or commitment to this small, struggling community. All of the talk about God coming as Redeemer was mere wishful thinking. A chill was beginning to encircle the hearts of many within the struggling community.

During the exilic period, Second Isaiah already had confronted the charge of divine indifference within the context of the processions of the Babylonian gods whose devotees boasted of the superiority of Marduk and Nebo over Yahweh. The prophet satirized those gods as mere blocks of wood incapable of speech or movement and showing warmth only when cast into the fire for burning. In contrast, Second Isaiah described Yahweh as a God filled with passionate concern for the abandoned people:

> For a long time I have held my peace,
>   I have kept still and restrained myself;
> now I will cry out like a woman in labor,
>   I will gasp and pant.
>
> (Isa. 42:14)

Effete pride and regal aloofness do not characterize the biblical God. Passion for justice, tender loving care that hurts at the sight of suffering, vulnerability, accessibility, involvement—all of these are of the nature of the God who reaches down to heal and restore. Second Isaiah searched for metaphors that convey this divine passion, and the result is language that can shock and offend, language invoking images of fearless warrior, disappointed lover, angry father, mother in the throes of labor pains.

Third Isaiah faces a community for whom the doubt concerning God's commitment to the well-being of the people has taken another form: They are in their own land, far from the Babylonian gods now humiliated before the superior might of

227

the Persians, but their land is withholding its blessing. The old doubts rise again: "Is the LORD's hand too short to save, his ear too dull to hear?" (59:1; cf. 50:2).

Disciple again takes cue from Master: Third Isaiah is drawn into action in imitation of the divine passion for the cause of captive Israel earlier described by Second Isaiah in the latter half of chapter 42. The people's cry, raised up to God by an angel in Zechariah 1:12, had to be answered: "O LORD of hosts, how long will you withhold mercy from Jerusalem and the cities of Judah?" The situation is far too urgent to justify continued restraint!

> For Zion's sake I will not keep silent,
> and for Jerusalem's sake I will not rest,
> until her vindication shines out like the dawn,
> and her salvation like a burning torch.
> (Isa. 62:1)

Yahweh's righteous impatience in 42:14–17 had taken form in a powerful counterattack on the forces of evil (see also v. 13) and in personal involvement in the deliverance of the captives from their oppressors. If we are correct in placing chapters 60—62 at a point early in the activity of Third Isaiah, chronologically not long after the return of the exiles in 538 B.C.E., chapter 62 can be seen as a turning point. The optimism conveyed in the reaffirmation of Second Isaiah's vision of restoration in chapters 60 and 61 is tempered in chapter 62 by another feeling. Somber intimations of impending crises begin to lead the prophet to a different posture, a more aggressive stance vis-à-vis those perceived as opposing God's purposes. The products of that stance have already been encountered in chapters 57, 58, and 59. They will be found as well in the final four chapters of the book. They do not offer light reading, but neither was the disintegrating community situation facing the prophet a light situation.

An aura of urgency runs throughout chapter 62. The change to come will be incisive, discontinuous with the oppressive structures of the past. "You shall be called by a new name," Zion is told. The old names recall the suffering and humiliation of defeat and exile.

> You shall no more be termed Forsaken,
> and your land shall no more be termed Desolate.
> (Isa. 62:4)

Third Isaiah follows Hosea, Jeremiah, and Ezekiel in utilizing the marriage metaphor to express the new name, that is, the new status of the people in relation to God:

> You shall be called My Delight Is in Her,
>   and your land Married.
>
> (Isa. 62:4)

The last verse of the chapter translates the metaphor into the classical biblical language of covenant:

> They shall be called, "The Holy People,
>   The Redeemed of the LORD";
> and you shall be called, "Sought Out,
>   A City Not Forsaken."
>
> (Isa. 62:12)

The assurances of God's protection and blessing that run throughout the chapter are interwoven with the motif of urgent appeal to the Lord to act. Verse 6 develops a picture of sentinels posted on the walls of Jerusalem who are to "take no rest" in giving God "no rest" until God completes the salvific act. The command of God to God's divine assistants to prepare a highway through the wilderness upon which the exiles could return to their homeland is echoed in verse 10, but the new setting gives the words a different significance. The journey, in the literal sense, has been completed; they are in Judah. But in a metaphorical sense, they have a long way to go. The Master's word becomes an admonition to persevere in both faith and hard work as instruments of God's redeeming purpose, never losing sight of the fundamental fact that hope ultimately resides not in human strength but in divine grace. Words taken from Second Isaiah again make the point:

> See, your salvation comes;
> his reward is with him,
>   and his recompense before him.
>   (Isa. 62:11; cf. 40:10)

At a point when the pain of delay and the burden of perseverance become heavy upon the people, a vision is reformulated in chapters 60—62 and placed at the heart of the struggling community. Lofty in its holy fantasy and elaborate in its hope, it nevertheless gives hints of the struggle of which it is a part, especially in chapter 62. It is entirely fitting that this beautiful, heartening vision should have been made the center-piece of the Third Isaiah corpus. It saves this section of the Bible from becoming hopelessly entangled in the vindictiveness that increasingly grew amidst the hardships and struggles of the restoration community. Even at the most bitter points of the battle, such as the portrait of Yahweh as bloody warrior slaying the nations in 63:1–6 or the description of the curse placed upon those perceived to be enemies within the community itself in 65:11–15, chapters 60—62 shed divine light on a dark human situation. In fact, where the situation becomes the most bleak, the light is seen to shine most brilliantly.

Isaiah 63:1–6
The Divine Warrior Comes

Biblical scholars typically divide into two "camps" over the question of which is more significant, the final canonical shape of a biblical book or the smaller units that were drawn into the final text but had an antecedent origin and function in the life of Israel. The position adopted in this commentary seeks middle ground in the controversy. Where units can be identified that precede the final edition of a book and can be placed with some degree of plausibility within a sociohistorical setting, there is much to be gained both in historical and in theological under-standing by studying these earlier, discrete compositions. At the same time, the literary form into which earlier materials have been drawn by tradents committed to preserving the literature handed down to them is also of great historical and theological significance. Stated simply, the more we can learn about every discernible stage of tradition, the richer our understanding of the biblical material will be.

This is certainly true in the case of Third Isaiah. We have just seen that chapters 60—62 took shape as God's word within a specific setting, the period immediately after the Edict of Cyrus in 538 B.C.E. But we have also recognized how these same chapters continued to proclaim God's word within their new setting as the literary center of the disparate and in part dissonant materials that have come to constitute Isaiah 56—66.

There is no need to judge the relative worth of original unit against canonical whole. We are tutored by the *entire* history of the living word of God.

What, then, is our opinion of the tradents who gave the final literary form to the materials of Third Isaiah? Are they among our biblical heroes? Jesus the Son of Sirach began his Hymn in Honor of Our Ancestors with these lines:

> Let us now sing the praises of famous men,
>   our ancestors in their generations.
>   (Sirach 44:1)

Abraham, Moses, and David, and many other people of stature, are celebrated, but nameless disciples such as those who edited the materials in Isaiah 56—66 are left in obscurity. That is a great pity, since their contribution to the sacred tradition is also deserving of praise. Let us try to imagine, for a moment, the nature of their labors.

We take Isaiah 63:1–6 as a case in point, a quite distinctive unit among the materials preserved from the disciples of Second Isaiah. It describes the God of Israel as Divine Warrior on a bloody rampage, in the name of vengeance and vindication, against Edom, representative of the nations that had destroyed and humiliated captive Israel.

Where does this poem fit in a collection that is offered as a summary of the message arising from the Third Isaiah group to the postexilic community? It certainly portrays a God who is passionately involved in vindicating a smitten people. Where is its proper place within the composition of Isaiah 56—66?

Chapter 62 portrayed the prophet as one who would not keep silent until the vindication of Zion would shine out "like the dawn." It spoke of sentinels upon the walls of Jerusalem who were to give the Lord no rest "until he establishes Jerusalem." In 63:1–6 the editors found a poem that dramatically depicts a God who does not retreat into divine obscurity, high and lifted above the messiness of human conflict. It is a poem celebrating the God who is moved to action in the face of injustice, a God who hears and responds to the pleas of the afflicted. It is not hard to see that experienced editors would find the poem creating a meaningful sequel to the image of sentinels "pestering" God until God acted on behalf of smitten Israel (62:6), and a fitting conclusion to the oath sworn by the

231

Lord, "I will not again give your grain to be food for your enemies, and foreigners shall not drink the wine for which you have labored" (62:8).

The Divine Warrior Hymn is not the only unit that seemed to follow meaningfully upon the appeal to God to act. Isaiah 63:7—64:12 is a lament that implores God to break silence and act to save the languishing community: "After all this, will you restrain yourself, O Lord? Will you keep silent, and punish us so severely?" (64:12). This too seems to be an appropriate sequel to the theme of chapter 62 that the prophet will not keep silent until God responds with decisive action.

The editorial decision was to place both the Divine Warrior Hymn and the lament after chapter 62 as responses to the urgent supplications for God to act. First came the hymn, replete with shocking imagery of righteous wrath, depicting a warrior God acting to vindicate those who had suffered under the cruel hand of the foreign powers. Then followed the long lament in which the community appealed anew to God to break the silence and to come down to save. As if to add further incentive to God, the lament includes a reminder of God's saving actions on Israel's behalf in past eras and a confession of sin. The latter is in harmony with the indictment directed against the unrepentant in 59:2: "Your iniquities have been barriers between you and your God, and your sins have hidden his face from you so that he does not hear." Thus chapters 63 and 64 were added to chapters 60—62 to create a long address to those who, even after the passing of the first generation of Second Isaiah's disciples, continued to maintain faith amidst further delays in the promised redemption of Israel.

Glimpsing behind the message formed by the editors to the antecedent units they incorporated into their text, we first consider the Divine Warrior Hymn in 63:1–6. It is important to recognize the traditional nature of the metaphorical language for God as warrior. Throughout the ancient Near East, it was customary to depict a nation's deity as a Man of War. In the song that celebrates deliverance from slavery in Egypt, early Israel drew upon this tradition to portray Yahweh as "a warrior" (Exod. 15:3). This usage persisted throughout the biblical period alongside other metaphors such as shepherd, mother, and judge. In contrast to them, however, the violence associated with the Divine Warrior creates serious difficulties in the mind

232

of the contemporary reader. How are we to understand the meaning and function of this hymn within its original setting?

Claus Westermann has pointed out that the question that opens the hymn can best be understood as one put by a sentinel (such as one of the sentinels on the walls of Jerusalem mentioned in 62:6) to someone approaching the city gate. God answers! "It is I, announcing vindication, mighty to save."

The central message of the passage is contained in this divine self-identification. It is a message that runs like a thread throughout Second and Third Isaiah. Second Isaiah begins with the announcement of God's advent:

> Get you up to a high mountain,
>   O Zion, herald of good tidings;
> lift up your voice with strength,
>   O Jerusalem, herald of good tidings,
>   lift it up, do not fear;
> say to the cities of Judah,
>   "Here is your God!"
> See, the Lord GOD comes with might,
>   and his arm rules for him;
> his reward is with him,
>   and his recompense before him.
>   (Isa. 40:9–10)

The theme is picked up in 52:8:

> Listen! Your sentinels lift up their voices,
>   together they sing for joy;
> for in plain sight they see
>   the return of the LORD to Zion.

It is continued by Third Isaiah in 62:11:

> See, your salvation comes;
> his reward is with him,
>   and his recompense before him.

Central to the hymn in 63:1–6, then, is God's own renewal of the promise that the order of justice that has been disrupted, causing horrible suffering within God's people, will be restored by God's own coming.

An ancillary theme, itself giving expression to a leitmotif already encountered in our commentary, is that the Divine Warrior comes *alone*. In 59:15b–20 the Divine Warrior similarly entered a world in which "there was no justice," where

233

there was "no one, . . . no one to intervene; . . . so his own arm brought him victory." Here a difference is discernible in relation to Second Isaiah. The announcement of the coming of God's deliverance in Second Isaiah was related to the military campaigns of Cyrus. The prophet of the exile claimed that there *was someone* who served as the human instrument of divine vindication. Cyrus defeated the Babylonian captors and issued an edict of release permitting the exiles to return to their homeland. Also according to Second Isaiah the Servant was God's chosen agent in establishing justice on earth. But here in chapter 63, God is "alone, and from the peoples no one was with me" (v. 3).

Behind this hymn in Third Isaiah we can glimpse a community that, even after having returned to Judah, continues to suffer economic and legal deprivation and subjugation under foreign powers. Scanning the world horizon as well as their own social landscape, they are unable to pick out what Second Isaiah saw, namely, a human agent of God's deliverance. What human figures have appeared as candidates have left disappointment in their wake. Sheshbazzar tried to rebuild the temple and failed. Zerubbabel, hailed as deliverer by his supporters, disappeared, perhaps as the result of Persian action in response to what was deemed insubordinate nationalism. Meanwhile, the faithful within Israel, that is, the servant people, suffered humiliation and abuse at the hands of their own leaders. So, was the promise of restoration as a people serving God announced by Second Isaiah and renewed by followers (chaps. 60—62) to be abandoned for despair? An ancient genre, available from Israel's earliest tradition, enabled the community to reply with an emphatic "No!" Through the Divine Warrior Hymn they could renew their trust in God's final victory over their enemies.

The metaphor they chose may not suit our taste as an appropriate vehicle for expressing God's saving presence in our world and in our lives. But only those are in a position to judge who live in circumstances similar to sixth-century Israel's, circumstances in which the powers of evil seem to have defeated every human agency of justice and in which the only remaining hope seems to reside in God's direct intervention. These are the circumstances that give rise to apocalyptic visions, visions that, if dreamed in the heads of those enjoying the comforts and securities of a prosperous society, violate the spirit of the biblical promises, but, if arising as a passionate and godly effort to

234

keep faith alive in the midst of human hopelessness, are important vehicles of God's word to the oppressed.

Isaiah 63:7—64:12
Where Are Your Zeal and Compassion?

We have noted above that the Divine Warrior Hymn in 63:1–6 and the extended lament in 63:7—64:12 amplify themes central to chapter 62, especially the theme of the prophet's not keeping silent for Zion's sake and the metaphorically formed theme of sentinels posted on the walls of Jerusalem giving the Lord no rest "until he establishes Jerusalem" (62:7). The literary coherence of the resulting text gives evidence of the theological sensitivity of the final editors.

As we did in the case of the hymn, so now in the case of the lament we shall seek to explain the meaning it had within its original setting before it was drawn into the larger literary structure of Third Isaiah. Once again we find the prophet seeking to keep God's word of promise alive in a period in which the community stands on the brink of losing its spiritual identity by attributing setbacks not to human unfaithfulness but to divine indifference. We see the prophet in the role of mediator, located between the two sides of an endangered relationship. In this role the prophet appeals to God on behalf of the people and to the people on behalf of God. With the candor of one committed both to God's honor and to the people's well-being, he pleads with God, accepts solidarity with the people in their sin by raising his voice in confession, and recalls the past in the effort to prompt both sides to break the tragic impasse.

The genre chosen for this purpose by the prophet is one that is familiar from the Psalter, the communal lament. Arising out of a situation of great need, the lament bases its appeal for God's help upon a recitation of God's merciful deeds in situations from the past when the people were similarly threatened. The theological assumption that underlies the lament is the steadfastness of God. Within Israel's understanding of the covenant, however, God's mercy was not construed in magical terms but in relational ones. God's protection could not be

235

taken for granted but was understood as the blessing granted to a people living in obedience to God's will. For this reason, confession of sin is an integral part of the lament.

The first verse of the lament begins where Israel's life with God began, namely, with God's "gracious deeds." One can sense how full the prophet's heart is for God's goodness through the heaping up of words for God's grace in one verse: "gracious deeds," "praiseworthy acts," "all that the LORD has done for us," "the great favor to the house of Israel," "his mercy," "the abundance of his steadfast love" (63:7). This is followed by attribution to God of an ingenuous assumption: "Surely they are my people, children who will not deal falsely"; and a conclusion, "and he became their savior in all their distress" (63:8–9a).

The simple purity of the relationship described in these first three verses assures the shock effect of the next verse:

> But they rebelled
> and grieved his holy spirit;
> therefore he became their enemy;
> he himself fought against them.
> (Isa. 63:10)

A state of idyllic innocence reminiscent of the Garden of Eden is thus rudely broken. God is generous beyond all imagining, reaching to save a people who possess no claim to worthiness, personally drawing them close and guiding them into a future filled with promise. But God does not indulge in the kind of permissiveness that would allow the relationship to become degraded into a human presumptuousness like that of an ungrateful and spiteful child. Rejected by those he loved, the grief-stricken God responds with the passion of one who was deeply committed to the relationship: God "became their enemy" (63:10). Just as impossible as an attitude of permissive indulgence abetting the decline of the people into ugly hardness of heart is an attitude of indifference reflecting passing fancy rather than steadfast love. In the effort to break the people from the prison of self-preoccupation, God acts decisively. The one who personally saved them (63:9) now personally fights against them (63:10).

The honest, emphatic confrontation has the desired effect. The self-containment and smugness of the closed consciousness that acknowledges no debts save the debt to personal resourcefulness is broken. Awareness of the historical dimension of life

236

is reopened, awareness of the fact that what Israel is can be explained solely in relation to God's gracious gifts of the past, awareness of the essential grounding of both individual and communal identity in the collective experiences of ages past. "They remembered the days of old" (63:11).

That remembrance did not consist of vague generalities. It was specific. It involved a specific individual named Moses living at a particular time and place in history. That is how God acted to deliver the ancestors of Israel, through a faithful human being, a *servant*. Remembrance of things past is not a coldly objective piece of scientific research. It entails involvement with the events recalled. In this case, the choice of Moses likely has meaning beyond his obvious place in tradition. Among those addressed by the prophet are Levites tracing their lineage to Moses. His name evokes vivid images of a time when the courage of one of their ancestors became the occasion for a breakthrough from humiliating bondage to the integrity of freedom. If the descendants of Moses showed similar courage, perhaps the miracle could be repeated!

One of the functions of the historical résumé in the lament was to create intolerable tension between things as they were in the recalled past and as they were in the present as a means of shocking alienated parties into an honest confrontation with the causes of the tragic impasse. Heightened tension thus laid the groundwork for an appeal to God on behalf of the people. It also moved the people to reflect on the reasons for the disparity. The key word creating the sense of tension here is the interrogative "Where?" It is used in a twofold manner.

The first "Where?" is an inquiry regarding divine presence in human history (63:11). The remembered past was a time characterized by God's presence in the midst of the people, saving them from the dangers that engulfed them. The present in contrast is a time of God's absence, a time of the soul-searching question, "Where?" The searing pain that accompanies that question has revisited the human race at times of untractable tragedy, most notably in modern times by the Holocaust. In *Night*, Elie Wiesel describes the agony of the experience of God's absence. A child hangs from the gallows set up by the SS. Someone is heard to ask, "Where is God? Where is He?" The child struggles between life and death for more than half an hour, and the same person asks again, "Where is God now?" Wiesel writes:

237

> And I heard a voice within me answer him:
> "Where is He? Here He is. . . . He is hanging here on this gallows." (Wiesel, pp. 61–62)

The true prophet does not seek superficial ways to dispel the darkness of desolation. Wiesel does not sweep the pain away with facile assurances. He obliges the reader to accept the contradictions of life as an invitation to the kind of reflection that breaks through facile human explanations. The prophet in our passage invites the audience to a similar confrontation with contradiction. He pictures the people guided by Moses: "Like a horse in the desert, they did not stumble" (63:13*b*). How different is the present situation of the prophet, as described, for example, in chapter 59: "We stumble at noon as in the twilight. . . . We all growl like bears." (59:10–11) This contrast drives home the spasms of pain underlying the twice-repeated question of 63:11, "Where is the one?"

The second "Where?" is more painful still (63:15). It goes beyond inquiry regarding God's absence to questions about God's nature and character. It asks, in effect, "Are the cynics in the community right in their claims that your arm is too short to save us, your ear too dull to hear our cries? Are the doubts regarding your power correct? Are the charges true that you do not care any longer about this people, that you have abandoned them to the forces of this world?" The honesty with which the prophet debates with God will come as a surprise only to those who forget the stories about Abraham, Amos, Jeremiah, and Job. The prophet, assuming the posture of a sharp prosecuting attorney, marshals all possible arguments against God. His recalling the fact that what God had done of old redounded to God's glory implies that the present inaction of God will lead to God's being discredited among the nations. Do we detect a hint of sarcasm in his appeal: "Look down from heaven and see, from your holy and glorious habitation" (63:15), for it raises the question of whether God is abandoning his personal style of involvement in the experiences of the people in favor of the comfortable repose of a heavenly palace? It is an appeal right to the heart of the God celebrated in worship as the God of might and compassion:

238

> Where are your zeal and your might?
> The yearning of your heart and your compassion?
> They are withheld from me.
>
> (Isa. 63:15)

The appeal is reinforced by the invocation of the most intimate of all of Israel's divine epithets, "You, O LORD, are our father" (63:16).

Spiritual anguish continues to surface as the lament continues: "Abraham does not know us and Israel does not acknowledge us" (63:16). Ostracized even from their own kin, they appeal for help like frightened children to the Father of them all.

The probing questions lead finally to the cause of their desolation. The one who has brought their adversity upon them is the very one upon whom they had been taught to depend for help in time of adversity. It is *God* who has made them stray (cf. Ezek. 20:25–26). In what could seem like a cruel mockery of their religious epic, Israel finds itself merged into the character of its arch villain, with heart hardened like the Pharaoh and with God fighting against them (63:17). The holy people who once fulfilled their vocation as "priests of the LORD" now see their sanctuary taken by their adversaries (possibly reflecting the loss of temple access on the part of the Levites to the Zadokite priestly leadership: (see Hanson, *the Dawn of Apocalyptic*). The people "called by God's name" has come to resemble the pagan nations.

The cumulative effect of the relentless series of contradictions culminates in an impassioned cry to God in heaven. Life has been turned upside down. The resources of the faithful minority seem exhausted. In 63:15 the prophet pleaded for God to *"look* down." But that is not enough in a situation in which chaos seems to engulf the earth. It is time for God to act, and to act incisively: "O that you would tear open the heavens and *come* down" (64:1). The images are violent, the kinds used throughout ancient Near Eastern literature to describe the arrival of the Divine Warrior for battle: mountains quake, fire burns, water boils. The bottom line of the appeal of the prophet is to God's honor (64:2). The key is reaffirmation of the sole sovereignty of God (64:4). And renewal of hope is based on the possibility of the people's recommitment in obedience through remembrance.

But how does a people open itself to the reentry of divine grace, forgiveness, and healing? The prophet gives the classical biblical answer, *repentance.* Accordingly, the prophet ignores for a moment the divisions that cut through the community and leads the entire people in a confession of sin (64:5*b*–7). Confes-

239

sion in turn clears the way for the people to cast themselves upon God's mercy. Confession washes them clean of the prideful thought that they can save themselves. Chastened, childlike, they place themselves at the mercy of the divine parent, to whom they appeal *in spite of* the shameful record of their past:

> Yet, O LORD, you are our Father;
>   we are the clay, and you are our potter;
>   we are all the work of your hand.
> (Isa. 64:8)

God is implored to consider once again the devastation of the cities of Judah, the desolation of Jerusalem, the ruins of the temple (64:10–11). And then the lament concludes with words that are among the most moving entreaties in the entire Old Testament. The prophet, moved by compassion to a sense of solidarity with the very ones he has severely castigated for wickedness and rebellion, addresses the heart of God:

> After all this, will you restrain yourself, O LORD?
> Will you keep silent, and punish us so severely?
> (Isa. 64:12)

The doubts, the contradictions, the tensions, the pains that have been expressed in the lament are not thereby resolved. But they are lifted up in one final impassioned plea to the only one who can help. Memory of God's gracious saving acts of the past remains intertwined with the hardships of day-to-day existence. In the act of lament and supplication, troubles do not vanish, but human vision is lifted above human helplessness to the heavenly parent. In such a situation, where no human parent deserving of the name could remain unmoved, is it possible to imagine that the source of love will remain silent?

Perhaps no one answered this universal human question as emphatically as Jesus in the parable of the unrighteous judge, who finally relented to the persistent pleas of the widow. "And will not God grant justice to his chosen ones who cry to him day and night?" Jesus asked. "Will he delay long in helping them? I tell you, he will quickly grant justice to them" (Luke 18:7–8).

Faith in God's commitment to justice and mercy has sustained God's people through the darkest periods of suffering in the past. Central to biblical faith is the confession that those who trust in that same God in their own trials will not be abandoned. Therefore, even when God seems to have with-

240

drawn, the suffering faithful individual and the stricken faithful community persist in directing their cries to the heavenly parent, "Yet, O LORD, you are our Father."

Isaiah 65:1–25
By Judgment and Salvation a New Heaven and Earth

The attention given to thematic unity on the part of those who did the final editing of the Third Isaiah corpus is again evident as we turn to chapter 65. The long lament contained in the previous two chapters lifted up to heaven the agonizing question, "Where?" and the desperate pleas, "Look down!" and "Come down!" As a separate unit, chapter 65 was originally written as a highly polemical salvation-judgment oracle, that is, a pronouncement combining a promise of salvation to the group within the community deemed obedient to God's will and a threat of judgment against others accused of turning to evil. Once it was placed after the lament, however, it came to serve an added purpose, namely, to provide an answer to the questions and complaints of the lament. For it opens with God's explanation of the bleak situation in which the foundering community finds itself:

> I was ready to be sought out by those who did not ask,
>   to be found by those who did not seek me.
> I said, "Here I am, here I am,"
>   to a nation that did not call on my name.
> I held out my hands all day long
>   to a rebellious people,
> who walk in a way that is not good,
>   following their own devices.
>
> (Isa. 65:1–2)

If there was to be a restoration to health, denial had to be replaced with an honest acknowledgment of responsibility. Not God's indifference but the people's rebellion caused the nation to stumble and fall. The evasive tactic of blaming God, which was only hastening the disintegration of community, was thus addressed through an expression of divine truth. The problem was self-centeredness, a preoccupation with "their own de-

241

vices" that excluded any consciousness of God's will. The theme is similar to the one developed at the beginning of chapter 59: "Your sins have hidden [God's] face from you." By centering on human schemes rather than on God's order of compassionate justice, the nation was falling into a captivity as destructive as any ever imposed on them by a foreign power. For God could not abide in a house of iniquity, and without God's presence Israel was lost.

By placing the lament and the salvation-judgment oracle in their present order, the editors thus preserved a classical prophetic lesson regarding human adversity. Repentance rather than blame and self-pity was called for. And there was a second part to that lesson: At a time when the afflicted community was being tempted to take flight into the apocalyptic vision of God breaking into human affairs to save the oppressed single-handedly and without human participation, the invitation to self-examination and engagement was issued. The call to justice and compassion and worship was renewed as the responsible way to get the nation back on the track to peace and security. The people were admonished to integrate into their institutions and social structures the justice and mercy for which they prayed to God. Israel's covenantal understanding of life by definition implied a participatory form of rule, with God's reign mediated through the responsible administration of justice within the land. While the signs of a drift away from prophetic engagement with human structures toward otherworldly dreams of divine intervention are present in Third Isaiah, the prophetic dialectic between God's sovereignty and human responsibility is maintained through the persistent call to servanthood, that is, to the vocation of serving as instruments of God's redemption within the day-to-day structures of society.

In the centuries that would follow, centuries in which the fortunes of the Jewish community were determined largely by foreign powers, it was often difficult for the people to persevere in the vocation of servant. Especially in times when those struggling to uphold *tôrāh* and worship found their efforts thwarted both by their own leaders and by the sponsoring foreign powers, it was very tempting to dissolve the dialectic in favor of flight into apocalyptic visions of a blessed realm unsullied by the political realities of this world. The Third Isaiah corpus marks an important crossroads in the history of biblical religion, since it balances the prophetic call to manifest God's reign within the context of everyday life with the invitation to focus attention on the God who arrives to save the righteous from a situation in which "there was no one to intervene" (59:16). Many beleaguered communities in centuries to come would fail to preserve that balance and would follow the path guided by apocalyptic visions of divine intervention unqualified by a sense of responsibility for the order of this world.

Having noted the theological significance of the position of chapter 65 within its larger literary setting, we now turn to describe its original function as a salvation-judgment oracle addressing two parties locked in a bitter inner-community struggle.

On this primary level, God's declaration that human sin rather than divine indifference explained the present suffering serves as the introduction to a sharply worded attack on the offenders. Verse 2 used general terms to identify that group, for example, "a rebellious people." Verses 3–4, constructed with a series of participial clauses, fill out the picture with vivid vignettes of people engaged in ritual practices associated with Canaanite religion that were condemned as abominations by Jewish law. Unauthorized sacrifice; ritual fellatio (an allusion well disguised in the received text of 65:3 but preserved by the Isaiah manuscripts of the Dead Sea Scrolls); necromancy; violations of *kosher*—such are the practices of a people "who walk in a way that is not good, following their own devices" (v. 2). To add insult to injury, they combine this shameless behavior with a "holier than thou" attitude (v. 5a). But God is not deceived by their hypocrisy and duplicity. Within a religious culture placing much emphasis on the burning of sacrifice and incense to create pleasant scents for the deity to whom they are offered, God bluntly repudiates their gifts:

> These are a smoke in my nostrils,
> a fire that burns all day long.
> (Isa. 65:5b)

The one who has been accused of not hearing and not responding announces that he will not remain silent in the face of such atrocity:

> I will not keep silent, but I will repay.
> (Isa. 65:6)

The solemn pronouncement of judgment that follows completes the customary prophetic speech pattern of indictment

(vv. 1–5) and sentence (vv. 6–7). But how will the sentence be carried out? In the case of the preexilic prophets, the threat of judgment was pronounced upon the entire nation and could take the form of an attack of foreign armies enlisted as instruments of divine punishment. But here the "latter-day" prophet is announcing God's sentence on only one segment of the population. Can the armies of a foreign nation be summoned by Yahweh to punish only a particular segment of the populace? The situation has become complicated and has placed strain upon the conventional forms of prophetic speech.

Within this complex situation an otherwise puzzling clause becomes comprehensible, "It is written before me" (v. 6a). The situation may be filled with ambiguity. The righteous may suffer while the wicked prosper. But clarity is preserved where it matters. Accurate records are being kept in heaven. Therefore the faithful can be confident that God's vindication will come. In ages to follow, in similar settings of community struggle and moral confusion, the motif of the divine book in which the names of the wicked and the righteous are recorded would persist as a source of hope for the perplexed.

In verse 8 a second metaphor is added, more exquisite than the first:

> Thus says the LORD:
> As the wine is found in the cluster,
>   and they say, "Do not destroy it,
>   for there is a blessing in it,"
> so I will do for my servants' sake,
>   and not destroy them all.

Through the painful experience of inner-community divisions the realism that, from the beginning, was a mark of prophecy has, in a certain respect, been deepened. A rather simplistic dualism between Israel and the nations has been modified by the awareness that Israel itself is a "house divided." Rash solutions to the problem of evil are precluded in a situation marked by ambiguity comparable to the presence of bad grapes in the cluster with the good. At a later point in Jewish history, Jesus used the comparable figure of weeds scattered among the wheat to make a similar point:

244

> The slaves said to him, "Then do you want us to go and gather them?" But he replied, "No; for in gathering the weeds you would uproot the wheat along with them." (Matt. 13:29)

It is precisely in the midst of spiritual confusion and moral dissonance that the faithful must remain steadfast.

Within such a confusing setting, however, the prophet does not abandon the people but remains as a beacon to guide them in the way of uprightness. This he does by keeping clear the divine standards whereby righteousness and wickedness are distinguished. In the service of this standard the prophet renews the promise of blessing to "my people who have sought me" (vv. 9–10), while at the same time pronouncing with equal clarity judgment upon "you who forsake the LORD" (vv. 11–12). Then in verses 13–16 the blessings and the judgments are blended into one litany of promise and curse. With these words Israel enters a new era, an era similar in many respects to our own, an era in which systems of value compete and contradictory views of the good abound and in which the people are lost without the guidance of those who see clearly the distinction between those "following their own devices" and "my people who have sought me."

The ubiquitous signs of moral decline notwithstanding, God has not abandoned the faithful to anomie. The twin pronouncements of salvation and judgment affirm the moral grounding of the universe. "But, O prophet," we can hear the people complain, "how can we know that justice and peace will be restored when all we see is the victory of our adversaries while we continue to suffer humiliation and defeat? When you deliver your divine word, 'The former troubles are forgotten and are hidden from my sight,' do you see something that we fail to see?"

We can picture the prophet closing his eyes, quietly reflecting, and then, after a period of silence, replying with the words in verses 17–25, words describing the life intended by God for all creation. But please! What purpose is served by this description of "new heavens and a new earth"? Is this not primary evidence for a Marxist analysis of religion as an opiate of the people?

It is terribly important that in answering this question one draw a clear distinction between two exercises of religious imagination. One dreams of shalom as an avenue of escape from real life with the effect of disabling people by breaking their will to act with courage and determination on behalf of God's order of justice. The other envisions shalom as an act of defiant affirmation that no power will thwart the fulfillment of God's righ-

245

teous purpose. The former leads to resignation and despair. The latter engenders hope. The former undermines social reform. The latter gives reform a clear focus by refusing to sacrifice justice to the logic of expediency.

The vision of the new heaven and the new earth fosters hope even as it elicits incisive action. It is simply not true that only programs outlining goals attainable on the basis of pragmatic logic are capable of moving people to action. Perhaps that is the case in movements that exclude a spiritual dimension, where the warning not to aim too high is in order, lest failure to reach the goal translate into a sense of defeat. For those whose identity is grounded in God's sovereignty the case is very different. No goal short of the restoration of all God's creation to its intended wholeness will satisfy the yearning of the Servant of the Lord. Shortfalls do not devastate the Servant, for the campaign for justice is not a personal project but a part of God's eternal purpose.

Our personal experience can aid us in understanding the contribution of the vision of the new heaven and the new earth to a life of involved commitment to compassionate justice. The medical doctor in Somalia, laboring in the midst of seemingly endless need, perseveres not by scaling down objectives to saving one infant out of ten but by working indefatigably out of yearning for the world in which there shall no longer be "an infant that lives but a few days" (v. 20). The relief worker in Bosnia steers the food-laden lorry up a dangerous mountain pass in commitment to the world in which "no more shall the sound of weeping be heard in it" (v. 19). Albert Schweitzer left the limelight of cathedral and university for the villages of Africa, Dag Hammarskjöld kept landing his United Nations plane in dangerous trouble spots, Mother Teresa maintained her ministry to the outcasts of Calcutta not out of programs designed on the basis of human pragmatics but out of a vision of a world in which "they shall not labor in vain, or bear children for calamity" (v. 23).

It will be a sorry world that takes a vision of God's new heaven and new earth out of its social justice equation. Of course many humanitarian efforts will continue to do their work on the basis of strictly rational criteria. The results will alleviate some human pain. But it is a sad prospect to think of a world bereft of servants who labor for no other reason than that God has called them to be agents of a love that is intended to restore

246

the dignity and wholeness of every mortal. For them, one promise in the vision is more precious than all others:

> Before they call I will answer,
>> while they are yet speaking I will hear.
>>> (Isa. 65:24)

The community of faith—whether it is in the form of a church, a synagogue, a mosque, or another assembly of worship—betrays its calling if it yearns for anything less than a human family so intimately connected with its source that when it calls, God answers! Only through this communion between the divine and the human can the community of the faithful offer to the world its unique gift, the gift of hope that will not be broken until that day when

> The wolf and the lamb shall feed together,
>> the lion shall eat straw like the ox;
>> but the serpent—its food shall be dust!
> They shall not hurt or destroy
>> on all my holy mountain,
>>> says the LORD.
>>> (Isa. 65:25; cf. 11:6–7)

Isaiah 66:1–24
Those to Whom God Looks

Chapter 65 ended with a picture of creation restored to its God-intended wholeness. All of God's creatures would live in harmony, and the place chosen by God for communion with humankind would display to the world the security and blessing that was God's intention for all people: "They shall not hurt or destroy on all my holy mountain, says the LORD" (65:25).

The vision at the end of chapter 65 reaffirmed for a people torn by political turmoil and economic hardship the goal toward which they were moving as a pilgrim people. It was a divine gift conveyed to them through the prophet that enabled them to see beyond human limitations to God's intentions and to resist the natural tendency to reduce expectations to present circumstances.

The beleaguered human spirit stands in need of being

247

uplifted through fresh visions of divine creativity. But visions take a turn quite opposed to encouraging courageous engagement if they become invitations to escape from involvement in the realities of life. At that point religion becomes an opiate as powerfully able to induce apathy and resignation as any narcotic. It is one of the marks of the Isaianic tradition that the eschatological vision of God's reign is repeatedly related to the realities of everyday life. The prophetic pronouncement in chapter 66 certainly returns to everyday life. It is a hard-hitting attack on those who would jeopardize Israel's future by substituting their human agendas for God's plan of universal salvation.

We shall turn to the specific message and setting of that pronouncement forthwith. But first it is important to recognize the theological design of the editors of Third Isaiah in the placement of chapter 66 after the vision of "new heavens and a new earth" in chapter 65. The God who created the universe as a good home providing for the needs of all its creatures would not rest until that day when it was restored to its rightful integrity. Nor would God look kindly upon human programs that sought to substitute empty ritual for the concrete acts of justice that were essential aspects of the divine order. Every effort to establish the blessed reign through human construction was doomed to failure, for it would come up against the God who could not be deceived by human idols and manipulative shrines.

The editorial integrity of the Book of Isaiah is illustrated by the tenacity with which the theme of fitting worship is maintained throughout the sixty-six chapters. The last chapter thus returns to the divine indictment on vain ritual that the reader encountered already in the first chapter:

> When you come to appear before me,
> who asked this from your hand?
> Trample my courts no more;
> bringing offerings is futile;
> incense is an abomination to me.
> (Isa. 1:12–13)

The reason why the ritual acts of the people are rejected does not become clear until the prophet describes the only proper basis of worship, namely, the life of moral rectitude. Offerings held high cannot hide from God the fact that "your hands are full of blood" (1:15). True worship must start with a true heart, and the true heart is revealed by acts of justice and mercy:

248

> Wash yourselves; make yourselves clean;
>> remove the evil of your doings
>> from before my eyes;
> cease to do evil,
>> learn to do good;
> seek justice,
>> rescue the oppressed,
> defend the orphan,
>> plead for the widow.
>
>>> (Isa. 1:16–17)

At the beginning, at the end, and repeatedly in between, the Book of Isaiah stresses the central importance of true worship. It is not trivial that the final chapter of the book revisits this theme.

True worship, as the keystone of the authentic life, hinges on proper perception. False worship, whether in the form of blatant idolatry or ritual charades, involves distorted perception. As expressed so clearly in Second Isaiah's irony-laden description of the Babylonians' worship of Bel and Nebo in Isaiah 46, there is something pathetic about idolatry. For human beings to think that through rituals of their making they can trick God into believing their hearts are pure is equally ridiculous. How fitting, therefore, that chapter 66 introduces its topic by raising the topic of worship above all human trivialities:

> Thus says the LORD:
> Heaven is my throne
>> and the earth is my footstool;
> what is the house that you would build for me,
>> and what is my resting place?
> All these things my hand has made,
>> and so all these things are mine,
>>> says the LORD.
>>> (Isa. 66:1–2)

Repudiated is the assumption underlying pagan cult worship that the deity is dependent on human gifts. In Egypt and Babylon, temples were constructed to provide gods with housing. Food and drink were offered to the gods to satisfy their hunger and thirst. Israel's God, by contrast, requires no physical offerings. All that fills the physical universe is God's own making. To think that God might need any part of this world's objects is to betray a badly distorted view of things.

What, then, is the proper objective of worship? The second half of verse 2 answers this question. What God seeks is a *rela-*

249

tionship with human beings, an honest and open relationship free of deception and manipulation. Thus the person receptive to God's initiative is one characterized by a pure heart and a deep longing for guidance and communion:

> But this is the one to whom I will look,
>   to the humble and contrite in spirit,
>   who trembles at my word.

Verses 3 and 4 apply the essential point that the first two verses have stated with poetic eloquence. First a list of sacrifices, viewed by the prophet as offerings designed to manipulate God into showing favor, are summarily equated with murderous and abominable acts. Then God threatens punishment upon those who, rather than responding to the divine initiative, seek their own way, the way of human cultic devices.

As is the case with most biblical passages, this one reflects a concrete situation within the community. It is a situation of bitter conflict. The prophet Haggai (Hag. 1:7–8) can be understood as spokesman for a group that views the rebuilding of the temple destroyed some sixty years earlier by the Babylonians as the key to the restoration of the community's vitality. The reasons underlying the intense vitriol whereby the prophet in Isaiah 66 identifies temple rebuilding and sacrifice with idolatry can only be speculated upon. It seems likely that rivalry between different priestly groups played a role. What is clear, however, is that the polemic became the occasion for a classic formulation of true worship that remains as valid today as it was in the year 520 B.C.E. True worship begins with the pure of heart, that is, with "the humble and contrite in spirit, who trembles at my word" (66:2). Or as another prophet expressed it earlier:

> What does the LORD require of you
>   but to do justice, and to love kindness,
>   and to walk humbly with your God?
>   (Micah 6:8)

Worthy of reflection is the question, What would be the nature of worship in our own day if the perspective of true worship described by Israel's prophets were reclaimed? What would be the characteristics of worship that began with the humble and contrite of spirit responding to God's call and trembling at God's word? As the various prophets whose voices were

250

blended into the present Book of Isaiah struggled to lead Israel back to the kind of worship that would prepare for God's return with universal peace and justice, so too the preachers who read and expound upon those words in our time are challenged to draw their people to acts of worship that are purged of human deceitfulness and filled with longing for God's presence.

For those who would hope that the vocation of proclaiming that word would bring assurances of prosperity and ease, the remaining words of the Book of Isaiah offer little consolation. Verse 5 instead indicates that faithfulness to God's word may bring rejection and scorn. Verse 6 adumbrates Jesus' announcement that he had come not to bring peace but the sword (Matt. 10:34). Accompanying the increase of the power of those who would supplant true worship with human schemes to manipulate God and control fellow human beings is the growing likelihood of conflict. Yet as sure as the pregnant woman would bring her child to birth, the purposes of God would prevail over every human challenge and God would establish the blessed reign planned from the beginning (vv. 7–13).

One might wish, at this point, that Isaiah 40—66, that prophetic corpus represented more frequently in the lectionary than any other in the Hebrew Bible, might end on a comforting note similar to the one with which it began in the first verse of chapter 40. Not so. That may have something to do with the contrast between divine understanding and human understanding: "As the heavens are higher than the earth, so are my ways higher than your ways" (55:9). While the Bible has through the ages been a source of profound comfort to the bereaved and disconsolate, it resists being placed in the role of matching human expectations. Scripture enters our lives not to confirm our prejudices, not even to confirm our most lofty assumptions, but to challenge and to purify. Perhaps this is the divine reason why the final verses of the Book of Isaiah do not end on the note that would allow us to complete our reading with a sigh of delight.

There is also a human reason detectable behind the harsh vindictiveness of verses 14–24. Verse 5 seems to indicate that the God-fearing ones who in verses 3–4 condemned the temple and its sacrifices as idolatrous were driven from the community by some of their own people who ridiculed their eschatological perspective. In the face of persecution, they of course could return to the vision of final redemption in chapter 65. But what

251

of the daily pain of seeing the wicked prosper while they continued to suffer humiliation. How natural to take comfort in the vision of God paying back his anger in fury (v. 15). Even in their hour of despair, however, God's mercy triumphs over God's wrath. While verse 16 announces,

> For by fire will the LORD execute judgment,
>   and by his sword, on all flesh;
>   and those slain by the LORD shall be many,

verse 23 proclaims,

> From new moon to new moon,
>   and from sabbath to sabbath,
>   all flesh shall come to worship before me,
>   says the LORD.

Odd, though, is the final verse. Concluding the magisterial Book of Isaiah with its celebration of the Holy God whose infinite love reaches out for lost mortals is a verse that holds up as an eternal memorial the worm-infested, smoldering bodies of those who have rebelled against their creator. Modern readers are not the first to flinch at the sight. According to the Masoretic notation, verse 24 is to be followed by the repetition of verse 23 in the synagogue.

The shocking imagery of the concluding verse states emphatically the dire seriousness of human beings cutting themselves off from the living God. It thus casts in bold relief the miracle that remains the centerpiece of the Book of Isaiah: Those who trust in God will be delivered from bondage and will be established in righteousness. Although our taste may have led to a choice of a more refined witness, it fits the realism of Hebrew Scripture that a worm has the last word as it urges us to recognize what is at stake in our response to the divine word that has come to us, namely, our eternal destiny. Maggot accordingly adds earthy confirmation to Moses' solemn admonition: "Choose life!"

BIBLIOGRAPHY

1. For further study

ACHTEMEIER, ELIZABETH. *The Community and Message of Isaiah 56—66* (Minneapolis: Augsburg Publishing House, 1982).

BEGRICH, JOACHIM. *Studien zu Deuterojesaja* (Stuttgart: W. Kohlhammer, 1938).

CLIFFORD, RICHARD. *Fair Spoken and Persuading: An Interpretation of Second Isaiah* (New York: Paulist Press, 1984).

CROSS, FRANK MOORE. *Canaanite Myth and Hebrew Epic* (Cambridge, Mass.: Harvard University Press, 1972).

ELLIGER, KARL. *Die Einheit des Tritojesaia* (Stuttgart: W. Kohlhammer, 1928).

FOHRER, GEORG. *Das Buch Jesaja.* Vol. 3 of ZÜRCHER BIBELKOMMENTARE (Zurich: Zwingli Verlag, 1964).

McKENZIE, JOHN L. *Second Isaiah.* ANCHOR BIBLE (Garden City, N.Y.: Doubleday & Co., 1968).

MELUGIN, R. F. *The Formation of Isaiah 40—55* (Berlin: Walter de Gruyter, 1976).

NORTH, C. R. *The Suffering Servant in Deutero-Isaiah* (London: Oxford University Press, 1948).

PAURITSCH, KARL. *Die neue Gemeinde: Gott sammelt Ausgestossene und Arme (Jesaia 56—66)* (Rome: Biblical Institute Press, 1971).

PREUSS, H. D. *Deuterojesaja: Eine Einführung in seine Botschaft* (Neukirchen-Vluyn: Neukirchener Verlag, 1976).

SHOORS, A. *I Am God Your Savior: A Form-Critical Study of the Main Genres in Isaiah XL—LV* (Leiden: E. J. Brill, 1975).

SPYKERBOER, H. C. *The Structure and Composition of Deutero-Isaiah* (Franeker: T. Wever, 1976).

STEINMANN, JEAN. *Le Livre de la consolation d'Israël, et les prophètes du retour de l'exil* (Paris: Editions du Cerf, 1960).

STUHLMUELLER, CARROLL. *Creative Redemption in Deutero-Isaiah* (Rome: Biblical Institute Press, 1970).

TORREY, C. C. *The Second Isaiah: A New Interpretation* (New York: Charles Scribner's Sons, 1928).

VOLZ, PAUL. *Jesaia II.* KOMMENTAR ZUM ALTEN TESTAMENT (Leipzig: D. Werner Scholl, 1932).

253

WHYBRAY, R. N. *The Second Isaiah* (Sheffield: JSOT Press, 1983).

ZIMMERLI, WALTHER. "Zur Sprache Tritojesajas." In *Gottes Offenbarung: Gesammelte Aufsätze* (Munich: Chr. Kaiser Verlag, 1963), pp. 217–33.

2. Literature cited

AUDEN, W. H. "September 1, 1939." In *The English Auden: Poems, Essays, and Dramatic Writings, 1927–39 by W. H. Auden* (Edward Mendelson, ed.; New York: Random House, 1977), pp. 245–47.

BERGER, THOMAS. *Little Big Man* (New York: Fawcett World Library, 1964).

BONHOEFFER, DIETRICH. *The Cost of Discipleship* (R. H. Fuller, ed.; London: SCM Press, 1948).

CLIFFORD, RICHARD, S. J. "The Function of Idol Passages in Second Isaiah." *Catholic Biblical Quarterly* 42:450–64 (1980).

DRIVER, S. R., and A. D. NEUBAUER. *The Fifty-third Chapter of Isaiah according to Jewish Interpreters* (London: James Parker & Co., 1877).

FRIEDLÄNDER, MICHAEL, ed. and trans. *The Commentary of Ibn Ezra on Isaiah* (New York: Feldheim, 1877).

HANSON, PAUL D. *The Dawn of Apocalyptic* (Philadelphia: Fortress Press, 1979).

———. *The People Called* (San Francisco: Harper & Row, 1986).

JACOBSEN, THORKILD. "The Graven Image." In *Ancient Israelite Religion* (P. D. Miller, Jr., P. D. Hanson, S. D. McBride, eds.; Philadelphia: Fortress Press, 1987a), pp. 15–32.

———, trans. and ed. *The Harps That Once—: Sumerian Poetry in Translation* (New Haven: Yale University Press, 1987b), pp. 392–94.

JOHNSON, DOUGLAS, and CYNTHIA SAMPSON. *Religion: The Missing Dimension of Statecraft* (New York: Oxford University Press, 1994).

LEVENSON, JON. *Creation and the Persistence of Evil: The Jewish Drama of Divine Omnipotence* (San Francisco: Harper & Row, 1988).

MacLEISH, ARCHIBALD. *J.B.: A Play in Verse* (Boston: Houghton Mifflin Co., 1958).

MUILENBURG, JAMES. "The Book of Isaiah, Chapters 40—66," Introduction and Exegesis. THE INTERPRETER'S BIBLE, vol. 5 (New York: Abingdon Press, 1956).

PRITCHARD, J. B., ed. *Ancient Near Eastern Texts Relating to the Old Testament.* 3d ed. (Princeton: Princeton University Press, 1969).

RICHARDSON, CYRIL, ed. *The Early Christian Fathers.* LIBRARY OF CHRISTIAN CLASSICS, vol. 1 (Philadelphia: Westminster Press, 1953).

VANAUKEN, SHELDON. *A Severe Mercy* (San Francisco: Harper & Row, 1977).

WESTERMANN, CLAUS. *Isaiah 40—66, A Commentary.* OLD TESTAMENT LIBRARY (D. M. Stalker, trans.; Philadelphia: Westminster Press, 1969).

WIESEL, ELIE. *Night* (Stella Rodway, trans.; New York: Bantam Books, 1982).

WILSON, EDMUND, ed. *The Shock of Recognition* (New York: Doubleday, Doran & Co., 1939).

YEATS, WILLIAM BUTLER. "The Second Coming." In *Collected Poems* (New York: Macmillan Co., 1933).